MULTICULTURAL EDUCATION SERIES

James A. Banks, *Series Editor*

D1594148

MUSIC, EDUCATION, AND DIVERSITY

Bridging Cultures and Communities

Patricia Shehan Campbell

TEACHERS COLLEGE PRESS

TEACHERS COLLEGE | COLUMBIA UNIVERSITY

NEW YORK AND LONDON

Published by Teachers College Press, 1234 Amsterdam Avenue, New York, NY 10027

Cover design by Patricia Palao. Cover photos (top to bottom, left to right): Highwaystarz-Photography, monkeybusinessimage, Wavebreakmedia, Tatyun, all via iStock; Alexandre Zveiger via Shutterstock.

Library of Congress Cataloging-in-Publication Data

Names: Campbell, Patricia Shehan, author.
Title: Music, education, and diversity : bridging cultures and communities / Patricia Shehan Campbell.
Description: New York, NY : Teachers College Press, [2018] | Series: Multicultural education series | Includes bibliographical references and index.
Identifiers: LCCN 2017044639 (print) | LCCN 2017045453 (ebook) | ISBN 9780807776742 (ebook) | ISBN 9780807758823 (pbk.) | ISBN 9780807758830 (case)
Subjects: LCSH: Music—Instruction and study. | Multicultural education.
Classification: LCC MT1 (ebook) | LCC MT1 .C223 2018 (print) | DDC 780.71—dc23
LC record available at https://lccn.loc.gov/2017044639

ISBN 978-0-8077-5882-3 (paper)
ISBN 978-0-8077-5883-0 (hardcover)
ISBN 978-0-8077-7674-2 (ebook)

Printed on acid-free paper
Manufactured in the United States of America

25 24 23 22 21 20 19 18   8 7 6 5 4 3 2 1

Contents

Series Foreword

In this eloquently written, informative, and engaging book, Patricia Campbell describes how music can enrich and reinforce the knowledge, skills, and values that students are learning across the curriculum. She also makes a compelling case for integrating music throughout the elementary and secondary curriculum because of the social justice and global perspectives and practices that music can infuse into the curriculum. In addition to being an astute and visionary musician and teacher educator, Campbell is also a singer, a pianist, and an ethnomusicologist who brings a cultural and inclusive lens to the pages of this highly readable and erudite book. Ethnomusicologists study "music in culture" and examine the ways in which music is a reflection of culture. Because of her keen cultural insights and vision, Campbell has a broad and comprehensive conception of music and music education. She views music as the cultural expressions of local and global communities and explains why school music should not be limited to the Western European musical canon, which she argues has too often dominated the study, teaching, and practice of music in the nation's schools. Campbell describes how music education can be made multicultural and global, and consistent with the realities of teaching students from diverse cultural communities.

Campbell explains why music should be a central and not a peripheral component of the school curriculum. Music can help students to develop and increase their skills in communication, cooperation, and empathy. It also can serve as a bridge across cultures, help to weaken cultural borders, and enhance cross-cultural interactions and understandings. Campbell maintains that music units and lessons should be implemented in culturally inclusive ways and should include music from global cultures and diverse communities, such as African American spirituals, Mexican mariachi music, country western, hip-hop, as well as Western European canon music. School music conceptualized and taught in the transformative and creative ways described by Campbell will incorporate the music of the cultures and communities of students from diverse groups and help them to attain "self-definition" because they will be validated and recognized in the school's music curriculum. Collins (2000) argues that it is essential for marginalized groups to attain self-definition in order to experience efficacy and empowerment.

When the school music curriculum includes the music of diverse communities, all students, in Campbell's words, are "seen, heard, and honored."

Elementary and high schools in the United States need to incorporate the teaching of music from community and global perspectives because of the growing population of students from diverse racial, ethnic, linguistic, and religious groups who are attending U.S. schools. Although students in the United States are becoming increasingly diverse, most of the nation's teachers are White, female, and monolingual. Campbell points out that the demographic characteristics of music teachers in the United States mirror those of other teachers.

Race and institutionalized racism are significant factors that influence and mediate the interactions of students and teachers from different ethnic, language, and social class groups (G. R. Howard, 2016; T. C. Howard, 2010; Leonardo, 2013). The growing income gap among adults (Stiglitz, 2012)—as well as among youth as described by Putnam in *Our Kids: The American Dream in Crisis* (2015)—is another significant reason it is important to help teachers understand how categories related to race, ethnicity, and class influence classroom interactions and student learning and the ways in which these variables influence student aspirations, behaviors, and academic engagement (Suárez-Orozco, Pimentel, & Martin, 2009).

Social class has a significant influence on music teaching and learning. Many low-income youth do not participate in school musical activities such as the jazz band or orchestra because they do not have the music knowledge and skills that many middle-class students have acquired from taking private instrumental lessons beginning at an early age. Music education programs are absent in many schools that serve urban low-income populations because of inadequate funding and because music often is considered an enrichment program that is peripheral to the teaching of basic skills in reading, writing, and arithmetic, which often is the focus in low-income city schools (Gorski, 2013).

American classrooms are experiencing the largest influx of immigrant students since the beginning of the 20th century. Approximately 21.5 million new immigrants—documented and undocumented—settled in the United States in the years from 2000 to 2015. Fewer than 10% came from nations in Europe. Most came from Mexico and nations in South Asia, East Asia, Latin America, the Caribbean, and Central America (Camarota, 2011, 2016). The influence of an increasingly diverse population on U.S. schools, colleges, and universities is and will continue to be enormous.

Schools in the United States are more diverse today than they have been since the early 1900s, when a multitude of immigrants entered the United States from Southern, Central, and Eastern Europe (C.A.M. Banks, 2005). In 2014, the National Center for Education Statistics estimated that students from ethnic minority groups made up more than 50% of the students in prekindergarten through 12th grade in public schools, an increase from

40% in 2001. Language and religious diversity also are increasing in the U.S. student population. The 2012 American Community Survey estimated that 21% of Americans aged 5 and above (61.9 million) spoke a language other than English at home (U.S. Census Bureau, 2012). Harvard professor Diana L. Eck (2001) calls the United States the "most religiously diverse nation on earth" (p. 4). Islam is now the fastest growing religion in the United States, as well as in several European nations such as France, the United Kingdom, and the Netherlands (J. A. Banks, 2009, 2017; O'Brien, 2016).

The major purpose of the Multicultural Education Series is to provide preservice educators, practicing educators, graduate students, scholars, and policymakers with an interrelated and comprehensive set of books that summarizes and analyzes important research, theory, and practice related to the education of ethnic, racial, cultural, and linguistic groups in the United States and to the education of mainstream students about diversity. The dimensions of multicultural education, developed by J. A. Banks and described in the *Handbook of Research on Multicultural Education* (2004) and in the *Encyclopedia of Diversity in Education* (2012), provide the conceptual framework for the development of the publications in the Series. The dimensions are content integration, the knowledge construction process, prejudice reduction, equity pedagogy, and an empowering institutional culture and social structure. Campbell describes excellent examples of how the dimensions of multicultural education and the related approaches to curriculum reform can be incorporated in the music education curriculum (J. A. Banks, 2016).

The books in the Multicultural Education Series provide research, theoretical, and practical knowledge about the behaviors and learning characteristics of students of color (Conchas & Vigil, 2012; Lee, 2007), language minority students (Gándara & Hopkins 2010; Valdés, 2001; Valdés, Capitelli, & Alvarez, 2011), low-income students (Cookson, 2013; Gorski, 2013), and other minoritized population groups, such as students who speak different varieties of English (Charity Hudley & Mallinson, 2011) and LGBTQ youth (Mayo, 2014). This book describes how the Western European canon has dominated the music curriculum and performance in U.S. schools and ways in which the music curriculum can be reformed to include global and diversity components. The book by Au, Brown, and Calderón (2016) in the Multicultural Education Series complements this book because it describes ways in which the perspectives, insights, and histories of communities of color have been marginalized and silenced in the curriculum of the nation's schools and in the curriculum studies discourse.

Campbell argues compellingly in this visionary and insightful book that the music curriculum can be a powerful bridge to cultural understanding. This is an important and timely argument because racial, ethnic, and religious conflict and animosity intensified after 9/11 and escalated after Donald J. Trump was elected president in 2016. Trump expressed anti-immigrant sentiments, issued an executive order that banned immigrants from seven predominantly Muslim nations (Chokshi & Fandos, 2017; Shear & Cooper, 2017), and made public statements that encouraged White nationalist groups to publicly flaunt racist behavior and symbols such as the Nazi swastika (Anderson, 2017). Improving race and ethnic relations in today's toxic racial climate should be a top priority for educators. School music programs can make a significant contribution to improving racial and ethnic relations in schools by enhancing cross-cultural understanding and interactions and engaging in what Campbell calls "musicking." When musicking occurs, students actively participate in global and community music activities and events with other students from groups who have diverse "roots, identifies, preferences, and past experiences." I am pleased to welcome this needed and imaginative book to the Multicultural Education Series and hope that it will experience the wide visibility and influence that it deserves.

—James A. Banks

REFERENCES

Anderson, C. (2017, August 5). The policies of White resentment. *The New York Times*. Retrieved from www.nytimes.com/2017/08/05/opinion/sunday/white-resentment-affirmative-action.html?_r=0

Au, W., Brown, A. L., & Calderón, D. (2016). *Reclaiming the multicultural roots of U.S. curriculum: Communities of color and official knowledge in education.* New York, NY: Teachers College Press.

Banks, C.A.M. (2005). *Improving multicultural education: Lessons from the intergroup education movement.* New York, NY: Teachers College Press.

Banks, J. A. (2004). Multicultural education: Historical development, dimensions, and practice. In J. A. Banks & C.A.M. Banks (Eds.), *Handbook of research on multicultural education* (2nd ed., pp. 3–29). San Francisco, CA: Jossey-Bass.

Banks, J. A. (Ed.). (2009). *The Routledge international companion to multicultural education.* New York, NY, and London, UK: Routledge.

Banks, J. A. (2012). Multicultural education: Dimensions of. In J. A. Banks (Ed.), *Encyclopedia of diversity in education* (Vol. 3, pp. 1538–1547). Thousand Oaks, CA: Sage.

Banks, J. A. (2016). Approaches to multicultural curriculum reform. In J. A. Banks & C.A.M. Banks (Eds.), *Multicultural education: Issues and perspectives* (9th ed., pp. 151–170). Hoboken, NJ: Wiley.

Banks, J. A. (Ed.). (2017). *Citizenship education and global migration: Implications for theory, research, and teaching.* Washington, DC: American Educational Research Association.

Camarota, S. A. (2011, October). *A record-setting decade of immigration:*

2000–2010. Washington, DC: Center for Immigration Studies. Retrieved from cis.org/2000-2010-record-setting-decade-of-immigration

Camarota, S. A. (2016, June). *New data: Immigration surged in 2014 and 2015.* Washington, DC: Center for Immigration Studies. Retrieved from cis.org/New-Data Immigration-Surged-in-2014-and-2015

Charity Hudley, A.H., & Mallinson, C. (2011). *Understanding language variation in U.S. schools.* New York, NY: Teachers College Press.

Chokshi, N., & Fandos, N. (2017, January 29). Demonstrators in streets, and at airports, protest immigration order. *The New York Times.* Retrieved from www.nytimes.com/2017/01/29/us/protests-airports-donald-trump-immigration-executive-order-muslims.html

Collins, P. H. (2000). *Black feminist thought: Knowledge, consciousness, and the politics of empowerment* (2nd ed.). New York, NY: Routledge.

Conchas, G. Q., & Vigil, J. D. (2012). *Streetsmart schoolsmart: Urban poverty and the education of adolescent boys.* New York, NY: Teachers College Press.

Cookson, P. W., Jr. (2013). *Class rules: Exposing inequality in American high schools.* New York, NY: Teachers College Press.

Eck, D. L. (2001). *A new religious America: How a "Christian country" has become the world's most religiously diverse nation.* New York, NY: HarperCollins.

Gándara, P., & Hopkins, M. (Eds.). (2010). *Forbidden language: English language learners and restrictive language policies.* New York, NY: Teachers College Press.

Gorski, P. C. (2013). *Reaching and teaching students in poverty: Strategies for erasing the opportunity gap.* New York, NY: Teachers College Press.

Howard, G. R. (2016). *We can't teach what we don't know: White teachers, multiracial schools* (3rd ed.). New York, NY: Teachers College Press.

Howard, T. C. (2010). *Why race and culture matter in schools. Closing the achievement gap in America's classrooms.* New York, NY: Teachers College Press.

Lee, C. D. (2007). *Culture, literacy, and learning: Taking bloom in the midst of the whirlwind.* New York, NY: Teachers College Press.

Leonardo, Z. (2013). *Race frameworks: A multidimensional theory of racism and education.* New York, NY: Teachers College Press.

Mayo, C. (2014). *LGBTQ youth and education: Policies and practices.* New York, NY: Teachers College Press.

National Center for Education Statistics. (2014). *The condition of education 2014.* Retrieved from nces.ed.gov/pubs2014/2014083.pdf

O'Brien, P. (2016). *The Muslim question in Europe: Political controversies and public philosophies.* Philadelphia, PA: Temple University Press.

Putnam, R. D. (2015). *Our kids: The American dream in crisis.* New York, NY: Simon & Schuster.

Shear, M. D., & Cooper, H. (2017, January 27). Trumps bars refugees and citizens of 7 Muslim countries. *The New York Times.* Retrieved from www.nytimes.com/2017/01/27/us/politics/trump-syrian-refugees.html

Stiglitz, J. E. (2012). *The price of inequality: How today's divided society endangers our future.* New York, NY: Norton.

Suárez-Orozco, C., Pimentel, A., & Martin, M. (2009). The significance of relationships: Academic engagement and achievement among newcomer immigrant youth. *Teachers College Record, 111*(3), 712–749.

U.S. Census Bureau. (2012). *Selected social characteristics in the United States: 2012 American Community Survey 1-year estimates.* Retrieved from factfinder2. census.gov/faces/tableservices/jsf/pages/productview.xhtml?pid=ACS_12_1YR_ DP02&prodType=table

Valdés, G. (2001). *Learning and not learning English: Latino students in American schools.* New York, NY: Teachers College Press.

Valdés, G., Capitelli, S., & Alvarez, L. (2011). *Latino children learning English: Steps in the journey.* New York, NY: Teachers College Press.

Powering Cultural Understanding Through Music

As in the case of J. S. Bach's *The Well-Tempered Clavier*, this prelude is a set of brief motifs, an introduction to the movements to come. The perspectives that tumble forth on these pages emanate from over 6 decades of my personal encounters in and through music. Some are linked to my half-century's work as a teaching musician, a card-carrying music educator by training. Some resonate with my having worked ethnomusicologically in the field of schools, classrooms, and communities in the United States; in extended stays in places like Bulgaria, Ireland, Germany, India, Mexico, Myanmar, Tanzania, Thailand, the United Kingdom, and on the land of the Yakama Nation; with colleagues and students in the comfortable armchairs of an academic institution; and with practicing teachers in their classrooms and rehearsal halls. Some emerge from conventional and continuing events, and as a result of late-breaking scenarios emerging in American schools and society. Encounters with children and youth, and with musicians and teachers, influence my thoughts and actions relative to music, education, and diversity. With fortuitous lived experience as an American musician, teacher, and scholar, I've had the advantage of weathering challenges through music and steering students of varied hues and views through music to find their own solace and a certain personal and communal power in musical expression, alone or together. I hold firm hope that music is an Rx for us all, regardless of race, class, or gender, and have good reason to believe that music solves and resolves many moments of discord, conflict, and incompatibility.

I'm captivated by the realization that music is essentially everywhere in the world, and that people want to sing it, play it, dance it, and listen to it. Intriguing are the musical expressions of elegant simplicity and exacting complexity, of short-lived expressive musical bursts and longstanding and continuing traditions, and the interests of people in sustaining heritage as well as people's earnest efforts to push the envelope to new sonic adventures. Beguiling are the genres of folk, popular, art music, and music of every other category and classification, and musical expressions that spring from the hearts of people of all colors and creeds. Fascinating are the ways in which the music that people make derive from their formal and school-based musical education, from their informal enculturative experiences at home and in the family, and from the liminal realm of music they know that is learned but not taught, that is felt but not deliberately and consciously thought. Captivating are the questions of music's considerable impact and power, its presence in times of joy and sadness, its role in shaping lives and growing human relationships, its sustainability in the face of all sorts of social and political changes.

This book follows on themes of music, education, and culture that run rampant in the fields of ethnomusicology and music education. Ethnomusicologists study music as a reflection of cultural identity and are intrigued with the concept of teaching as a political act; their pedagogical work is influential at the tertiary level for ways in which they help to broaden the perspective of music majors and prospective music teachers to the possibilities for musical expressions in the West and throughout the world. For music educators who work in elementary, secondary, and tertiary teacher education programs, aspects of music education practice have encompassed questions of cultural diversity and social justice for decades, so much so that the acronym MCME (or McME) is widely used to refer to multicultural music education, even as other derivations of multicultural, intercultural, and global studies of music have been associated with teaching models, methods, and movements: CDIME (cultural diversity in music education), WMP (world music pedagogy), and SJME (social justice and music education). Within the distinctive fields of ethnomusicology and music education, there is a shared desire to attend to the interface of music, diversity, and democracy in schools; to design and deliver a balanced diet of curricular studies in music; and to ensure access and equity to musical experience and study for all children and youth.

The challenge of educating citizens to think and act effectively in a multicultural society is a shared one, such that it takes the efforts of teachers across all subjects (and at all ages and stages of student development) to realize the aims of an all-encompassing multicultural education. Music is a powerful means of defining heritage, developing intercultural understandings, and breaking down barriers between various ethnic, racial, cultural, and language groups. There is a considerable history in the United States and internationally of musically educating all children in schools, although this history is rolled back in the face of budgetary crises that question education in the arts as central to a comprehensive education plan. In recent decades, where music has been in place, there has been steady development in the integration of a broad variety of the world's musical cultures within elementary and secondary schools (and in teacher education programs). Less evident is documentation of music's potential to impact other dimensions of multicultural education, such as the knowledge construction process, prejudice reduction, an equity pedagogy, and an empowering school culture. Furthermore, in most venues, the realities of cultural diversity in music education do not always match the impassioned articulations, even though there are model programs and projects working to advance the principles of music and multicultural education in schools.

The intention of this volume is to provide insight to educators of music, the arts, and other curricular subjects, all of whom seek the realization of multicultural aims, on the role of music in the curriculum as a powerful bridge to cultural understanding. The book serves to document some of the key ideas and practices that have influenced current music-educational practices in schools (with occasional reference also to the related arts, especially dance) and raises key issues coming from well-grounded scholarship in ethnomusicology and cogent evidence from research, policy, and practice in shaping education in music (and education through music). It argues for school experiences in the performance, composition, and listening analysis of art, folk/traditional, and popular expressions as avenues for developing knowledge of local and global communities. Featured are an examination of world music pedagogy as a pathway to knowing music and culture, and a study of the issues of bimusicality, authenticity, context, and school–community intersections that complicate the teaching and learning of world music cultures. Informal and formal learning practices will be examined for their synergy (and also the tensions between them), and music of oral cultures will be discussed in light of curricular programs intent upon developing notational literacy. The presence of musical communities is acknowledged for their potential contributions to school music programs, and efforts in applied ethnomusicology (through the employment of community music techniques), are described for their work in highlighting local music and musicians, culture bearers and heritage musicians who, as "insiders," are rich resources in the expressive practices of their cultural communities.

Unlike previous publications on multicultural music education that are tuned solely to the provision of diverse music "materials" (songs, instrumental pieces and musical selections), this book addresses philosophy and practice from the distinctive and overlapping perspectives of music education and ethnomusicology, while also keeping the essence of multicultural education very much in mind. The multiple dimensions of multicultural education and the levels of curriculum reform (from "contributions" to "social action") are acknowledged, too, in assessing the impact of musical study on student respect for difference as well as the recognition of similarities across cultures. Importantly, the uniquely powerful phenomenon of the shared musical experience is dissected for its impact in developing solidarity, mutual support, and social cohesion, and recommendations are offered for the integration of music into specific classes as well as throughout school culture at large.

The readership of this volume is likely to be undergraduate and graduate students in music and music education. Students of the arts, as they can be integrated into curricular practice, also may find relevance in some of the components and chapters. For undergraduate students in the process of thinking through the foundations of music in schools, this book introduces the central tenets of diversity in the content and method of music education for all elementary and secondary school students (rather than only the privileged few). Graduate students of music returning for advanced studies—many of whom may not have had occasion to ponder the meaning of diversity and democracy within their teaching experience—may be enlightened about efforts thus far to multiculturalize the music curriculum. Readers will be pressed to consider the further potential for accomplishing goals of diversity awareness and democratic action through music.

There are eight chapters in this book, including an introductory chapter that provides a brief summary of music's place in human life and in school settings. Chapters emanate from the premise that music's potential is considerable for shaping student understandings and valuing of diverse populations. They offer perspectives on music as a weighty way forward to the principles and practices in place, partially realized, or in need of development for music within curricular programs of elementary and secondary schools, and in the preparation of educators in music and other subjects where music can find its place as an effective tool for addressing diversity. There are chapters detailing the nature of musical diversity, the history of music of local and global communities in schools, ethnomusicological principles as they flavor and fit music education policy, and transmission processes in musical cultures as they are relevant to offering students full-fledged musical experiences that go beyond "the song" to broader and deeper conceptualizations of music. There are also chapters on world music pedagogy as a multidimensional instructional process, the collaborative roles of culture bearers and teachers as insiders to music and classroom cultures, and a reckoning with the realities of teaching music with multicultural principles in mind.

Ubuntu (Zulu for "I am because you are") signifies an embrace of the many in our lives who make us who we are and to whom we are indebted for their contributions to our understandings and perspectives. My heartfelt thanks to all good people I have known for the inspirations and influences in my life. To my parents, who had curiosity and open-hearted respect for everyone in our neighborhood and in our extended community. To the folks of Cleveland, Ohio, in my growing-up years of listening to and learning from one another in the schools we attended, the churches in which we engaged in prayer and community service, the high school in the midst of the integration efforts that happened uneasily at first but very surely and with every good intent, and the citywide events meant to honor and celebrate national, cultural, and community pride. While Cleveland circa 1960 was not a perfect union of peoples of so many diverse backgrounds, we who were then in our childhoods gained valuable lessons from listening, watching, and engaging, thanks to the help of sensitive and respectful parents, teachers, and other responsible adults. Ubuntu!

I wish to give thanks to the bright lights in my journey as a musician, teacher, and scholar: to Jonas Svedas, my Lithuanian piano teacher, for 10 years of his artistic inspiration in opening to me the world of J. S. Bach, Mozart, and Debussy; to Evangeline Merritt, who helped me to find my voice for singing Fauré and Rossini (which I took back into my lifelong interest in singing Anglo-American folk songs); to William M. Anderson, Terry Lee Kuhn, Virginia Mead, and Terry Miller, my doc-mentors at Kent State University, who started me into the shift from music teacher to music teacher educator and music scholar; to Barbara Reeder Lundquist, whose understanding of music and human relationships comes shining through every lecture and lesson she has ever given, and every sit-down conversation that we've had—from Seattle to Seoul, and from the University of Washington (UW) to the University of Dar es Salaam.

I am grateful for my colleagues at UW, beginning with my editor, James A. Banks, visionary scholar in the building next door to my own School of Music. I'm honored to contribute a volume to his distinctive series amid the collection of prestigious authors he has gathered, even as I'm continuously inspired by his tremendous wisdom and endless scholarly energy. Many thanks to Brian Ellerbeck and Lori Tate, editors at Teachers College Press of Columbia University, for their careful shepherding of this work along the way to publication. I'm grateful to Steven J. Morrison, Shannon Dudley, Christopher Roberts, Marc Seales, and Christina Sunardi for their commitment to teaching music for the sublime experience that it is, as well as for developing multicultural understanding through performance and academic courses. Many thanks to my pathbreaker-colleagues, especially Lee Higgins, Huib Schippers, Bonnie C. Wade, Jennifer Walden, and Trevor Wiggins, for the experiences and passionate exchanges we've shared over the years on music, education, and culture.

I am humbled by the thoughtful work over many years by seasoned teachers, some of whom became graduate students at UW and then moved on to university positions to likewise do the good work of raising culturally responsive teachers: You know who you are, and you are much appreciated. I'm deeply grateful to Charlie Campbell, and to Andrew: you two who have lived the ideas with me over the years, prompting and pressing me to articulate more clearly and to put my words into musical and teaching action.

May this work help you, the reader, to know how music is necessary for us all for what it can do in our schools to strengthen the spirit and bring communities together.

CHAPTER 1

Musical Engagement as Human Need

Music's role in the multicultural education of students is as undeniable today as it is longstanding and far-reaching across the United States, Canada, and much of the rest of the world. There is growing acknowledgment of music's important role in the lives of children and youth, and thus the recommendations are strong for making a place for music as a subject of study within the school curriculum. Music teachers provide group lessons, ensemble experiences, and experiential classes in school programs, offering listening, performance, and creative composition and improvisation opportunities, and they are increasingly clued in to the importance of music in developing the cultural—and multicultural—understanding of their students. Called "music educators" and "teaching musicians," they are trained and certified in music and its pedagogy, and meet state-mandated qualifications similar to those prescribed for teachers of all subjects. They care to develop the expressive-creative skills, understandings, and values of all their

1

students, and the professional literature is encouraging them to do so in as many musical styles as they can muster. Educated in tertiary-level music education programs and certified by departments and ministries of education, music teachers have a unique edge in the work they do: They have the power of music, in all of its diversity, to make a solid impact on the holistic development of elementary and secondary school students.

This chapter defines and discusses music, the musicking act, and musical diversity, and considers the presence and power of music in life, in society, and in education. Music is described as consisting of its sonic properties (of melody-rhythm-timbre-texture-form) and also as an integrated conceptualization of sound, behavior, and values. The act of making music is acknowledged as humanly necessary. Music's powerful impact on the intellectual, social, and personal development of children and youth is recognized, as is its track record in achieving wellness, social cohesion, and community. The simple fact of music in daily life is underscored through a set of scenarios descriptive of music as meaningful to individuals from infants to elders, and this evidence of the human affinity for music (across a variety of sociocultural settings and circumstances) leads to one of many justifications for the curricular inclusion of music in schools. Not surprisingly, the study of music in its many guises leads to the chapter closure on thoughts concerning the realization of multicultural understanding through musical experience in the school curriculum.

Music, Deeply. It was breathtaking, like time standing still, almost, and yet the music was all about time, unfolding in sound. The whole of the evening was beautiful, sometimes subtle, sublime, there on my first trip to Severance Hall with my father. We had been given a pair of free tickets to hear the Cleveland Orchestra, conducted by the great Hungarian maestro, George Szell. For both of us, it was our very first live symphony concert, although I was 12 and he was 41. We had no words, just ears wide open and eyes that glistened with emotional awe that we could not verbally articulate. I still recall the palatial ambiance of the well-lit, marble-floored lobby, the scent of perfumed ladies with shoulder capes of fox heads biting fox tails, the feel of crushed velvet seats in the first balcony, and the sound encircling us, sometimes transparent so that we could hear every tone and tune, sometimes sounding like all sounds were sailing from a single instrument. It was the 3rd movement of Beethoven's Symphony No. 9 that had engulfed us. The strings were so absolutely in melodic unison as they wove their meandering way through the work, and the purity of the winds and horns was like none we'd ever encountered from street bands we'd heard in holiday parades. All at once, the regal feel of the concert hall was converted to a sense of reverence and devotion befitting a visit to an ornate cathedral. We were mesmerized, as if the hand of God was reaching out to us through the music. *Adagio Molto.* I was singing it inside in its many recurrences and variations, and the melody stayed with me. We left the concert in a state of euphoria, and as we walked our way across the wet sidewalks back to the car, we each re-membered the melody of the movement and sang it aloud, together, again and again, all the way home.

Music sparks deep sentiment in the moment of its performance and set-tles into remote places within human memory. For me, the Irish "trad" music at Miltown Malbay was heart-stopping, as was the music of the Bulgarian gaida players in Plovdiv, the mariachi music in Guadalajara, the percussion-heavy rhumba sound in the crowded basement dance club in Havana, the taraab con-certs of oud and violin in Zanzibar, the St. Louis blues of Henry Townsend, the Indo-Celtic fusion that master *tabla* player Zakir Hussain once brought to Seat-tle, the mastery of Burmese slide guitarist U Tin in his home studio in Yangon, the high lonesome bluegrass sounds of Ralph Stanley and the Clinch Mountain Boys at Beanblossom, Indiana. It doesn't end. It's all breathtaking, and I nearly lose my head every time in the sounds of so many fine musicians in the world. Music is a powerful phenomenon, and I'm convinced that it is the responsibility of educators to make musical experiences available, in all of their diversity, to all students to know, deeply.

DEFINING MUSIC

"Music" conjures up thoughts of its sonic properties: a lyrical melody, a com-pelling rhythm, the texture of a melody and its countermelody, the formal organization of returning and repeating sections of a melody, the timbre of a smooth-as-silk soprano voice or a nasalized yet resonant double-reed oboe. The science of music, and the pleasure of music as well, is in its sound. Music is a sonic thing of great beauty, a sound-reflector of humanly felt emotion.

To some fans and followers, music is extreme high art, as in the case of a dynamic symphony by Ludwig van Beethoven, an intoxicating saxophone solo by John Coltrane, or the heady melodic filigree of a Thyagaraja vocal form from southern India known as *kriti*. In these cases, music is beautiful for its propensity to lift listeners out of the everyday activity and into a dif-ferent (and often sublime) reality. For some, music is viewed as an activity meant for full-on participation, an occasion for people to raise their voices together in song, or to join with their instrument in group expression. Music is a social activity, an opportunity for making something beautiful together. For many, music is a solo listening activity, a part of one's daily life, and they tune in to music while driving, exercising, riding a bus, preparing a meal, or performing household chores. A definition of music is often in the ear of the beholder, even as it is also fashioned by its function, and depending upon the individual and the community to which he or she belongs, music is variously defined.

In the Western world, the word *music* may bring to mind violinists, pi-anists, flutists, singer-songwriter guitarists, and hip-hop artists. In addition to performers, the image of music may include the composer who carefully crafts and creates symphonies and string quartets that are new and personally expressive. Western art music composers themselves may speak of their music as an imitation of life, or of nature, or of the deeply internalized spiritual or psychological essence of an individual life. They may refer to a state of mind, a specific event, or a person as inspiring their compositions, and they may clarify how their music expresses their particular feeling. Some composers will argue a different stance, though, noting, as Igor Stravinsky did, that music is absolute sound and not in any way "referential" (Craft, 1994). Music is about the craft of the composition, the structure, the logical piecing together of germinal sonic motifs into a full work of sonic art. Beyond art music, however, composing happens in the hands of songwriters and hip-hop artists who creatively express their perspectives and positions through a combination of text in verse with melodies and/or musical "beats" or rhythm tracks. Whether expressive of particular ideas or not, composers join performers as those whose professional calling is music, creating it as composers and re-creating it as performers.

Consider *music,* the word, and its various linguistic equivalents. This English-language word is related to the Latin *musica,* the French *musique,* the German *Musik,* the Spanish *música*, the Russian *Myzyka,* the Gaelic *ceól,* and the classical Greek *mousike.* In Slovenia, the word is *glasba,* in Hindi, *sangeet,* in Shona, *mumhanzi,* in Samoan, *pese.* *Musiqi* is the Arabic rendition (which applies to instrumental music but not to sung poetry or chanting parts of the Qur'an; this variant of the word is found all the way down the Swahili coast of East Africa). Some cultures employ separate words for vocal and instrumental music, as in Macedonia's use of *pesne* (song) versus *muzyka* (instrumental music). Sometimes, music is so all-encompassing of the performing arts of vocal and instrumental music, dance, and drama that an umbrella term such as *ngoma* is used as in the case of parts of sub-Saharan Africa, or *saapup* by the Blackfoot nation of Montana, or *Gesamtkunstwerk* by the 19th-century opera composer Richard Wagner. Among the Kaluli people of Papua New Guinea, music is located within a five-part taxonomy of sound—speech, poetry, song, bird-song, and weeping (Feld, 1982). In still other cultures, there may be no word at all for the phenomenon of music; in these places, music just *is.*

Music is a pan-human phenomenon, even as it is named and conceptualized differently. In addition, there are cultural constructions of music that pertain not only to its sound but also to musical behavior and the ideas that undergird and inspire music (Nettl, 2015). The very act of making music is a specific kind of human behavior, and there are many ways to behave in this musical act. Consider not only that behaviors vary among musicians who sing and musicians who play various musical instruments, but also that there are different standard practices associated with vocal and instrumental performance that are deliberate and as regular as ritual. Musical behaviors vary from culture to culture, from one genre to the next, and even across musicians. Some performers stand while others sit on chairs or floor spaces, some group together to follow a conductor while others read one another's breath rhythm and gestures in order to know when to start and stop (and how to phrase a musical idea). Some musicians are very still, concentrating their movement in the fingers that play upon the holes of fiddles, lutes, the keys of clarinets and the valves of trumpets, while others are visibly active in the nod of their heads and the dip, bend, and sway of their bodies. Ritualistic behaviors are involved in musical performance, including how performers dress, how they enter the venue or onto the stage, and how they are acknowledged (and how the musicians themselves acknowledge audience response). As for musical ideas and values, people in various places perceive music as sacred or secular, secret or shared, pure and untarnished or of mixed styles, meant to be performed only by the highly trained or by all who are interested and regardless of previous experience or training. Music, then, is sound, behavior, and values, a truly integrated phenomenon altogether, but one that is variously treated from one culture to another.

MUSICKING AS A PROCESS

Alone or together, people make music because they must: They sing, they dance, they play, and they listen. Music is a uniquely human trait, a fundamental prosocial feature of all people in every society, and an opportunity for the involvement of individuals and communities in expressive artistic practice. Across time and distance, in cultures and communities now and in their past history, musical involvement has remained a vibrant and vital quality of the human condition. Music invites people to produce and to listen thoughtfully, and it necessitates a keen logic that mixes well with emotive sensibilities in order to perform, participate in, and make sense of music that is beautiful, meaningful, and essentially expressive.

Christopher Small (1998) coined the term *musicking* to refer to the act of making music and to engaging as a participant in a musical event—as an active listener or as a dancer whose movements respond to music's expressive qualities, rhythms, and various formal qualities. In Small's view, musicking includes also those who enable and facilitate a musical event as part of a sociological whole, so that stagehands, lighting specialists, and ticket takers in a concert hall are also important to the musicking entity. It can be argued that another important category of enablers are the educators who sequence pedagogical experiences for their students to learn to perform, create, and listen and respond to music. The main matter of musicking, however, is that the accent on music shifts from the age-old Western meaning of music as object—a musical instrument, for example, or the notation of music—into its significance as action and process. Further, musicking refers to music as more than the final performance, but as participatory behavior that is as alive in rehearsal as it is in the final public concert. In musicking, every progressive stage of musical engagement is as important as a finished musical product (e.g., a performance or a recording).

For children and youth, and for teachers who are charged to work with them in schools, musicking is meaningful because it emphasizes the active involvement of students every step of the way. They are participants in making the music (of any style), whether vocally or on instruments; in receiving as listeners both live and recorded music; and in responding to music in ways that involve them in stylized dance or free and interpretive gestures and movements. For many students, music needs to be not just a product resulting from labor-intensive and rigorous practice (although producing a refined and polished performance is certainly within the realm of reason for those who desire it). Music needs to be a musicking experience, an activity and an opportunity for students to be drawn into music in such a manner that they feel genuinely accepted for what they musically know, coming from various homes and neighborhoods and from near and far in the world, and for what they can do across a spectrum of skill levels. Musicking stipulates that all children and youth can find meaning in "sonic art," as listeners, and can contribute successfully to a musical enterprise, as performers and composers. Musicking offers a wide-open invitation for all students to enter into the social act of musical participation, regardless of their roots, identities, preferences, and past experiences.

UNDERSTANDING MUSICAL DIVERSITY

Music is not a universal language. Nor is it a variety of separate languages, totally indistinguishable and without overlapping meanings. Rather, music is an array of learned sonic dialects, some familiar since birth and others far afield from an individual's experience. There are as many musical expressions as there are cultures, and thus music's diversity expressions parallels that of language and culture, close and far from one another. Those within a culture "get it": They know the music of their culture, and this music is meaningful to them because they have been enculturated and socialized to understand its sonic structures, behaviors, and values. If they've grown up in a culture that has provided them with opportunities to listen to and learn to perform African American gospel music, they will know gospel music more deeply than those without such experience. Similarly, if they have been exposed to and educated and trained in mariachi music, they will know mariachi music. Likewise, the same can be said about those who listen to and learn the *pattala* (xylophone) music of Myanmar, the Pakistani praise song called *qawwali,* and the music of the Turkish *saz* (plucked lute). Music is understood more fully by those who have learned to play (or sing) even a single selection, or who have been guided to learn to listen for its essential features, than by those who've had no opportunity to study it. Cultural outsiders to a musical style, and those with little to no education in the style, will come up with contradictory impressions of the music or may be entirely confused as to its logic and thus its beauty too. In order to understand the music of Morocco or Mali or Melanesia, it's necessary to learn elements of its practices. Playing and also understanding music plucked on a three-stringed Japanese *shamisen* (lute) or a Bolivian *charango* (lute) requires training. With its discrete differences across cultures, music of every culture takes time and energy to understand and value.

In interesting ways, music continues to be performed over time within a musical culture, often with variation that reflects the fluid interests of performers and their audiences. For those engaging in the musical education of students in schools, musical understanding is complicated, then, by the tremendous historical evolution of music. Which music does one teach and learn, not only across the world but also within a given musical culture? Western orchestral music is different today than it was in the 18th century (we need only compare a symphony by Mozart to one by Mahler or Martin). American popular music has undergone rapid change from the 1920s to the 1940s, and from 2000 to now. Country music has evolved from its 1940s hillbilly style through its country western period of the next 30 years, and from the sounds of Johnny Cash and Loretta Lynn to Garth Brooks and Alison Krauss. As well, despite its prominence and popularity today, hip-hop has gone through considerable evolution from the time of Grandmaster Flash in the late 1970s to the sounds of Jay Z and Kendrick Lamar. Music is not static, although older music may be respectfully re-created and studied alongside an acknowledgment that expressive potentials are evolving with the presence of new technological possibilities—new instruments, new recording devices, new multimedia possibilities. Some performers are insistent on playing the preludes and fugues of J. S. Bach as they were sounded on the 18th-century clavichord, on "period instruments," while others may adapt Bach to high-tech electronic reproduction, or to the Chinese *zheng* (zither), or Guatemalan-style marimbas, or Senegalese 21-string *kora* (harp), or Trinidadian steelpans. On the other hand, some music intentionally may be preserved intact, as in the case of Japanese *gagaku*, an orchestra that dates to the 8th century A.D. and has weathered exceptionally well for over a millennium. For students, musical understanding of a genre, within a culture, is ever more complete when its historical evolution is acknowledged and studied. This concept of an evolving genre, of living traditions, is recognized, but it is challenging for teachers who may accept this ideal but are faced with limited time for growing their students' musical understanding of genres and styles across time.

In the culturally diverse populations of our schools, children and youth have in their ears, their minds, and their bodies the music of their home and family experiences. Musical diversity abounds in schools, if we consider these experiences together: *banda,* beatboxing, *bhajan, cai luong,* chicken scratch, *conjunto,* country western, gospel, hip-hop, K-pop, polka, pow-wow, reggae, *rondalla,* salsa, *son jarocho, tamburitza,* zydeco, and so many more art, folk, and popular music genres. A recognition of students' musical cultures can make for an excellent launch into a course or program, as the sources for musical diversity are there within the lives of the students. Whether they perform the music themselves, or are experienced listeners, or are connected to family members who make the music, students often are intimately connected to music that is meaningful to them by virtue of their identity, their birthplace, and the surrounds of their community. Often, the music of their evolving youth identity may not match the music of their parents and grandparents, so that there again is a further diversity. Mexican youth, for example, may be drawn to reggaeton, while their parents and grandparents may prefer a mariachi's *canción ranchera* expressions. In developing an education in music that is genuinely multicultural, teachers do well to tap into the experiences of their students, who, group by cultural group, may bring many generationally determined genres forward for exploration. Altogether, students and their families represent a diversity of musical cultures worthy of exploring together, leading to a wide array of rich and meaningful musical experiences.

Musical understanding, then, one of the goals of a musical education, has its challenges and just rewards. Questions emerge even in the first steps of selecting the music to study and experience, and to perform. Within a single culture, be it Bolivian or Burmese, Venezuelan or Vietnamese, which music, from what period, as performed and preferred by which subculture within the nation, should be selected? The diversity of musical expressions that results from a wide spectrum of cultures across the world is increased when considering the extent of musical diversity within cultures. The sheer quantity of musical styles initially may overwhelm teachers and work to hamper attempts to feature many genres. At the same time, an awareness of the many splendors of music across place and time also may engross and captivate the attention of teacher and students alike, leading them to discover together the extent to which music has been shaped by humans' capacity to express themselves in unique and myriad ways.

MUSIC'S IMPACT

Music's influence on the human psyche is considerable. J. K. Rowling was one among many who, in her widely read tome, *Harry Potter and the Sorcerer's Stone* (1998), penned these words about music: "Ah, music. A magic beyond all we do here!" "Here" was the fictional Hogwarts School, but the remark makes the important point that music has an allure, an enchantment, and it is certainly well suited to the students at a school for an affluent and privileged (fictional) population. Music has power and capacity, and embraces and impacts a widespread set of moods, emotions, and feelings. Music is about love, joy and sadness, life and death, together- and alone-ness, even loneliness. It invites reflection and meditation, allows us to wallow in our worries and to work through troubled times. It creates communal feeling and offers a sense of oneness. In *Music Grooves,* Charles Keil (Keil & Feld, 1994) described the manner in which people become consubstantial as they join together in making music and suggested that they enter into a communion with one another, a *communitas,* a deeply physical feeing and fully emotional attachment. Steven Feld, writing in the same book, noted that among the Kaluli of Papua New Guinea, the making of music together results in what is called *dulugu ganalan,* a lift-up over feeling, in which petty differences between people dissolve into wordless sounds and grooves. Music lifts us up, encourages us, and puts us on a pathway to health and well-being.

Because music expresses and connects to human emotion, it also runs the spectrum from positive to notably negative messages and influences. As powerfully productive as it is, music can be hard-hitting and unsparing, too, especially when it is expressed through extreme volume, the high frequency of screeching pitches, and the rough timbres and textures of winds, brass, strings, and percussion instruments. Music is capable of delivering messages of exclusion and violence both in its sonic essence as well as in lyrics it carries, and has served unnervingly as an instrument of torture and humiliation (Fast & Pegley, 2012; Ross, 2016). An admission of the misuses of music by captors of prisoners in times of war does not reduce music's importance, but certainly offers another view of music's uncanny power.

Music has been described poetically, even as its impact also has been studied scientifically (Theorell, 2014). More often than not, music makes us feel good, which is evidenced by the activation of the endorphins, the euphoric bonding that transpires, and the synchronization of heartbeats and breathing rhythms. Music affects the mind and the body, the way we think and feel. It has been found to regulate the emotions, and it also has been recognized as effective in reducing anxiety, fighting depression, and boosting the immune system (Bicknell, 2009). Particular musical features, in particular musical pieces, may impact chemical processes in the body that effect cognitive, emotional, and physical change. For example, upbeat music with fast-paced rhythms may serve to excite us, while slower music at a softer volume works as a sedative to settle us down and relax us. Music that is paired with memories of particular people and events may trigger nostalgic memories, goosebumps, or even chills down the spine (Theorell, 2014). Listening to music, and particularly to music that is personally valued by the listener, has been found to reduce the heart rate and blood pressure in heart disease patients (Bradt, Dileo, & Polvin, 2013).

Music is powerful for its capacity to move us into and out of the ways we think and do, and for how it affects our thoughts, feelings, and behaviors. Not only listening but also acts of singing and playing can make a difference in psychological well-being, a refined sense of focus and attention, working memory, and the executive functioning of the brain. Children who undergo musical training appear to have better verbal memory, reading ability, and pronunciation of second languages (Merrett, Peretz, & Wilson, 2013). Musical training correlates with or may even be the direct cause of plastic changes in auditory, motor, and sensorimotor integration areas. Rhythmic entrainment, which happens through vocalization (chanting and singing), movement and dance, and in the process of learning to play an instrument, is key to honing the temporal processing of information—any information, on any topic (Miendlarzewska & Trost, 2013)—a quality vital to logic and reasoning. While the benefits of music for full-on brain development are yet unclear, it appears fairly obvious that auditory and fine motor skills develop through musical training, and that the transfer of these abilities to phoneme discrimination and general intelligence is strongly evident.

Making music in a social context appears to increase communication, cooperation, and empathy between and among group members (Koelsch, Offermanns, & Franzke, 2010). The theory that music originally developed as a source of social cohesion is widely embraced, and the multiple prosocial results of musical involvement are hailed as important outcomes (Theorell, 2014). These outcomes may differ with the age of the individual, and yet the social benefits are nonetheless present. Adults, especially older adults, are drawn to music for its therapeutic dimensions, as a source of meaning and both social and personal growth, an intense and inner experience. Children and youth see music as a way of connecting with friends, escaping bad moods, releasing pent-up energy, and occasionally finding a private "personal space," especially in their free-listening time. Music is formidable in its impact, and experiences in performing, creating, and listening offer a sense of power, even as we move through life and the fulfillment of social, sensual, and spiritual needs.

LIVING MUSICAL-CULTURAL EXPERIENCE

Music is a constant in everyday life. People spend a considerable chunk of their waking hours listening to it; responding to it in movement, gesture, and groove; and singing, chanting, whistling, and playing it on instruments (and sometimes on non-instrument objects that have the capacity for sound-making, like tapping out rhythms on available surfaces such as buckets, cans and tabletops). Music is a vehicle for knowing culture, a way to understand the self, the other, and the relationships between them. Music is reflective of the individual, the group, and the all-encompassing metaculture. That music is alive and well, and very present in our lives regardless of age, race, gender, circumstance, and social status, is a fact. Some cases of people's interactions and involvements with music are documented below. These accounts offer multiple perspectives on culture, because the cases depict music in particular times and places, and within specific cultural contexts, as it is experienced and as it is learned both through formal music-educational means as well as informally. Music knows no bounds, as these stories suggest: It permeates human life from infancy onward, through stages of advancing age, and into the golden years of the elderly.

Early Music

Little Lonnie is cuddled there in his bassinette, barely 3 weeks old, swaddled in soft blue sleepers, supine and cozy. His mom and dad have read the parenting manuals and have listened to family members and friends, all advising them to share the music they love as soundscape for their new son, "from day one." Lonnie's newborn hair is dark, tufted, and slightly wet with sweat. His glassy eyes are open wide and glistening, his eyebrows furrowed in concentration on the synthesized sound of stringed instruments that move in a slow progression of minor-keyed chords. To the ringing music-box timbre of a treble melody, he looks straight ahead with his eyes welling up in tears. He shifts his glance and head upward. Slowly, he turns his head right and then left, and brings himself to settle his gaze heavenward again as the melody soars, now raising little fists to his neck, his fingers opening and closing in slow motion. Can he comprehend the musical meaning, as it was intended by the composer? Will he respond to all music with such curiosity and spirit, coming at him from his family, his community, and the wider world? Will he be drawn to art music, folk and traditional music, popular music? Will he take to an instrument, with his family's encouragement? Does it matter? For him and for now, the music has reached him and has evoked in him a profound emotional response. Now, at well into 2 minutes of the looped musical track, little Lonnie yawns and closes his eyelids. He has concentrated and now finds contentment, and drifts off to sleep.

A Musical Language

James is just 2, standing in his purple print jammies with his back against the living room sofa, rocking rhythmically from side to side to the beatbox track. His father sits next to him, eyes cast downward, nodding in time to the beatbox groove, injecting an occasional "ah" and "yo." James is musically alive, his left hand moving expressively into the air at chest level. His utterances are articulate and intentional, high-pitched and running in one phrase after another, precisely observant of the spaces in the music where his words can flow: "Ah dah-doo inna aye dee dee," "Ah yoo yabba ooh ee," and "Ah yo ah yo ah yo dah-doo." The phonemes of his utterances are not translatable, but the meaning and mood are straightforward: James is expressing flat-out joy and flow in the rhythm he is riding. He's hip-hopping as only a talented 2-year-old can, his vocal expressions and his bouncing little body locked to the beat, the subdivisions of the beat, the syncopations and polyrhythmic textures in the mix of percussive instruments and voices he hears. "C'mon," says the father to his little boy, and James gently grabs his father's sleeve, locks into his father's recurring head nod, and then follows into another round of hip-hop mastery as he rhythmically babbles his secret syllables while rocking and gesturing. His formal language is at least 50 words, so says his father as the beatbox track fades away and James curls himself up into the shape of a little ball. But when a good beat comes on, James again will abandon the formal vocabulary and release his own musical expressions in the phonemes of his choice, bouncing away as he goes. Music is there for him, prior to (and in spite of) the language he's at the edge of knowing.

A Welcome Ritual

Mr. Waugh is a powerhouse in his classroom. In his particular way of welcoming his 5th-grade students, he sets the tone for his genuine interest in their well-being through routines characterized by movement that is rhythmic to watch (and sometimes to listen to as well). Mr. Waugh can groove, and he does so daily with his students. Dressed in well-tailored dress pants, a white shirt, striped tie, and silk vest, he scans the line of students that forms outside his classroom door. They're stationed head-behind-head against the cinder-block wall, awaiting their chance at a hand-clapping routine that each one has devised with him individually, an imprint of who they are and what their interactive relationship is with him. They feel the connection with their teacher, who looks them squarely in the eye as the student's own personal signature handshake takes off. Sometimes their movement is full-bodied, and head, shoulders, knees, toes, and torso are in rhythmic motion together, and the routine is a shared musical ritual. Mr. Waugh describes the necessity of the greeting ritual for his students, noting that "the gestures we make are beyond a simple 'hello.' We've figured our 'welcome' out together, and this is a daily routine. There's an unspoken tribute to the groove of a hip-hop maneuver that makes 'the connect' for us and ensures that we are in this learning venture together." With student investment in a lively ritual that is inherently musical, Mr. Waugh then can deliver students to the learning they will do in his classroom. He builds trust and gives joy to his students from the outset, and they radiate a kind of controlled energy that follows them into the classroom and into their focus on the academic work they will accomplish.

Jazz Dream

In their 3rd-period daily rehearsal session at JFK High School, the "boys in the band" (plus one girl) at first may appear raggle-taggle but they are musically fierce. They are an 18-member jazz band, dressed in their daily wear of jeans and t-shirts, horns and saxes honking away to a tight groove coming out of the "engine room" trio of piano, drums, and bass. They take private instrumental lessons in school from district-funded contract teachers, and they're in full force for extra before-school rehearsals with their expert and earnest band teacher, Mr. Marshall. They're a mix-and-match of kids coming through a school system that cares about access by all its students to education in the arts (equivalent to, rather than left behind, student access to education in math and science, language arts, and the social sciences). These jazzers have each made the grade, passing auditions, honing skills through home practice, and playing the gold-standard pieces of Duke Ellington and Cole Porter at a level far beyond what most mid-teens can muster. They come from an urban neighborhood of low-income, single-parent, and nontraditional families, and they are drawn together by a dream to play jazz, the school-approved "music of cool." Mr. Marshall finds ways, through district funds and private donors, to ensure that all kids who want to play, can play, and finds the funds necessary to support their lessons, instrument rental, reeds, concert apparel, and travel to festivals. The students are collectively a rainbow of races, ethnicities, and religions, and they are driven to become something musically special, both alone and together. Taking skillful solos on "Night in Tunisia" and "Body and Soul," it appears that these JFK High School musicians may be well on their way to "living the dream" through their embrace of jazz in all its high-end American artistry.

Drum!

It's Thursday evening, and the small fellowship room in the steam-heated basement of an old neighborhood church is filled with a group of mostly White 30-somethings, about a dozen women and a handful of men, dressed in after-work casual attire. They are seated shoulder-to-shoulder in a tight semicircle, each with a brightly colored drum directly in front of them. They are the African Drum Class, imitating the rhythmic phrases played on a small strapped-on drum by their teacher, an energetic young woman dressed in a long and flowing tie-dyed turquoise dress. She plays an eight-beat rhythm, and they play it back immediately (and precisely). The adult drummers are functioning as a single organism, entirely in sync with one another, and fully attuned to the quick pace of their leader's rhythm. The imitation exercise is continued with successive members of the group taking the lead role, and each lead player is acknowledged with applause and smiles. The teacher next turns to call-and-response tactics, playing one phrase, expecting full-group imitation, followed one by one with eight-beat improvisations that likewise are imitated by the group. Around the room they go, and the flow is remarkably musical, each drummer taking a turn. The group is on fire, their leader runs a few new rhythms by them with specific drum strokes, and there's a conscious sense of collaboration afoot as the percussive sounds pitch forward. The players seem to fall into a trance, until one woman sends off a smile that is caught by a full section of players who beam back at her their own radiant joy. In a lull between exercises, two women are overheard discussing ways in which these rhythms are seeping out into their own teaching in two local middle schools as openings, closings, and transitions that can be tapped and clapped between academic activities.

A Choral Union

The adult choir at their local church draws Lisa, LaBelle, and Melanie together every Wednesday night and Sunday morning to sing and to socialize. Now in their 50s, with their children gone from their homes into professional careers and child raising in families of their own, the women have time to develop new interests and involvements. It was a natural move for them, as long-term parishioners, to volunteer their voices to learning, at the midweek rehearsals, the music that is sung at the 10 a.m. Sunday morning Mass. The three friends join others in the mixed group of some 30 voices, where women outnumber men by a ratio of four to one and the majority of singers are in their 50s and 60s (but are joined by several singers in their 20s). They sing in unison the standard liturgical music of the Proper of the Mass, including the *Gloria*, the *Credo*, the *Sanctus*, and the *Agnus Dei*, as well as contemporary Catholic service hymns such as "Let There Be Peace on Earth," "Ubi Caritas," and "On Eagle's Wings," along with older standards like "Panis Angelicus" and "Ave Verum Corpus." LaBelle presses the group to diversify and has made progress as the repertoire expands to include "Steal Away," "Soon and Very Soon," and "Deep River" (which she leads from the piano to ensure that "folks got the rhythm"). Lisa treasures the time to join "in prayerful song," as she calls it, while LaBelle and Melanie agree that the rehearsals are "invigorating exercise" (complete with vocal warm-ups and physical warm-ups) and are "a good bit social," including chat time, a few jokes from the good-humored choir director, and a stop afterward by the three friends for dessert and a drink. They enjoy the singing and like to be actively engaged in parish activities as an important part of their culture of faith. The choir sings together, if not always completely in tune, and there is a sense among them that they constitute a "choral union" for the greater good.

* * *

These stories tell of the lure of music, its appeal and enticement across age, occupations, and stations in life. Some listen, while others are drawn to full participation. Music of many styles, both mediated and live, has seeped into these people's lives. Across the life span, music ebbs and flows, becomes a force, fades away, and returns again. The diversity factor is in play in these accounts of everyday people, whose preferred musical styles emanate from their home and family surrounds, and from their curiosities with music that appears in their life, beckoning their engagement. Music crosses cultures, even as it empowers cultural identity, and thus it is there, nonthreatening, all-embracing, and meeting many needs.

MUSIC IN EDUCATION

In the 2016–2017 protest of the construction of the Dakota Access Pipeline (DAPL), *Mni Wiconi* (Water is life) was the Lakota rallying cry (Weston, 2017). As water is essential for life among the Lakota—and for all of humanity—so, too, is music key to making life worth living, and to living life to the full as thoughtful and sensitive (and musical) beings. Music's place in the education of children and youth is ensured when music is viewed for its deep and abiding benefits in the holistic development of children and youth, and as a critical means of their artistic expression, social–emotional connection, and cultural understanding. Music is an essential human need, and a carefully considered program of musical study offers music's full benefits to learners of every age.

The study of music has a long and accomplished history in educational institutions. It took its place in European universities of the Middle Ages, appearing alongside arithmetic, geometry, astronomy, grammar, logic, and rhetoric as central to a balanced liberal arts curriculum. Music was studied by university students for its theoretical principles, its acoustical components, and its own particular logic and order. Those who fashioned the strong classical education in universities maintained that music's placement was guaranteed not only for its technical features, arguing that geometry involved the same ratios as those found in music, but also for its capacity to purify the soul. Meanwhile, the performance of music was nurtured by cathedrals and churches, convents and monasteries. Orphanages became the precursor of conservatories (or *conservati*, meaning "saved"), where orphans and foundlings in Italian cities such as Naples and Venice were offered lessons in singing and on instruments. By the 18th century, conservatories were fully established so that performers in Italy, Germany, France, and elsewhere could be trained on every European classical musical instrument, while musical study of a theoretical nature was continued as critical core study in universities. Music remained central to a strong liberal arts education as one of the quadrivium subjects through the centuries and was foundational to the education of leaders for the church, civil service, law, and medicine (Mark, 2008).

While a musical education, whether taken at the university or through conservatory training, had become the mark of an educated citizen in Europe, musical study eventually emerged as an offering to school students. Particularly in more-advantaged private schools in Europe and in North America, students were offered opportunities in vocal music and instrumental training, and school choirs and orchestras began to make their appearances. By the 19th century, common schools in the United States were offering free public education for all children of a city, neighborhood, or region (Mark, 2008). Emphasis was on reading, writing, and arithmetic, with studies in history, geography, and algebra and geometry soon following. Through the advocacy of music's role in moral instruction (due partly to the song texts that were featured) and in the physical development of the lungs (for singing) and the articulatory senses, music made its way as a common core subject for study in American elementary schools by the close of the century.

For two centuries in American schools, music has contributed to the holistic education of young people and to the development of their expressive-artistic selves. Music has played a powerful part on the palette of key curricular components for growing the capacity of young people to think, to feel, to create, to get along with others in communal musical experiences, to make something beautiful, expressive, meaningful. As a subject for study, music often appears in school programs alongside courses in math, language arts, and the social sciences to advance the intellectual and socioemotional development of children and youth in elementary and secondary schools. The study of music is a curricular "given" in many school settings and is mandated in elementary school, or even through eighth grade, by many state departments of education. It appears as an important area of elective study in secondary schools and sometimes is required for graduation from high schools as well as for university admission. Educators are viewed as responsible for ensuring that all students have access to music, so that none are excluded from the opportunity to become expressively and artistically educated.

Yet sometimes music does not make the grade and is excluded as a subject for study, especially in school programs that gasp for breath due to budgetary restrictions. Then, band, choir, orchestra, and every other kind of music-educational venture is dismissed with an apology that "we just can't afford it." Music and all the arts—visual art, dance, drama—are put on the chopping block, referred to as peripheral to the core curriculum, unnecessary "frills," and unfit to be counted among the common core subjects. All the images of joyful children in performance mode as singers, players, and dancers, of listening intently and deeply to music's many dimensions under the guidance of specialist teachers, of composing and improvising music of their very own creation, are dismissed as extraneous and expendable. The challenges are considerable in persuading school boards and curriculum specialists of the right of all children to an education in music, despite the data that support the benefits of musical study to children's holistic development.

All people, from every walk of life, deserve music in their lives. They deserve opportunities to listen to it, as well as to become musically expressive singers and players. Music merits a central place in the education of all children and youth in schools, for developing the imagination, for venting emotions, for providing leisure and lifetime skills. Sometimes music is included in the school day in a mandatory way, while sometimes it is an elective course of the student's own choosing. Sometimes musical study is just not available to children or youth, when it is cut out of or cut back from the curriculum, particularly when school finances call for a tightening of the budget.

But the study of music is not an exclusive privilege. Rather, it is a responsibility of educators to decide to keep music with the set of common core understandings and skills that bring wonder and joy to every child. As a curricular offering, music offers children a chance to move from where they musically are *au naturel*, coming from so many home and family settings, to the rich array of skills, understandings, and values that offer them an individual and collective identity. Music plays many roles for students, and a school curriculum inclusive of music is more than just the continuation of a key constituent of a liberal education. Music bridges cultures, and the songs children sing, the pieces they play on so many varied instruments, the dances to which they learn to move in stylistic rhythms, positions, and formations, engage them in holistic ways of understanding their world. Nearly a century ago, "Music for every child" appeared as the banner cry of the fledging but fast-growing Music Supervisors National Conference, an American-based organization (and the predecessor of the Music Educators National Conference and the National Association for Music Education); its meaning is every bit as significant now as it was then. Given that music is a human need, and a human potential awaiting the nurturing of specialist teaching musicians, the study of music of the world's cultures, local and around the globe, is beyond question. Music is life, and musical study is very much key to a more balanced lifelong engagement.

Even while the struggle continues to ensure that music is a strong and solid presence in the school curriculum, the question of whose music will be featured is an ongoing one that sounds only more loudly as school populations become more diversified and as recognition grows in schools and societies of our kindred selves and our interdependence on one another in communities and across the globe. An historic Panel on World Music was commissioned in 1996 by the International Society for Music Education to examine the place of the world's musical practices in education. Led by ethnomusicologist Bruno Nettl, the panel offered a policy statement that hailed the critical need for music teachers to preserve and teach "the music cultures of human society while developing creative and competent musicians for the contemporary world." The recommendations of this panel of ten educators, ethnomusicologists, performers, and composers, were multiple, including:

1. That any musical education, including of course the study of individual musics, repertoires, and instruments, take as a point of departure the existence of a world of musics all of which are worthy of understanding and study.
2. That exposure to local musics, Western art music, and as much foreign music as possible be part of the formal music-educational curricula of all nations; and further that special attention be paid to the musics of ethnic and social groups constituting the national population.
3. That a minimal background in understanding a selection of musics of the world's cultures be part of all teacher education curricula.
4. That music education methods in the teaching of the world's musics be formulated in such a way that the aesthetic integrity of the musics, and when possible their authentic process of transmission, be fully respected. (International Society for Music Education, 1996)

The oft-quoted report of the panel was influential in the development of curricular policy far and wide across the world, even while the challenges were considerable in making change happen. Various national and international organizations and institutions followed suit in declaring the importance of diversity in musically educating young and old, including the National Association for Music Education, the American Orff-Schulwerk Association, the Organization of American Kodály Educators, and the College Music Society. Policy articulations have come forward from these groups, and manifestations of a valuing of musical and cultural diversity have shown themselves in the conference calls and program content at annual meetings, and in some of the publications of their members. The ideals were set in motion late in the 20th century, and yet the awakening and application of these recommendations in the everyday practices of school music programs is a gradual process still seeking full realization.

MUSIC AS A BRIDGE

Schools do not exist in isolation, nor do their curricular programs function without attention to student needs, to the views and values of their families, and to communities that surround and impact them. Music joins other curricular subjects that are enriched through links to communities.

Rarely do effective schools separate from their neighborhoods, and teaching faculty may well be connected to various local and virtual communities of like-minded schools that share similar philosophical missions. School–community partnerships help to create, and serve to confirm, relevant content and learning styles that fit the experiences of children and youth at home, in the family, and in outside friendship groups. Students may spend parts of their days in specific locations of home and school, but their learning continuously unfolds understandings that are paired with and build upon previous knowledge. While the connections between schools and communities vary, the outcomes of these links are notable and well worthy of efforts by teachers to ensure.

Music is a bridge to cultural understanding. Although cultures and communities have unique means of musical expression, many musicians recognize that music transcends arbitrary cultural boundaries to offer a common understanding of the human condition. Collaborations among musicians assert that music bridges the divides that have arisen artificially from diverse races and ethnicities, religions, and political beliefs. As proof of the bridge, consider the various collaborative projects that successfully have joined individuals and their communities together across a spectrum of diversities for purposes of musical and artistic expression and of human understanding through the shared community that is created: the Jerusalem Academy of Music and Dance's performing ensembles of Israeli Jewish and Arab musicians, the West–Eastern Divan workshop every summer in Spain for young musicians from Israel and the Arab world, and the Fez Festival of World Sacred Music that features performers of mystical songs from Azerbaijan, Sufi music from India, and Baroque church music from France. Some of these collaborations are intended for the promotion of dialogue and the creation of a culture of peace, while others that give primary attention to the music itself ultimately land at the same outcome of creating mutual respect for the individuals involved (as well as for their cultural communities).

One of the more prominent bridge-making efforts through music is the Silk Road Ensemble. Described as an ensemble of musicians that co-create art, performance, and ideas, this Grammy Award–winning project comprises performers and composers from across 20 nations and cultures. Internationally acclaimed cellist Yo-Yo Ma formed the ensemble of musicians from throughout Asia, Europe, and North America, and their spectacular cross-cultural musical expressions are captured on six recordings and a documentary film. The ensemble takes its name from the historic network of trade—of silk, curative herbs, religion, and cultural ideals—that stretched from China to Korea and Japan in the East, through Central Asia, Turkey, and Italy in the West, and to India in the South. The cultural connections through music are educational in the efforts of the Silk Road project to provide education in and through music to school students in New York City's public schools and through affiliations with Harvard University and residencies at the University of California, Santa Barbara, the Art Institute of Chicago, and the Aga Khan Museum in Toronto. The Silk Road initiative is aimed at promoting multicultural artistic collaboration, and it inspires and invites replication and development of similar projects that can connect schools with a diversity of musicians, composers, and artists who live in communities nearby.

Music is a human need, widely available, and highly successful in connecting cultures, communities, and schools. It deserves a place in the school curriculum, because a musical education ensures children's capacity to grow more musical through study and experience, and to become acquainted with people and cultures through the music they make—listening to artists, joining musically with them, and learning from them. Delving into the expressive artistic practices of cultures and communities can only enrich the musical, social, and cultural benefits of a musical education to students. With an embrace of multiculturalism, music teachers have a unique opportunity to celebrate music as life, music as cultural identity, and music as a means of knowing the world nearby and across the globe.

CHAPTER 2

The Changing Nature of School Music

This chapter is adapted from P. S. Campbell, "Music Education," in the *Encyclopedia of Diversity in Education*, edited by J. A. Banks, 2012, reproduced with permission of Sage.

An evident clash of cultures recently transpired within the realm of the primary professional organization of American music educators, signaling a discouraging state of affairs at the helm with regard to music, education, and diversity. This regrettable incident, briefly recounted, provides the backdrop for a review of school music across three centuries and of music teaching and learning in the United States from colonial to contemporary times. The chapter offers an understanding of music education from its first appearance as an Anglo-American effort to its embrace of European musical ideals, and to more recent efforts, partly successful, to envelop the musical expressions and music-learning practices of various American groups as well as the planetary possibilities of music as a world phenomenon. The rise of multiculturalism is noted as it has influenced curricular development in school music, and aspects of a long and winding road of philosophical discourse within music and education fields are briefly noted as they relate to this historical précis of the nature of school music as both longstanding and conventional, while also responsive to societal and demographic changes. An historical glance at the evolution of music as a curricular component lends perspective, and a focus on how aspects of diversity have been realized in pioneering school music programs may help in understanding some of the sources and development of today's challenges in crafting policy that plays out in practice.

Historical Artefact. As people accumulate the wisdom of many years, some refer to themselves as an artefact. They recognize that while they are not really "an object produced by human craft," they may well grow into functioning as an historic relic, the remains of a time gone by, and even an auspicious source of information on time and place. With age and experience, people can become historical artefacts, communicating details of a particular time, as well as cultural artefacts, conveying facets and features of a place and people. I'm an artefact.

In taking stock of a half-century of changes in school music culture, I'm astonished to have lived a long history in what seems like a flash of moments, and to have experienced societal change, musical visions and revisions, and educational reform. Like other elders whom I have known, I cannot name the date of my metamorphosis into a kind of historical and cultural artefact—but suddenly I've assumed the role. My life as music student dates to the middle of the past century, and so much of my professional life as a music teacher is situated within the period in which the United States developed from a system aimed at a thoroughly monocultural music education to one that, at its most successful, meets multicultural and intercultural aims. "White flight" was in motion in my early life, but my family stayed firm through the wildfires of demographic change. I can recollect personal stories and images of growing up in the time of the Civil Rights movement, and of racial disquiet in the schools I attended, and the grave inequities experienced by classmates of color. I was in awe of my

African American classmates: Their spirituals and gospel songs captured and conveyed their endless struggles for freedom, justice, and equity, struggles I would never know. Janeen and I stood side by side in the soprano section of our high school choir, both of us with our big voices and intense musical interest, but we all knew who could rock the spirituals like Aretha, and I was drawn to the syncopations she moved, the slides in and out of pitch she could create, and the polyrhythmic feel she could get going with her claps, head-nods, and pops that was absent from my own singing.

Ten and 20 years onward, by the 1990s, there were circumstances in which American school music teachers and university professors alike were receiving directives to diversify the content of their music programs. These were often ignored as irrelevant, but I recall some who were recognizing the need to globalize and to multiculturalize, and who were eagerly seeking resources. Some teachers were transcribing UNESCO-issued recordings of the world's cultures to Western notation, a few were locating Africans who were giving lessons in African drumming, and still others were searching out songs in foreign languages to sing (unfortunately, sometimes in their English-language translations). There were some shining-star teachers, too, who were laboring tirelessly to configure ways to reach children and youth from all sorts of home and community circumstances in their school music classes, planning dynamic learning experiences in the music of West Africa and South Asia, and sending the message that all of these musical cultures were theirs, "ours," and open to everyone to experience.

In order not to appear myopic, relying on my own first-person stories, I suggest a review of the literature to piece together historic change in American society, its schools, and school music content and repertoire. Still, artefacts like me have stories humming inside, and we await the invitation to reveal personal perspectives on critical periods in the development of multicultural sensitivity through music.

PROFILING DIVERSITY

In the spring of 2016, a controversy grew within the American arts sector, triggered by the remarks of the executive director of the National Association for Music Education (NAfME) at a meeting of arts service organizations convened by the National Endowment for the Arts. The remarks sat squarely within the topic of race in America when, in response to a prompt about the challenges facing arts organizations on matters of diversity, inclusion, and equity, Michael Butera made the statement that he could not take action to diversify his NAfME board. He explained the lack of diversity on his board (and in the NAfME membership of 130,000 music teachers) as due to the fact that "Blacks and Latinos lack the keyboard skills needed for this field," and suggested that music theory was a difficult subject of study for minorities—as if to say that they could play music but did not have the capacity to know music analytically. According to some of the seven colleagues at the table with him, there were immediate responses by way of challenges to the statement (McCord, 2016). However, these colleagues were unable to pursue the meaning of the comments when Butera angrily walked out of the room, well in advance of the meeting's scheduled end time. While he had announced earlier that he would need to leave the meeting before it was officially closed, it was the manner and force of his pushback on his colleagues' questions on changes by his organization to accommodate diversity that concerned them. The NAfME executive abruptly departed, leaving no opportunity for a conversation to explore ways and means of shaping a more inclusive structure for this powerful professional organization and reasonable channels for practicing and responding to diversity initiatives in school music programs.

An immediate and collective roar rose up from officers and members of many arts education organizations, including Chamber Music America and the League of American Orchestras, along with multiple voices of NAfME members. There were accusations of (and denials from) the executive director and plenty of shock and awe to go around. Some voiced their confusion that groups of people were singled out as not sufficiently skilled to meet the needs of the profession, while others wondered why in the world keyboard skills were even necessary to conduct a string ensemble, support children's vocal development, teach wind and brass instruments, and guide young listeners into understanding Mozart. While the executive director was placed on administrative leave so that allegations could be investigated, it was announced 24 hours later that he and the NAfME board had agreed that he would not be returning. At the same time, the board announced that a new executive director (Michael Blakeslee, a veteran of the organization for 30 years, although not a woman or a member of a minority group) would take the reins and bring the organization into focus on issues of inclusion and diversity in all matters of music education.

The incident had touched a nerve among members of this historic organization. NAfME was founded in 1907 as the Music Supervisors National Conference, then was named the Music Educators National Conference (MENC), and finally slipped into its current name in 2012. It is an organization of American elementary and secondary school music educators, along with tertiary-level music teacher educators, who are dedicated to the presence of music education in core school curriculum in the United States, and operates on the basis of its century-long slogan, "Music for every child; every child for music." Despite a continuing although sometimes low-profile attention in the field to issues of diversity, inclusion, and equity, these issues were suddenly palpable. Deeply concerning to the membership was the Grand Canyon–like gap that continued to exist between the rhetoric and reality of the American music education system, not only within NAfME but within K–12 schools and in the preparation of musicians in university programs for school-teaching positions. A call rose up and is continuing to be voiced, demanding a substantive conversation on what music is taught, to whom and by whom, in public and private schools.

The provision of access and opportunity in music, and in all the arts, to all students has become a centerpiece of strategic planning within the professional organizations like NAfME, and in schools and universities as well, and initiatives are more evident now than even a generation ago for making bands, choirs, orchestras, and music teacher education programs look like (and sound like) America in all of its diversity. Still, it's a considerable journey ahead, for an organization that was envisioned at the beginning of the 20th century, to fill the needs of a 21st-century American school-aged population of unprecedented diversity. Similarly, the challenges are considerable for transforming school and university music education programs whose ideals for a musically educated population are rooted in the early 19th century (or earlier).

The development of music as a curricular subject in American schools was shaped by musicians with familial and cultural connections to Europe. The founding ideal of preserving the art music of European masters through transmission and teaching remain strong almost two centuries later, and British-based church hymns from colonial times have had some staying power in the selection of song texts of moral and ethical value to young singers in vocally based programs. Efforts in music education to respond to immigration flows and civil rights are evident, and the journey of jazz to the mainstream of secondary school music offerings is a case in point. So, too, has been the rise of folk songs and dances of many lands over the past century. Even "nonconventional" ensembles such as mariachi, Zimbabwean-styled marimbas, and steel bands have come to the fore of curricular inclusion, in some regions, in the hands of pioneering educators. Yet the concern is real that some of the change may be a gloss, a flirtation with "musica exotica," such that considerations of the broader spectrum of music as a diverse set of expressive practices—and of music as sound, behaviors, and values—have been given small notice. The blatant (and false) statement of the executive director might not have arisen if there had been a full-fledged grasp of the urgency of response to questions of diversity and inclusion, and an awareness of the historical evolution of professional attention to multicultural and global perspectives.

EARLY AMERICAN-STYLE MUSIC LEARNING

Just as music has been prominent in the history of the world (and in all corners of the world), so, too, is the teaching and learning of music a phenomenon to behold across the ages. In the United States, musical styles, contexts, and functions have been documented since the arrival of the asylum seekers from England who sought their religious freedom. (It must be noted that prior to the arrival of Europeans in the New World there was plenty of music among the "First Nations," the Native Americans, but details are not known as to the sound or transmission system in place. Nor is there much detail as to how music was taught and learned in other oral cultures, including those of enslaved Africans in 18th-century American settlements and towns—although some evidence does exist of the music's qualities and characteristics.) Early Anglo-Americans of the colonial period sang their psalms in Protestant church services, and some with curiosity as to how the melodies might be sustained across the generations took an interest in helping singers to learn these songs as they were intended to be sung. Indeed, the education and training of singers in the new-world churches were wrapped around issues of orality, aurality, and notational literacy—learning by ear or by signs and symbols, by note or by rote, from impassioned preservers, some of whom were musically accurate and proficient.

The singing masters associated with the transmission of Christian church hymns were writing their history from 1700 onward as they journeyed on horseback to makeshift singing schools in rural and urban areas across the eastern seaboard, the middle west, and the south. Well-documented are the songs and scriptures they taught, and their tunes and tune books. This early means of a musical education existed in barns and in tents rather than in schools, and adults and children came together in the evenings with their singing masters, who were there to introduce repertoire and demonstrate healthy in-tune singing style. The notation of old tunes and new song compositions by singing masters led to a need for group lessons in note reading, and so the pedagogy of singing was expanded to develop notation-literate singers who could lift their voices in congregational song on Sunday mornings. They learned to sing a repertoire of psalms and songs through the notes that preserve them. Music and music education were alive and well at the dawn of the American nation, but the particulars of most communities are not available. However, adults as well as children were involved as a community who worked their days away and offered prayers of thanksgiving and for good harvests and protection from the elements. Early American-style music transmission and learning were mixed, sometimes "semiformal," and exploratory of what could work to preserve and pass on the songful prayers to yet another generation of hymn singers.

A SONGFUL START WITH A EUROPEAN TWIST

The musical education of children and youth in American schools was established formally in Boston by singing teacher Lowell Mason in 1838 as a songful presence within the school day. Singing was central to this first venture into music as a curricular subject and was established on the basis of three counts: the moral messages of the song texts, the physical exercise (of the lungs and other vital organs), and its intellectual stimulation (via its contribution to a strengthening of the memory), since songs for performance typically were learned through notation and then memorized. School administrators and school board members were equally drawn to these extramusical rationales rather than to the argument of music for music's sake, or that music be taught for its sheer beauty and expressive value. Still, efforts to promote music education for the masses, rather than for the talented few, were heard and heeded.

Lowell Mason was well-known as a hymn collector, including compilations of Anglo-American–styled Sunday school music such as, in 1835, *Juvenile Lyre: Or, Hymns and songs: Religious, moral and cheerful, set to appropriate music. For the use of primary and common schools.* He initiated the "Better Music Movement" in his efforts to bring European song into schools, particularly through the 1844 publication of the *Manual of the Boston Academy of Music* (which was an edited translation of a German collection of school songs). He was fiercely opposed to the folk-like fuguing tunes of Anglo-American composers William Billings and Daniel Read, which featured dance rhythms with independent but occasionally intersecting contrapuntal melodies. Likewise, he excluded the popular modal melodies of folk traditions, such as shape note and sacred harp singing, from the collections for use in schools. Mason favored European-flavored songs and their rule-based compositions for choral and instrumental ensembles in print and in school practice, and the American folk tunes that he viewed as crude and undeveloped were left out of the school music programs he fashioned.

Within a few decades of its launch in Boston, vocal music education became a common curricular practice in elementary schools from Boston to Cincinnati, and southward to Savannah and Atlanta, as children learned to sing by rote and by note a repertoire of European-based folk songs and traditional hymns. Despite the presence of spirituals, field hollers, blues, and other Black-based genres in African American communities in the deep south, these song styles were left out of the approved repertoire of songs and singing practice in schools. Instead, school music in the time of and following the Civil War continued to feature English translations of European songs and other English-language songs, all of which were selected for texts that celebrated beauty, friendship, peace, and good cheer. The Old World of Europe was seen as the source for music of highest intellectual and moral value, while the music of new-world Americans was perceived by pioneering school music supervisors and teachers as much less sophisticated and unworthy of inclusion.

School choirs, bands, and orchestras began to appear in secondary schools by the late 19th century, and experiences of the music of Beethoven,

Brahms, Mozart, and Mendelssohn rapidly developed for the aesthetic-expressive education of adolescents. Of course, students of this era frequently discontinued their schooling beyond the compulsory age of 10 (or 12), and opportunities for furthering their formal musical education also disappeared. Many Americans were singing sacred and secular music in their communities far beyond the realm of schools, and a few joined formal singing societies in cities like Boston and Philadelphia. Within the formal curriculum, Lowell Mason and his contemporaries agreed that music of the German tradition was of the highest quality so that even the new compositions they were writing for schoolchildren resembled the structures and sentiments of German-origin (and some Italian, French, and British) art music. The first music textbook series, *The Song-Garden,* published by Mason in 1864, consisted of songs by Mozart and Beethoven, and German and Swiss folk tunes. The lack of a presence of American folk music in the standard repertoire for schools, as well as the unwavering homage to European composers and genres, settled in and shaped the opening chapter of music in American education.

SEALING THE LEGACY OF EUROPEAN MUSIC

For nearly a century past the first appearance of music in schools, music educators focused their efforts on singing, notational literacy, and music appreciation. Standard works by European composers such as Bach, Mozart, and Beethoven constituted the repertoire of musical study in elementary and secondary schools, and composed works for school-aged singers and instrumentalists were decidedly European and Euro-American in flavor. A pedagogical sequence was evolving, too, that led to the development of a wide array of graded music textbooks and summer training sessions that would enable classroom teachers to learn scientific and systematic methods for teaching music. Spearheaded by Luther Whiting Mason, a superintendent of music in the Boston primary schools, the design of detailed lesson plans came into use for teaching songs by rote, even as learning by note brought up the other side of a professional debate on the value of the two approaches. Learning by rote, it was argued, developed the aural skills even though it required a strong musician to model the music accurately, while learning by note brought with it the tools for translating centuries of notated music and guaranteed that students could become independent musicians once outside the sphere of their music teachers' influence. While each method has its benefits, notational literacy triumphed and the interest by music teachers in aural skill development markedly diminished from this time forward.

With the invention of the Victrola, and the marketing of the Victor-Victrola Talking Machine after 1900, listening lessons offered homage to the master composers, too, as operatic and orchestral masterpieces by Verdi and

Wagner could be carried right into the music classroom. Although there was a range of recorded styles that included blues, early American jazz, and folk, art, and ritual music from China, Egypt, India, Japan, Korea, and Turkey, Western art music was standard fare for school use among the early recordings. Listening lessons eventually extended beyond the European masterworks, via educational programs on radio as well as through recordings, but there is scant evidence of listening lessons attendant to musical diversity before the mid-20th century.

Choral music continued to make minor inroads as a secondary school venture in the late 19th and early 20th centuries, arising naturally from the vocal emphasis given to music education in elementary schools. Exported music from recent composers such as Brahms, Schubert, and Wagner was making its way into school classes and rehearsals, even as oratorios and other great works of Bach and Handel were heralded and held in very high esteem. Although group violin lessons and school orchestras were coming into being gradually, instrumental music study was mostly a private tuition-based, after-school activity in the 19th century. Violin makers, and makers of clarinets, flutes, and trumpets, were kept busy with requests to outfit music-educational precursors to in-school activity, including community orchestras and bands (there were about 10,000 brass bands nationally in the golden age between 1865 and 1920). At the end of World War I, bandsmen from the battlefields in France and Germany were hired as music teachers in American schools to work with young wind, brass, and percussion musicians in concert and marching bands. Church choirs and touring orchestras intent on the performance of European art music also influenced the organization in schools of glee clubs, mixed choirs, and instrumental ensembles. An increasing number of secondary schools were staffed by specialist teachers in choral and instrumental music. Still, it bears mentioning that public schooling for all students at the turn of the 20th century did not extend beyond the elementary grades, and most students who attended high schools at that time were urban-based, middle-class Whites. Further, since racially segregated schools were the norm in this period, many children of color were attending schools where formal music programs were absent from the curriculum and where instrumental music rarely was offered.

FORBIDDEN "FOLK" MUSIC

Despite the distinctively original expressive forms of some American communities, Western art music forms continued to prevail as the principal curricular content in school music classes well into the 20th century. Soundings of "others" were beginning to appear in neighborhoods of immigrants, and a celebration of "exotic cultures" at the Chicago World's Fair of 1893 brought together in re-created villages performers from far-flung places like

Java, Japan, and Egypt who sang, danced, played, and offered arts and crafts from their far-away homes. Meanwhile, established communities of African Americans in the first decade of the 20th century were developing blues and jazz, shaping sacred music, learning classical music, writing operas (such as Scott Joplin's *Treemonisha*), and performing in symphonies and on the Broadway stage.

The first recordings of Black musicians began to appear in stores at the turn of the 20th century, paving the way for the massive popular music industry that was to come. Referred to as "race music," pioneering jazz masters like Jelly Roll Morton, Bessie Smith, Fletcher Henderson, and Louis Armstrong were far too musically sophisticated to be labeled as "folk" and were developing avid Black and White fans through their recordings and live performances. Later generations moved early jazz forms into swing music as personified by Duke Ellington, which was followed by the bebop of Charlie Parker and Dizzy Gillespie and the "cool" jazz styling of Miles Davis, Ornette Coleman, and John Coltrane. None of this music was "folk," yet it was also forbidden much as folk music genres had been excluded from the curriculum.

Although their presence was notable in the United States for centuries, Mexican Americans sang and played music mostly for themselves, in their own communities, from *corridos* and *rancheras* to the developing regional expressions such as Tejano-styled *conjunto*. Yet despite the sizable Mexican-heritage population in vast territorial areas of what are now California and the American southwest, as well as through a flow of immigrants from Mexico to work in the development of irrigation projects and in planting and harvesting, the music of Mexicans rarely was represented in the recording industry or in schools before the 1930s. Likewise, Puerto Rican folk music genres, from *bomba* to *plena*, were enjoyed by millions of people of Puerto Rican descent living in the United States (especially in New York City and surrounding areas), but made slow progress beyond the local communities. Similarly, other Latin American communities made their own music for themselves, and the industry and education sectors were late in recognizing the value of their diverse expressions. An intrigue with indigenous Native American expressions, developed through the excursions of early ethnomusicologists like Alice Fletcher (1915) and Frances Densmore (1918/2001) to tribal grounds early in the 20th century to record songs and instrumental pieces, rarely was channeled to the public; their recordings were deposited into archives, libraries, and museums.

In schools, the musical expressions of African Americans (and of Latin Americans and Native Americans), whether folk, jazz, or any other labeled style, generally were classified as "primitive" and ill-suited for curricular inclusion. Indeed, the designation of "folk music" implied, often inaccurately, a minimalist or simplified expression when compared with the sophistication of art music. Spirituals, called "slave hymns," had been forbidden as musically crude and morally corrupt, and even the praise of Antonín Dvorák, world-renowned Czech composer, was ineffective in persuading Americans of their musical merit. A performance by the Fisk Jubilee Singers at a convention of the Music Supervisors National Conference in 1922 was an impressive first encounter, for many music teachers, with the power and sophistication of their choral music, after which spirituals began to surface on the concert programs of school choirs. Other African American popular music forms did not fare so well, however, and were forbidden in the curriculum, including all jazz-related styles. Their associations with saloons and ribald establishments caused concerns by educators that the music itself was cheap, vulgar, and immoral, and thus potentially ruinous to young people. Likewise, gospel music was argued to be too religious for school inclusion, even while the sacred cantatas of J. S. Bach had already found a foothold in secondary school choir repertoires. The wild rhythms of the Jazz Age were summarily excluded from the schools, and in the 1920s neither the Charleston nor "the shimmies" were permitted on school grounds. Even when jazz finally was allowed into some schools in the 1950s as an extracurricular club activity in which students met after school to rehearse for the school dances at which they would perform, the ensembles were referred to as "dance bands" rather than jazz.

FAR AND AWAY SONGS

Folk music of a variety of origins was understood as interesting but not fully appropriate for the enlightenment of young people as expressions of high culture. When millions of immigrants began arriving in America at the end of the 19th century, so, too, did their songs, dances, and instruments, which were performed regularly outside schools for ceremonies and celebrations at churches and community gatherings. In schools, a gradual awakening of interest in the broader palette of musical styles and cultures revealed itself in classrooms where immigrant populations were prominent. From the 1920s onward, "far and away songs" were surfacing in these school classrooms and were translated into English (and sometimes their melodies and rhythms also were changed from the way they would have been sounded and heard within their places of origin). The folk songs were part of the unwritten lore that included folktales, proverbs, and riddles, all of which were transmitted orally, but as they were converted to school use they were put into print, including the conversion of songs and tunes into Western staff notation that could be integrated into notation-heavy school music programs intent upon meeting music literacy goals. Until mid-century, Western Europe remained the principal source of folk music that was meant to diversify the music curriculum, so that music of the Baltic and Balkan nations in the Eastern European reaches was deemed a serious stretch from a more familiar repertoire.

Along with the songs they shared, arriving immigrants were bringing "folk dances from around the world" that ranged from Irish set-dancing to German-style polkas, Greek *tsamikos,* Italian tarantellas, Swedish *hambos,* and Croatian *kolos,* engaging children and youth in settlement houses, community centers, and local schools. Folk dances were accessible to all, as there were no struggles with language in learning to perform them. The increased interest in the early decades of the 20th century in eurhythmic movement, gymnastics and calisthenics, and modern and creative dance further boosted the presence of folk dances in music programs. As technology became available, 78 rpm recordings were played for children in physical education and music classes to provide them with the authentic instrumental music to accompany their rigorous movements in pairs, lines, and circles. Children danced and sang to these recordings, and European folk music found its place alongside the art music of master composers.

A curiosity was growing among teachers and textbook producers for a more varied music repertoire, although before mid-century little curricular development was forthcoming of the array of musical expressions from Africa, Asia, or elsewhere. Integrated and interdisciplinary lesson units were sometimes in play, too, folk songs with geography, history, and literature content. The growth of European folk music in schools was aided by the advent of specially produced recordings of "the world around song," so that as schools were equipped for it, teachers could share Irish, or German, or Italian music alongside the works of Bach, Beethoven, and Brahms.

A LATIN AMERICAN AWARENESS THROUGH MUSIC

A surge of interest in Latin American music arose in the 1930s, much of it due to the Good Neighbor Policy established by the Roosevelt administration that directed cultural exchanges with the countries of Central and South America. Invitations by the State Department brought many artists and educators from Latin America to the United States, even as American music educators traveled south to Mexico, Brazil, and Argentina. Musicologist Charles Seeger, who was born in Mexico City and spent his formative years there, was called upon to deepen his involvement in Latin America in the service of music education. In his "Pan American" years, Seeger worked with MENC to establish exchanges between Latin American and U.S. performers, composers, and educators. South American educators were invited to write articles for the monthly magazine *Music Educators Journal,* and conference workshops occasionally featured Spanish-language songs and folk dances. Some of the works of this period were more musicological than directly relevant to practicing teachers, as attention was directed to the identification of scholarly collections of recordings, the development of scholarly journals (and the music component of the *Handbook of Latin American Studies,* 1943–1950), and the founding of institutes and councils for inter-American research in music. Meanwhile, Seeger advocated the use of Latin American songs and listening experiences in schools, and textbook companies in the 1940s responded to an urgent demand for materials that included those songs and listening selections.

Yet outside of the occasional school orchestra that could tackle a work by Mexican composer Carlos Chavez or Silvestre Revueltas, or a rare band that could play a bolero, rhumba, or other dance form on their winds and brass instruments, music educators often demonstrated their attention to the music of their Latin American neighbors by having students sing "The Mexican Hat Dance" or "La Cucaracha." Meanwhile, the considerable populations of students whose families traced their roots to Mexico, Puerto Rico, the Dominican Republic, Cuba, other parts of the Caribbean, and Central and South America took their places in music classes that were taught, as before, by Western art–trained White teachers who continued in the legacy of largely European art and folk music repertoire. The brilliance of Latin American music remained largely under cover, awaiting translators and intermediaries to integrate this music into university programs of music teacher education and out into the schools.

MUSIC FOR WORLD PEACE AND CIVIC RESPONSIBILITY

By the mid-20th century, a number of events were seeding music curricular change in American schools, not the least of which were rapid transformations in transportation and communications. Societal change was fast and furious, seemingly more so than the 19th-century period of industrialization, and likely greater than efforts earlier in the 20th century to Americanize waves of immigrants into a unified whole. As Americans pulled out of World War II, they were drawn into a Cold War with the Soviet Union that powered a fierce competition for domination of nations and cultures, of land and water rights, and of the quest for satellites in space. From an American presence on various fronts in the war years, previously little-known peoples and places in the West, the Pacific, and well into Africa became known, and curricular interventions were reflecting these worlds. The close of the war energized music educators to seek means for achieving international understanding and world peace, and music was viewed romantically as "the international language." UNESCO established the International Music Council, which in turn set up the International Society for Music Education (and the International Council for Traditional Music) in 1953 with the intent of fostering the presence of world music cultures for performance and study in elementary and secondary schools, and in universities as well. Curricular policy statements in music education were advocating the importance of knowing "music of the world's peoples," and elementary school textbooks were shifting to the presentation of musical cultures through authentic field recordings.

On the home front, the racial inequities that continued across all facets of American society were fueling the formulation of the Civil Rights movement—movements of pride and power in the 1950s and 1960s that gave voice to a harsh history of unequal treatment by White-dominated American society of African Americans, Latin Americans, and Native Americans. When calls for "Black pride," "Brown pride," and "Red pride" went unheeded and built up frustration, pride morphed into power (Black, Brown, and Red), and a struggle for justice rose up that was impassioned and sometimes violent. All mid-century vectors were pointing to the need by American educators to address issues of diversity, equity, and inclusion. The unconstitutionality of a "separate but equal" policy that had guaranteed inherently unequal treatment (along with devastation brought on by wars and conflicts of this period) set off enough alarms to convince educators to reconfigure curricular goals of peace, global awareness, and multicultural understanding. At the same time, an awareness of homemade American music was developing, and musical folkways were giving way to popular music idioms like rhythm-and-blues and rock-and-roll. For most teachers, this "youth music" had been hands off and not fit for schoolwork, even though these forms might have been a window into the sensibilities and understandings of their diverse student populations, and so change came slowly to the acceptance in the curriculum of further musical styles removed from the legacy of Western art music.

UNIVERSITY STUDIES OF WORLD MUSIC CULTURES

With the founding of the Society for Ethnomusicology in 1955, the curiosity of university faculties in performance, historical musicology, music theory, composition, and education was aroused, causing them to wonder about the musical expressions of "the other" and to find some possible relevance in the study of music as a world phenomenon by undergraduate music students. At UCLA, the University of Washington, Wesleyan University, UC-Berkeley, the University of Michigan, Indiana University, and the University of Illinois, the doors were opening in the 1960s and 1970s to studies in the music of India, Japan, and Indonesia, and the ears of music majors (many of them prospective music educators) were opened to a wide spectrum of the world's musical cultures. Gamelan "orchestras" of bronze xylophones and gongs became iconic statements of tertiary-level programs seeking diversity in their content; they were exemplars of high-art Asian music, along with the occasional Japanese *gagaku,* Filipino *kulintang,* and Thai *mahori* ensembles, that began to appear in courtyards or rehearsal rooms to draw students directly into music-making experiences. Some music education students became intrigued with opportunities to learn solo instruments such as Japanese *koto* and *shakuhachi,* Korean *kayagum,* and Chinese *pipa,* if only for the purpose of a deeper understanding of the logical structures and sonorities of new genres (even as most could not imagine having the budget to buy instruments for use by the schoolchildren they one day would teach).

Interest also was developing in universities about the musical traditions of the African continent, particularly as the roots of African American styles could be traced to sub-Saharan African musical features. Visiting artists from Ghana, Nigeria, Senegal and elsewhere in West Africa were invited by university music departments to form drumming ensembles and to lecture on the musical cultures of their communities. Students of music and music education were enlightened about the *ngoma* tradition in which singing, dancing, and drumming are equally valued, even as they were learning to think and act in ways that required their keen attention to rhythmic precision, physical involvement in synchronous movement, and interactive and communal performance. Gospel choirs began to appear at universities, too, although more often within the realm of student activities than as a scheduled course within university music departments.

Latin American music, especially *musica tropical,* blended into the repertoire of jazz ensembles, and Mexican mariachi became a presence on selected campuses in Arizona, California, and Texas. More rarely, a university within driving distance of a reservation found a way to support the residency of a Native American singer, flutist, or drummer. Within several decades of curricular transformation, a balanced diet of musical experiences was seen as achievable in an undergraduate program, although most music programs remained then (and now) European-styled conservatories steeped in the study of Western European art music. Those music students seeking teaching certification in select university programs that diversified their performance and academic offerings were developing a broader palette of musical understandings. They were often keen to collect songs and rhythms, if not full-out instrumental practices, that might be featured, sometimes in modified form, in the education of school-aged children.

ALL-INCLUSIVE MUSIC EDUCATION

With the ways in which technology, communications, and transportation were drawing distant points in the world closer together, music teachers were challenged to rethink repertoire and pedagogical approaches, particularly with the advent of multiculturalism in American society. An all-inclusive music education was bandied about by experienced music teachers (especially in university programs of music teacher education), whose earnest commitment to musical and cultural diversity, and to the ideals of multiculturalism as it could be interpreted within music curriculum and instruction, inspired an assortment of persuasive advocacy essays, teaching materials, and research studies, and an array of clinical presentations at conferences, symposia, workshops, and working sessions in the United States and internationally.

The Tanglewood Symposium of 1967, a gathering of musicians, educators, and corporate leaders, prompted the shifting of policy from European-based musical content to an all-inclusive curriculum comprising popular music, jazz, and music of the world's cultures. The rhetoric of the Declaration published a year later was eloquent, and some were impassioned by the possibilities, but the reality is that few were prepared to work into their school programs the content and method of a more global view of music. Among the memorable statements were those by ethnomusicologist David P. McAllester (1968), who questioned how educators could "go on thinking of 'music' as Western European music, to the exclusion of the infinitely varied forms of musical expression in other parts of the world" (p. 67). He recommended the use of African songs in singing sessions and made note of world music ensembles in university music programs as well as model school programs where children could experience the songs and dances of Israel and various sub-Saharan African cultures. A statement in the Declaration arguing for the inclusion of diverse musical expressions in the curriculum is a memorable and much-quoted recommendation: "Music of all periods, styles, forms, and cultures belongs in the curriculum. The musical repertory should be expanded to involve music of our time in its rich variety, including currently popular teen-age music and avant-garde music, American folk music, and the music of other cultures" (1968, p. 139). Tanglewood galvanized some in the profession to begin to seek and find music to enrich the standard repertoire. It fired up the production of educational materials that could address the need for musical diversity in classes for children and youth.

In the professional literature, labels were ascribed to the movement to diversify the music curriculum, including "multicultural music education," "multiethnic music education," "global music education," "teaching world music," and "cultural diversity in music education." (More-recent labels with overlapping aims include "world music pedagogy," "cultural diversity in music education," and "social justice in music education.") Central principles were articulated: to engage students in the performance and directed listening of music in its multiple manifestations; to teach cultural understanding through the study of music, musicians, and their musical values; and to respond to the identities and interests of individual students within the school community. Musical diversity gradually was gaining a toehold in teachers' discussions—if not actions—of the content of the music curriculum.

Path-breaking "world music educators" served the Tanglewood cause by contributing to the reform of repertoire in textbooks and recordings, especially in the 1970s and 1980s. They modeled content and method of songs and singing styles, polyrhythmic percussion ensembles, folk dancing, and listening experiences that were part analysis and part participation. When district mandates were requiring secondary school band, choir, and orchestra directors, as well as elementary music specialists, to develop broader cultural understandings through music, especially late in the 20th century, the next crop of world music educators engaged in the dissemination of songs, dances, and instrumental pieces, and contributed as well as to the proliferation of multicultural materials in textbooks, on recordings, in "culturally inspired compositions" and arrangements, and through the Internet. These educators joined with ethnomusicologists, culture bearers, and artist-musicians of a grand variety of musical expressions to offer workshops and summer courses for teachers to learn selected musical cultures beyond the Western art music they knew best from their university studies. In selected schools, music educators were experimenting with "African drumming ensembles," steel bands akin to those in Trinidad, and floor-sized marimba ensembles modeled after those found in a handful of sub-Saharan African cultures.

CONTINUING COMMITMENTS TO MUSIC, EDUCATION, AND DIVERSITY

A symposium organized by ethnomusicologists in 1984 stepped aside from questions of repertoire to emphasize instead the manner in which world music cultures are taught and learned. Called the Wesleyan Symposium on the Application of Social Anthropology to the Teaching and Learning of Music, specialists presented on music transmission systems on the African continent, in Bulgaria, among the Hopi, in Iran, and across Polynesia. While there was little provision of curricular content for classroom use in these presentations, the symposium paid tribute to music teaching and learning, the wide-open inclusion of adults and children together in music and dance at cultural ceremonies and celebrations, and the use of ethnomusicology as a teaching tool in discovery of the musical and cultural identities of students in schools. The clamoring had begun among teachers for "music materials," but the ethnomusicologists at this symposium were directing necessary attention to the importance of not just the music but also the culture-specific and cross-cultural behavioral practices, even "rituals," of music teaching and learning.

Two professional groups (MENC, now NAfME, and the Society for Ethnomusicology) and a museum, the Smithsonian Institution, conspired to co-sponsor the Symposium on Multicultural Approaches to Music Education, in 1990. Intended as a three-day event, ethnomusicologists, music educators, and museum curators developed and carried out a series of sessions meant to model the implementation of music in a multicultural school music curriculum. The music of four cultural groups was featured in lectures, demonstration lessons, and pedagogical analysis, embracing definitive features of the music of African Americans, Asian Americans (with attention to Chinese-heritage Americans), Hispanic Americans (particularly Americans whose heritage was traced to Cuba, Puerto Rico, and the Dominican Republic), and Native Americans. The symposium was held on the heels of one of MENC's best-selling publication, *Multicultural Perspectives in Music Education* (Anderson & Campbell, 1989), which was a hefty compilation of age-appropriate lesson plans and ethnomusicologically accurate descriptions of music in a sampling of the world's cultures. This book proved pivotal to the profession, both as a statement of the value of multiculturalizing school music programs as well as a means of specific songs, dances, and instrumental pieces that could be taught to children and youth; second and third editions were published in English and Chinese. The symposium not only sampled several of the lessons in brief, but closed with a Resolution for Future Directions and Actions that confirmed a professional commitment to teaching the music of local and global cultures in schools and in university music teacher education programs, and vowed to encourage accrediting groups to require broad multicultural perspectives for education programs at all levels and in all contexts.

In Europe, a collection of educators, artist-musicians, culture bearers, and ethnomusicologists began meeting in 1992 on the topic of "Teaching World Music"; they soon were joined by Americans tussling with the challenges of multiculturalizing and internationalizing their music programs in schools, universities, and conservatories. In fact, the group collectively referred to themselves as "TWM: Teaching World Music," switching a decade later to "CDIME: Cultural Diversity in Music Education." There are no officers or offices associated with this group, but there is a definitive sense within this network of musicians, educators, and scholars of what they need to know and share with regard to the pedagogy of world music. They meet every 18 months to 2 years, depending on who may be interested in hosting them, in places like Amsterdam, Basel, Brisbane, Dartington, Helsinki, Kathmandu, London, Malmo, Seattle, Singapore, and Sydney. The CDIME gatherings have featured panels, papers, lecture-demonstrations, and workshops on topics of oral transmission, formal and informal education, school–community connections, and pedagogical issues relative to musical diversity and culturally responsive teaching (and learning). Participants share an interest in fostering diversity in the musical education of students of every age and meeting the challenges of teaching musical cultures with integrity. Earlier concerns for authenticity, representation, and context have been joined by considerations of intercultural competence, recontextualization, and even transnationalism. A number of participants have published their pedagogical work in books, recordings, and other media, and one compendium of chapters, *Cultural Diversity in Music Education* (Campbell et al., 2005), that raises challenges while also offering solutions to the practice and theory of world music in educational application.

A second Tanglewood symposium was organized under the auspices of Boston University in 2007, where a small cadre of invited educators and scholars met to take stock of global perspectives in music, its transmission processes, and changes over four decades in the manner in which music is produced, consumed, and understood. Tanglewood II (2007) gave rise to insights on ways that public and private schools might take full advantage of four decades of technological, intellectual, social and cultural transformations since the original meeting. The Declaration called for attention to developing the means to "engage all children as musicians" and to offer a musical education for children, youth, and prospective teachers in university programs that "meets the demands of an evolving musical society." While less oriented to the impassioned call of the first Tanglewood for diverse repertoire and pedagogical approaches, attention was drawn to music as a powerful mode of human expression as well as to the importance of equity and access by all to musical instruction and participation regardless of age, religion, class, nationality, race, ethnicity, disability, culture, gender, and sexual orientation.

Various national and international organizations have created panels, commissions, and study groups to work through the development of music, education, and multiculturalism, so that philosophical and research-based conceptualizations could be worked into practice. Among the efforts was the establishment by the International Society for Music Education of the ISME Panel on World Musics, which crafted a policy statement in 1994 that inspired conference sessions on models of world music teaching for many years to come. Among the panel's recommendations were that "any musical education . . . take as a point of departure the existence of a world of musics all of which are worthy of understanding and study," and that "exposure to local musics, Western art music, and as much foreign music as possible be part of the formal music educational curricula of all nations; and further that special attention be paid to the musics of ethnic and social groups comprising the national population" (Campbell, 1994a, p. 66). A recent effort by another international organization, the International Council for Traditional Music (www.ictmusic.org), is calling attention to issues of music education, diversity, and nondiscriminatory practices relative to students, teachers, musical expressions, and curricular content through its establishment in 2017 of the Music, Education and Social Inclusion Study Group. Comprising ethnomusicologists, heritage musicians, and educators, this group is delving into issues of identity in education, transmission practices, social inclusion, and other broad issues at the confluence of scholarship and practice.

PRINCIPLES IN THE PRACTICE OF MUSICAL DIVERSITY

While considerable progress has been made historically in diversifying content and method in American music education practices, the funding crisis in the arts has limited the capacity of music educators to fully embrace the tenets of a multicultural or world-oriented curriculum. Since the turn of the 21st century, many music educators are making every effort to hold on to their programs, shoring up against the erosion of longstanding traditions in band, choir, orchestra, and conventional song-based elementary music programs. Opportunities for professional development in selected world music cultures, more readily available to teachers through grant-funded projects a generation ago, have decreased, and the luxury of retraining, of having the time, energy, and funding to learn a second or third musical culture, appears to be in recession. A backlash to the movement to multiculturalize the curriculum has arisen in the post-9/11 period, as music educators have drawn their attention back to the traditional repertoire of standard school ensembles that is based in European and Euro-American practices. One pervasive position in the music education profession is the belief that students require a long and intensive training in a single culture's music to enable their performance of it, and thus many music educators continue to view those instrumental and choral-vocal traditions that are based in Western European art music sensibilities to be the logical first choice for the curriculum. (After all, this art music is still the principal focus of education and training in undergraduate programs in music.) Given dwindling time for music within the school-day schedule, a monocultural approach remains widely in practice to sustain the repertoire of the historical school music culture, alongside the multicultural-lite treatment of music beyond the West; accordingly, music from just about anywhere else in the world may sound more like a generic Western-influenced school brand of music than like music from its place of origin. Some of the experimental world music ensembles of several decades ago are increasingly marginalized (if not already disappeared), because a retreat to standard historic and conventional practices appears to be the natural regression-to-the-mean response by many in the face of fiscal and sociopolitical constraints.

Yet despite the obstacles, there are exemplary models of music education practice attendant to matters of musical and cultural diversity. The emergence of a community consciousness has motivated music educators to be in touch with musicians living locally, and gospel choir singers, Irish fiddlers, Puerto Rican salsa-style percussionists, Japanese koto players, and Native American singer-storytellers have served as resident artists in schools, providing up-front and personal experiences with music and musicians. In this way, informal and formal learning circumstances are wedded, and students are offered personal and communal expressions of artistic, social, political, and cultural concerns from a wide span of the world's musical cultures. There are pockets of promising practices, and yet deep reckonings with diversity, equity, and inclusion have yet to transpire in many schools. Ironically, while contemporary performers of folk, world, jazz, and art music represent various races and identities, music teachers are overwhelmingly White, music is entirely absent from the programs of many underserved urban school populations, and the content of the music curriculum is sadly not aligned with the array of dynamic sounds available locally and globally. The story of music, education, and diversity is left undone, and the slogan "Music for every child; every child for music" remains unrealized and unfulfilled.

The challenges are real for crafting a music curriculum that embraces the music of local and global communities, and the interests and needs of children and youth of a variety of circumstances. Key to the development of effective learning pathways in music is that they are resonant with the origin cultures of the musical selections as well as with the cultures of students. The changing nature of school music requires teachers who will live up to the realities of musical diversity, demographic changes, and global connections. This, alongside the fashioning of values for more-inclusive professional organizations, may help meet the challenges of transforming school and university music education programs for the 21st century.

An Artefact's Story. An historical artefact can conjure up images from her childhood memories, with meaningful messages attached. At a time of small-box, black-and-white TVs and newsprint comic books, ca. 1960, I was a fan of Superman. He had curly dark hair like my Dad, he liked smart girls, and he could fly. I loved the opening music to the Saturday morning show, which would call us from breakfast to a spot on the living floor in front of the "box." It was orchestral music, full of lush strings and bold brass "victory" sounds that messaged great strength, which gave way to the voice-over of a male baritone pronouncing my idol as "faster than a speeding bullet, more powerful than a locomotive, able to leap tall buildings in a single bound." Pure fantasy, of course, but just the sort of hero some of us were weaned on in that time, and with theme music that conveyed courage, adventure, and wisdom. I recall a comic book image, too, that became "signage" of the era, plastered on the walls of schools and gyms: Superman, standing on the ground in his blue, red, and yellow warrior garb, a smile on his face, his index finger pointing upward, his red cape catching the breeze as it unfurled behind him. He was radiating bright yellow rays, and he was surrounded by a group of adolescent-aged boys in cardigans and khakis, one hugging a basketball and another leaning on a bicycle with his letter-sweater in view. He was facing a girl with her hands clasped demurely behind her, and his strong hand was gently patting the head of a young Asian boy. The word balloon above him hung there in the radiant bright yellow rays: "And remember, boys and girls, your school—like our country—is made up of Americans of many different races, religions, and national origins, so . . ." The sentence was completed in black print at the bottom of the cartoon square, "If YOU hear anybody talk against a schoolmate or anyone else because of his religion, race or national origin—don't wait: tell him THAT KIND OF TALK IS UN-AMERICAN." And there was a white-on-dark-blue banner at the very bottom of the page that read, "HELP KEEP YOUR SCHOOL ALL-AMERICAN!"

The message of the superhero had staying power for me, and in my mind I had joined the familiar musical theme to the message, steering me to a sense of connections between musical power and cultural equity. A half-century since the time of Superman, we might wonder: Are all children so impressionistic at an early age? What do they learn from an image, a program on TV, a sequence in a film, a thought on the Internet? How do we work with mediated images, separating so much chaff from the wheat? How do we balance the good, the bad, and the ugly, using negative matter as teaching moments? How do we supply positive perspectives atop images of violence, abuse, abandonment, and uncivil society? Can real and fictional heroes, and political leaders, model moral behavior and respect for all cultures? Finally, what are the musical works and songs that bring a shared sense of freedom, justice, honor, and reverence for all the world? Can the act of music-making help to dissolve negative connotations of difference through the sort of social bonding that develops among those who sing, play, and dance together?

CHAPTER 3

Educational Intersections of Ethnomusicological Ideals

The convergence of the fields of ethnomusicology and music education is examined in the chapter. Music educators view ethnomusicology as an affiliated and relevant scholarly discipline that provides potential musical content for the shaping of more diversified musical experiences in the curriculum, while ethnomusicological studies in transmission and learning processes are also present although not often recognized, but which are relevant to the work they do in schools. Continuing efforts at the cusp of the two fields are noted for contributing to musically and multiculturally educating students in university programs, and school music practices are acknowledged for their direct line to enlightened teacher education programs and professional development courses where ethnomusicological ideals and "world music materials" are substantive and relevant. Attention is turned toward interests by ethnomusicologists in music education practice, and efforts by music educators in their adapting of ethnomusicological methods, theories, and concepts to questions of teaching and learning. A discussion ensues of concepts out of ethnomusicology that are deemed relevant by music educators in their development of policy and practice: *bimusicality* (and multimusicality) regarding the entrainment of musicians in the nuances of music in various practices; *authenticity* as it pertains to musical details to be preserved in teaching/learning music; *representation* as to which music is featured from a community but with precautions as to essentializing and stereotyping; and *context* (including the decontextualization and recontextualization of music as it is studied outside its community of origin).

Crossroads. I watched from afar the unfolding of a program in music education studies at the University of Washington that was replete with diversity principles. Working in the midwest, I was captivated by the vision of Professor Barbara Reeder Lundquist for a more multicultural approach to music education that she had set in motion since her time as a graduate student there in the 1960s. She had been a student of Robert Garfias, founding professor of the ethnomusicology program at the university, and was well-attuned to the works of James A. Banks and his colleagues in the university's Center for Multicultural Education just next door. Barbara had come to work in music teacher education from successful school-teaching experience in the multicultural central district of the Seattle City Schools, and she returned there to teach with relish and by choice ("I had many questions about teaching kids, and had to get back to them in order to learn from them"), taking leave for three years from her position as university professor in the 1970s. She developed the first-known African drumming ensemble in a North American school (ca. 1965), working daily with kids who learned from her via oral-aural processes and who played with energy and verve. With the proximity of the programs in ethnomusicology and multicultural education, Barbara was inspired to work steadily and with enthusiastic conviction of the need to shape a program in music teacher education that would be sensitive to urban cultures, popular (as well as art and folk) music, and a global array of musical practices and cultural perspectives. Standing at the crossroads of the fields in a time of deep need for new ideas about repertoire and how to teach it, Barbara Reeder Lundquist crisscrossed the fields of ethnomusicology and education with style and a dynamic spirit in bringing about the inevitable development of multicultural music education. While she was fashioning the field, I was enrolled at Kent State University's Center for the Study of World Music. There I found myself, unknowingly at first and then jubilant on recognition that my PhD program of study was shaped through the collaborative efforts of intersecting faculty in music education (William M. Anderson, Terry Lee Kuhn, and Virginia Mead) and ethnomusicology (Terry E. Miller and Halim El-Dabh), all of whom facilitated my journey into music, education, and multiculturalism. As life courses sometimes dovetail, it was not so very much later that I found myself on the Washington faculty with Barbara, co-teaching with her, fitting the insights from my studies with fine mentors at Kent State with her trademark high-energy and razor-sharp music-educational flair. Anchored in the work of my intersecting mentors, I've enjoyed the privilege of working with this tempest of a master music teacher and feel propelled to stay the course at the intersections of the fields.

SOFT BOUNDARIES AND BORDER CROSSINGS

Despite the unique natures of the two fields, where ethnomusicology involves the study of music cultures while music education concerns the music teaching–learning process, the conditions for border crossings have never been better. Ethnomusicology increasingly is leaning toward public humanities and practical matters in the application of ideals to public-sector and community projects, while music education is drawn to ways of responding to the challenge of increasingly diverse student populations in a time of demographic changes in society and schools. Although the borders between the fields appear to remain firm in some "siloed" academic contexts at the tertiary level, the boundaries between the fields are frequently soft so that the intersections of specialist scholars and teachers of music have been intensifying. Fresh from journeys across their own disciplinary boundaries, specialists in both fields are weaving ideas from one another's works into their own. Moreover, there is evidence of a harmonic convergence between the fields, as one field draws from the other and breathes new life into the next ventures that arise.

Ethnomusicologists have ventured into territories traditionally belonging to music education. Some have written practical manuals or short articles that offer content and approaches for teaching music of particular cultural groups. A few have written lengthy descriptive analyses of transmission, teaching, and learning processes, or have served on panels and commissions devoted to diversity issues in music education policy and practice. Some have been active on the teachers' workshop circuit, engaging inservice teachers in the development of techniques and repertoire for use in their classrooms and ensembles. Some are involved in teaching summer courses in world music cultures, and long-standing school music classes and ensembles are expanding their repertoires at record rates due to the collaborative teaching of ethnomusicologists and music education specialists. A few ethnomusicologists have collaborated with music educators in assorted instructional projects, teaching materials, and curricular plans, and more rarely in research. Knowingly and unknowingly, some ethnomusicologists have been influenced by music educators through these collaborations, growing more applied as they learn how the expressed needs of teachers for diversity, equity and inclusion may be satisfied. With and without collaboration or tribute paid to the scholarship of music educators, some ethnomusicologists are studying the very raison d'etre of music education, the teaching and learning processes of master and aspirant musicians. In shifting their professional lens from the study of music alone to the study of music-makers, ethnomusicologists have developed a participant-observation approach to research that has turned them into students of a musical system: They are learning from the masters, and by this very act have been drawn into questions of music's pedagogy, training, and educational systems.

Border crossings, it seems, are happening in both directions, and the cross-fertilization of the fields is bringing them closer together. Within the realm of academic research, there is now a small cadre of music education scholars worldwide who are utilizing an ethnomusicological method in their pursuit of questions relevant to music learning and instruction. The pathways across the music education border to ethnomusicology and back clearly have been cut, making way for new understandings of music, teaching and learning, and research inquiry.

INTERSECTIONS AT THE UNIVERSITY LEVEL

Music in higher education has not kept pace with dramatic changes in society. Four-year BA and BM undergraduate degree programs are tailored toward individual lessons on a principal instrument (be it piano, voice, or any of the orchestral instruments); ensemble performance experiences in university orchestras, choirs, symphonic bands, and various chamber groups; and academic courses in music theory and history. For those students preparing to teach music in schools, there are music education methods courses for teaching vocal-choral, instrumental, and classroom music in elementary and secondary schools; field experiences in schools; and supervised student teaching internships. This university music curricular plan recalls the 19th-century conservatory model and is held intact through accreditation by the National Association of Schools of Music, whose aim since its founding in 1924 has been the education of musicians who can advance classical Western European music in their work as performers in homegrown regional orchestras, opera companies, choral societies, and wind bands, and as teachers in schools. Despite music's centrality to all cultures and societies, the core aspects of undergraduate music study have remained largely insulated from relevance to diverse cultures and the influences of technology. University music schools and departments continue to give almost exclusive emphasis to Western European classical music.

There are notable exceptions to Eurocentric programs in higher education music studies, and a half-century of experimental courses and the introduction of new ensembles are proof positive that musical diversity can be woven into the preparation of university music students for work as performers, composers, and teachers. Early on, university faculty with specializations in music education and composition were especially receptive to hiring ethnomusicologists for their programs who might establish ensembles to perform world, folk, and traditional music. They were intrigued by and sometimes enamored of the benefits of having on board music scholars who could expand student perceptions of music and open student awareness to the musical world beyond the symphony halls and opera stages. They recognized the significance of the philosophical stance that some societies held, for example, those in West Africa and the Pacific, on the pan-human capacity for music-making, and were drawn to the optimistic belief that all students, from music majors to those majoring in history, chemistry, and math, could find a place in the music-making experience. They were drawn to the communal nature of some of the world's ensembles as relevant and befitting the original premise of the common school's educational equity, that "what's good for some is good for all." They found appealing the importance of collaborative social experiences in the gamelan or a West African drumming group; as in the case of traditional school bands, choirs, and orchestras, some faculty applauded the noble goal of teaming together for a united musical effort. Globally conscious music educators, including those who recognized that diversity awareness begins on campus and in local communities, joined with ethnomusicologists with interests in music teaching and teachers, and together they began to assert their position of the need for music education students to be enlightened about the diverse musical expressions that could be taught and learned.

Separately but coinciding with the efforts of music education faculty, composition faculty were exploring dimensions of world music for the sonic potentials of "strange" gongs and xylophones, drums, shakers, bells and stamping tubes, multistringed lutes and harps, and one- and two-stringed fiddles. Composers were eager to explore new instruments and to pair them with Western European orchestral instruments in new ways. Some were in awe of performance techniques and were inspired to play familiar instruments in new ways, or to tune them to pitches they had not considered previously. More than a few composers joined their campus gamelans, or independently drifted into studios of visiting artists from Japan, Nigeria, and the Pacific Islands, to discover through performance and dialogue just what made the music of a place "tick." More than other members of a music faculty, composers made their way regularly to concerts on campus and in the community featuring artists from Africa, Asia, and the Americas. As they sought to combine Western and world instruments, elements, and structures, they also recognized the need for hiring heritage musicians as adjunct and affiliate faculty to teach the Japanese flute, Yoruba *dundun* (talking drum) of Nigeria, or polyphonic choral music of Fiji, Samoa, or the Cook Islands. Along with music educators, composers enthusiastically made cases for the creation of permanent faculty positions for ethnomusicologists who could direct ensembles and lead the campaign to open students' ears to the wide world of sonic possibilities.

Ethnomusicologists on faculties of music today may be administratively placed within a department's music history and theory faculty, connected as they are academically to some aspects of musical and cultural analysis of music genres and practices. But in fact ethnomusicologists frequently are hired as a result of cases made by music educators and composers whose valuing of music of the world's cultures runs long and deep. University faculty of music education, in particular, have their ears fixed to local music and musicians; to the popular music of youth culture and the array of children's oral-tradition songs, rhythms, and singing games; and to the music across the world that serves as gateways into cultural understanding. Joined by composers whose intrigue continues with the world's expressive possibilities, music education faculty are striving to stretch music majors' experiences with music beyond the Western classical canon. Still and all, following decades of experimentation, faculty in music history, theory, and performance studies typically defend the merits of Western art music as first and foremost, and declare their accommodation of "other music" as optional study that should only follow or support the foundational Western art music courses of a music-major program. Hope for diversity in university music programs comes from news of exemplary programs that press for innovation and reform, and that view Western music as just one of a constellation of musical cultures for students to know well through university study and experience.

A Manifesto in Motion. The quest continued for diversity in university programs in music when in 2013–2014 the College Music Society's Task Force on the Undergraduate Music Major (TFUMM) was established as a group of eight college and university music faculty from across the United States. Their efforts resulted in the release of a report referred to as the "Manifesto for Progressive Change in the Undergraduate Preparation of Music Majors." The group's exchange across dimensions of artistic practice, pedagogy, scholarship, leadership, and innovation was dynamic and productive, and discussion was keyed to the relevance of programs in music to the social circumstances of contemporary society and the fit of an education for music majors to the work they will do in society and its schools, and in changing communities and cultures. The Manifesto recommends ways in which diversity, creativity, and integration can serve as frameworks for a recrafting of four-year degree programs. Seen as an ongoing deficiency in the education of music majors is its ethnocentric orientation, in that large numbers of music majors graduate with little or no hands-on engagement with music beyond European classical repertoire and without a nod to the multicultural communities that surround them. Thoughtful reflections are offered on the study of world music cultures, with particular attention to music of the African diaspora, including jazz and other African American music genres, and the roots of much American popular music in African societies in which music is sung, played, and danced. Moving beyond superficial mention, the Manifesto has inspired an outpouring of publications and more than a few advances in the reform of undergraduate and graduate degrees in music that are more broadly encompassing of a breadth of cultural manifestations (Sarath, Myers, & Campbell, 2017).

Dramatic changes within the realm of music teacher education unfold as awarenesses of demographic change, and of musical evolutions, become apparent. In universities where ethnomusicology programs are well established, music education faculty seek to work a world cultures survey course and participation in a world music ensemble into curricular offerings for their undergraduate students. In some university programs, music history courses have extended to history-and-culture courses, and music theory courses occasionally journey to the intricacies of the Indian *raga, tala,* and *sargam* system of sight-singing, to polyrhythms from West African cultures, and to the rich harmonies of Georgian choral works. University faculty are now arranging for guest appearances in their methods courses by ethnomusicologists and visiting artists who might provide a demonstration of a musical instrument or genre as illustration of more musically inclusive school repertoire. Early programs in ethnomusicology at UCLA, the University of Michigan, and the University of Washington have led the way in these curricular developments, and Kent State University's establishment of its Center for the Study of the World's Musics was a model that balanced program of Western and world music for prospective teachers seeking degrees and certification. In many music teacher education programs nationally, there is increasing enthusiasm for the inclusion of local and global music practices, and individual courses are being designed to provide students with experiences in performing, composing, and improvising, and to lead music education majors through the very teaching/learning processes that can be taken forward to elementary and secondary school music programs.

While the interweave of diverse musical realities over a four-year music education plan is ideal, it has become standard practice to offer a single course in multicultural music education, or world music pedagogy, social justice, or inclusion. The challenge of just one course is to be able to provide full exposure, experience, and education in the issues and their translation to teaching and learning practice, when "inclusion" is a tall order that may require covering bases as disparate as special needs, gender and sexuality, and all the world's music cultures. A distribution of some of these topics into selected methods courses across the entirety of the degree program is reasonable, while a single course in a credit-intensive program may align itself well with the pedagogy of diverse global and local musical expressions.

One classic course of this nature is called Ethnomusicology in the Schools, which represents the efforts of a music education faculty involved in integrating principles and practices of ethnomusicology with multicultural and global education studies. The course has been in place for 40 years at the University of Washington and has shifted from an introduction to an array of ways in which music is conceived and perceived, with the accent on African and African American practices, to a course that features a broader span of world music cultures as well as an aggressive thrust into the realities of teaching in a community removed from the lives of university students. The course components involve a set of 30 in-class experiences, individual out-of-class assignments, and an off-campus, week-long residency in a community to sample-teach music of many cultures while also learning the music of the local people by listening and "doing" music, that is, singing, dancing, and playing the local traditions. Much is made of "listening to the world" across 59 selected tracks (with an identification test to follow), developing a music-culture curricular unit for implementation with young learners in a school, learning 30 traditional songs by ear from recorded sources (with no notation), and participating in a week-long, live-in residency of music teaching and learning in a poor rural community with significant populations of Mexicans, Mexican Americans, and Native Americans. The course is intended to ensure that, as a result of participatory experiences in music and teaching, prospective teachers will think globally and act locally in music and through music, expand their musical repertoire, learn through the oral transmission process, and develop relationships with students in a cultural-multicultural community far from campus.

The task of raising up musicians who are broadly trained in music is a daunting one, comparable to the mission of developing responsible citizens who think and act with sensitivity to the diverse perspectives of a multicultural population. University programs are notoriously slow to change, and honored traditions of content and process die hard while new visions take time to embrace and enact. The intersections of ethnomusicologists with music educators (and composers) were historic even as they are continuing, and the benefits of these intersections to music education in a time of tremendous musical and cultural diversity warrant our continued effort.

SERVING INSERVICE TEACHERS

Teachers regularly seek professional development so as to stay attuned to their content knowledge and pedagogical effectiveness, and music teachers are determined to know more music, more of music's interface with technology and the media, more pedagogical twists and turns that communicate to learners of differentiated modalities. The multicultural mandates in their schools and districts bring music teachers together to Saturday workshops, weekend and summer courses, and the music they feature is frequently the direct result of research by ethnomusicologists that has been carefully vetted "fit" for school use by leading music educators. A first generation of inservice clinicians appeared at the time of the Civil Rights movement and continued for decades after to offer teachers resources and insights into ways to teach the music in various school music settings. William M. Anderson, Barbara Reeder Lundquist, Sally Monsour, and James Standifer knew about "multicultural music" materials and methods, often through their own school-teaching practices, their testing and trialing of pedagogical ideas, and their collaborations with ethnomusicologists, culture bearers, and artist-musicians. In their workshops from the 1960s onward, they introduced teachers to African American blues, spirituals, and gospel, and led them to play, on instruments or through body percussion, the complex layered rhythms of sub-Saharan African music from individual cultures in Ghana, Senegal, and the Gambia. They facilitated sequential listening to the classical music of India and Indonesia, opening the window to singing Hindustani raga-like melodies while clapping *tala* rhythms and playing Javanese gamelan melodies and gong phrases on available classroom instruments. They offered opportunities to sing Arabic-language folk songs and dance in circle- and line-formations to the music of Lebanon, Jordan, Syria, and cultures of the Arabian Peninsula. In their time, they often introduced music, in their workshops, to teachers who had never before heard these unfamiliar styles despite their four-year and graduate degrees in (Western art) music.

The dissemination of world music cultures, and their pedagogy, continued via workshops and clinical activity through the heyday of multicultural music education in North America in the 1980s and 1990s, as it persists today. Often, this second generation of workshop leaders were graduates of those very teacher education programs that had successfully melded ethnomusicology into their standard methods courses. Among American music educators active during this period in clinical demonstrations of methods and materials for teaching the world's musical cultures were Bryan Burton, Ellen McCullough-Brabson, Mary Goetze, Doug Goodkin, Rita Klinger, Marvelene Moore, Mary Shamrock (and myself). They offered sessions, particularly to teachers of secondary school choirs and elementary school vocal and general classroom music, on teaching music cross-culturally and in culture-specific units such as Native American social songs and dances, choral song in African, African American, and Maori styles, and adult music and children's games from China, Ghana, Japan, Indonesia, Israel, Vietnam, and Zimbabwe. They were featured in school districts and at national and international meetings of the Music Educators National Conference, the American Choral Directors Association, the American Orff-Schulwerk Association, the College Music Society, the Organization of American Kódaly Educators, and the International Society for Music Education. Except for chiefly instrumental music education gatherings, such as the annual instrumentally-based Midwest Clinic where conference programs are intent on sustaining and celebrating the longstanding American concert band tradition, school music repertoire was beginning to change through the efforts of multiculturalist music educators. Ethnomusicologists such as Michael

Bakan, Mellonee Burnim, Han Kuo-Huang, Dale Olsen, Portia Maultsby, Tim Rice, and George Sawa were among those who offered workshops to teachers alone or in tandem with music educators on the music of their training and field study—African American gospel song, Balinese gamelan, Chinese *luogu* (drum and gong ensemble), Andean flutes and pipes, Bulgarian dance music, and Middle Eastern *maqam*-based melodies. A third generation of music educators, including Carlos Abril, Sarah Bartolome, Amy Beegle, Lily Chen-Hafteck, David Hebert, Juliet Hess, Karen Howard, Vicki Lind, Constance McKoy, Christopher Roberts, Amanda Soto, Brent Talbot, is leading the way in culturally responsive music pedagogy, social justice projects in music, and pedagogical approaches that feature diverse musical expressions in music ensembles and classes.

Beyond the music-making experiences of so many workshops, a kind of professional development occurs in symposia and conferences that are especially designed to attend to relevant issues of music, education, and culture. There are boundary-breaking moments in the progress made in diversifying music education practices and policies, from Tanglewood (see Choate, 1968) to the meeting on "Music Education and Social Inclusion" under the auspices of the International Council for Traditional Music (www.ictmusic.org). (See Chapter 2 for descriptions of these and other events featuring intersections of ethnomusicology and music education.) In these venues and circumstances, the professional development is in the mostly verbal exchange in presentations relevant to curricular frameworks, the postulations of philosophical ideals into practical application, and the descriptions and analyses of pedagogical models. Ethnomusicologists are drawn to these gatherings to imagine changes in the way of repertoire and pedagogical approach, and the unique cultural perspectives that are gained through musical study and experience; their collaborations with music educators is continuing progress in clarifying multiculturalism as it can be meaningfully tailored to the education of music teachers.

CROSS-OVER SCHOLARSHIP

Among the topics of mutual interest between ethnomusicologists and educators are those of music transmission, teaching and learning, music cognition, the musical cultures of children and youth at play, in social interactions, and in their informal play. Rice (2003a) documents the considerable extent of studies by ethnomusicologists on music teaching and learning; the rise of interest in scholarship on children's musical cultures is reflected in works by ethnomusicologists Tyler Bickford (2017), Andrea Emberly (2014), and with Mudzunga Juniah Dahvula (Emberly & Dahvula, 2014), and Amanda Minks (2013b). (See Chapter 6 for attention to the topic.) Further, the mind–body and music–dance dualities have captured the interests of ethnomusicologists such as Charles Keil and Steven Feld (1994), even as movement and dance are also central to music pedagogical processes espoused by influential pedagogues such as Emile Jaques-Dalcroze in school music teaching (Campbell & Scott-Kassner, 2017).

In classic fieldwork and the musical ethnographies that have resulted from it, the participant-performance approach to research quite naturally has placed ethnomusicologists in the position of students learning repertoire and techniques from artist-teachers of *sitar* and *sarod, mbira, kora,* and instruments of the *gamelan.* Early ethnomusicologists like Mantle Hood at UCLA and Robert Garfias at the University of Washington institutionalized within the field of ethnomusicology a performance approach to musical understanding. Hood (1971) subscribed to the concept of bimusicality, testimony to the importance to ethnomusicologists of learning a second culture, and he vociferously claimed that the well-trained ethnomusicologist should be able to function musically in two cultures (or more) as a result of training. Garfias conceived of a visiting artist program for students so that they might learn the music from short- and longer term resident musicians in the manner in which it is traditionally learned and taught (Averill, 2004). Likewise, David McAllester and Robert Brown developed the ethnomusicology program at Wesleyan University with the intent of featuring world music performance as a pathway to learning music and culture. One of the pioneers in the development of fieldwork techniques within ethnomusicology, John Blacking (1973) suggested that engagement in the performance of a musical tradition functions as a research technique and as an aid to musical and cultural understanding. Referring to his early experience in playing blues with blues musicians, Jeff Todd Titon (1992, 2015) claimed that he was "doing ethnomusicology before he studied ethnomusicology," learning about music and musicians by sitting alongside them and playing. To be sure, the view held by ethnomusicologists is logical—that the acts of performance and of learning to perform not only develop bimusicality but reveal insightful understandings of the music, musicians, and musical culture.

For scholars within the field of music education, there are significant influences, particularly in the past 20 years, from ethnomusicology's fieldwork approach and techniques. The scope of music education research is decidedly diverse in its content, since music is taught and learned in many circumstances and settings. The scholarly methods for this research are also multiple, spanning all manner of inquiry, and now running the full gamut of quantitative and qualitative methods, whereas they once were predominantly musicological (through the 1950s) and then experimental. In fact, experimental research in music education was prominent for over three decades, as the field was full of concepts and methodological design from the parent field of psychology (and its subfields of perception and cognition, age-based developmental stages, memory, motivation, and identity). An emergence of qualitative approaches to research came at

the turn of the 21st century. Music education scholars now utilize ethnographic techniques borrowed from ethnomusicologists (who in turn had
borrowed from anthropologists), and students in graduate research programs in music education are pursuing questions of social process and
cultural relevance to musical expressions, classrooms, schools, and neighborhoods—ethnomusicologically.

Trailblazers in the application of the ethnomusicological method to music education were seeking understanding rather than explicit explanations,
and so interviews, observations, and the examination of material culture
from journals to instruments were set into motion. Gregory Booth (1986)
studied the pedagogical techniques of master instrumentalists in India, and
his descriptions of the verbal and nonverbal behaviors of their teaching, as
well as the ambiance of their lessons, are the result of extended fieldwork
there. His transcriptions of master–student interactions at lessons, and musical segments during these lessons, are centrally located in ethnomusicological method. Ramona Holmes (1990) explored as a participant-observer
the aural-oral techniques of a fiddle player in the teaching of beginners in a
community outreach program, which led her to the development of a template for aural instruction applicable in many teaching contexts. Her ethnomusicological process featured transcriptions of class sessions, including
relevant musical segments of the fiddle teacher's demonstration and student
attempts to imitate and emulate their model. The work of both of these
scholars is notable as early examples of the method employed, as are the
backgrounds of their experience and training that led them to their blended
research endeavors: Both had been public school teachers, active musicians
(Booth a *tabla* player and Holmes a fiddler in the Estonian and Celtic traditions), and students of formal ethnomusicology coursework.

Other ethnomusicologically based music education research followed.
Kari Veblen (1991) identified traditional musicians in Ireland whom she
could observe and interview, and stayed close as a participating member
of the Irish musical community there through the course of her study. The
work of Rita Klinger (1996) on culture bearers in the classroom is notable
for the manner in which her living within the community of the school and
the sponsoring organization was able to bring ethnographic insight as to
the nature of school residencies of Native American singers and storytellers. Sheila Feay-Shaw's (2002) study of the transmission of Ghanaian music
by master musicians and music teachers is likewise ethnomusicological in
nature, as she was first a participant-performer in the lessons of one musician and then an observer of the lessons and classes of other musicians and
teachers. In fact, her rich account of her own struggles to learn complicated
cross rhythms demonstrates the reflexivity that has emerged as an important dimension of the ethnomusicological method. In a study of bicultural
sensibility, Amanda Soto (2012) examined the bimusical identity of Mexican American children in a bilingual/bicultural school as they navigated

between different musical and cultural spheres present in their daily lives. She documented the school and home influences of children in the making of their bimusical identity and found children's repertoire to be a mix of Spanish-language children's songs, mediated popular songs, mariachi music, church songs, and songs of the standard school repertoire. Karen Howard (2014) designed a music-culture project to offer as a 14-week exploration by fifth grade students of musical cultures from Africa and the African diaspora. In a study of the synchronous aims and practices of music education and multicultural education in an ethnomusicological manner, she described in colorful detail the daily class journeys into musical cultures unknown to the children, which, assisted by visiting culture bearers, met standard age-appropriate musical and sociocultural learning goals. Important works by Deborah Bradley and Juliet Hess are challenging some of the ways in which Whiteness is operating as racism in music education: Bradley (2012) dissects the frequent use of an old saw like "music is a universal language" as perpetuating a monocultural view of repertoire by excusing the need for teachers to teach music beyond their comfort zone, while Hess (2014) draws attention to the bifurcation of music in the academy as Western classical music and Other (world) music, thus marginalizing Other as an unnecessary frill to the classical curriculum.

The arrival of handbooks on topics within subfields of education and ethnomusicology is further evidence of a cross-section of specialists in the two fields working together to seek answers and resolve issues. While editors may claim one field or another as their home territory, multiple authors have contributed scholarly chapters on their particular expertise. *The Oxford Handbook of Children's Musical Cultures* features 37 chapters that provide accounts of children's musical interests and needs, and their formal and informal means of learning music, in cultures as diverse as the Papago indigenous people of northern Mexico, members of a children's choir in a village church in Sierra Leone, and young North Indian brass players in their father's wedding band (Campbell & Wiggins, 2013). In another handbook, *The Oxford Handbook of Applied Ethnomusicology* (Pettan & Titon, 2015), a set of chapters offer insights on areas of practice such as music and cultural policy, advocacy, education, and contemporary practices of music in peace and conflict resolution, museums, libraries, and archives. Still another handbook on community music (Bartleet & Higgins, 2018) provides insights on the value and meaning of music in communities, and describes myriad ways in which community music functions as a pedagogical pathway through music to tolerance, friendship, and love. Finally, *The Oxford Handbook of Music Education* (McPherson & Welch, 2012) offers enlightening chapters on a wide variety of topics from music education in early childhood to vocal and choral music, instrumental music, and school ensembles, and features a thoughtful article by senior ethnomusicologist Bruno Nettl (2012) on music and culture, comparative study, and traditions and transmissions.

PUBLICATIONS "UNDER THE INFLUENCE" AND "IN COLLABORATION"

Beyond the scholarly works, a host of publications are appearing to feed the practice of teaching music as a human phenomenon and as a multicultural/intercultural experience. There have been resources offered by large textbook publishing corporations and a flurry of books from World Music Press (see below) designed to offer "multicultural music materials" to teachers. Magazine articles have been written with lesson plans, notation, and annotated discographies, and several books of curricular materials, as well as advocacy for diversifying curricular content, have been published by MENC (NAfME). Fueled by the expressed missions of the multicultural movement, *Multicultural Perspectives in Music Education* (Anderson & Campbell, 1989, 1996, 2010) was the effort of educators working with ethnomusicologists, featuring co-authored chapters that opened with an ethnomusicologist's introduction to a cultural region such as East Asia, Europe, sub-Saharan Africa, the Middle East, or Latin America, followed by lesson plans designed by a music educator. Just prior to this publication, *Sounds of the World* had been published by MENC as a series of five sets of cassette tapes produced by ethnomusicologist Karl Signell and a teacher's guide written by music educators and ethnomusicologists. This resource was a misnomer of sorts, because all performers were living in the United States, although they looked homeward in their musical reflections of their first culture. The five sets were Music of East Asia, Music of Eastern Europe, Music of the Middle East, Music of Latin America, and Music of Southeast Asia.

Ethnomusicologists were moved to the limelight in a series of eight influential interview-articles for the *Music Educators Journal* in 1994–1995, later published as *Music in Cultural Context: Eight Views on World Music Education* (Campbell, 1996b). The proposal had received a lukewarm reception by staff members of the Music Educators National Conference, as objections initially were voiced as to "the disconnect" between ethnomusicology and music education, but a persuasive argument was waged and won partly on the basis of the promise of a developing partnership that this publication would foster. Interviews were designed, conducted, and transcribed, and introductory remarks were fashioned, resulting in monthly articles that illuminated assorted principles of teaching the world's musical cultures, while also providing explicit information on culture-specific musical practices that were the expertise of the featured ethnomusicologists. The articles were compiled as chapters in a slim volume for future use, and alongside the interviews were lesson plans with musical examples and resource lists, a framework for studying music cultures, a summary of issues raised by ethnomusicologists, and a resource list of books and various media. Research-active ethnomusicologists were selected for their depth and breadth of insight on a particular culture and/or region, including David P. McAllester (Navajo), Terry Miller (Thailand), Bruno Nettl (Iran), Anthony

Seeger (the Brazilian Amazon), Bell Yung (China), Christopher Waterman (the Yoruba in Nigeria), Mellonee Burnim (African American gospel), and Steve Loza (Latino, especially Mexican). From the interviews came a clear sense of the pathway forward for multiculturalizing and globalizing music education in ways that would apply ethnomusicological principles to music curricular experiences in elementary and secondary schools. Ten practical recommendations for teachers were offered then and are still relevant now:

1. Blend the "old" with the "new" by holding to tried-and-true repertoire in school music programs while integrating unfamiliar and diverse content as well.
2. Listen repeatedly to the music, so to grasp the stylistic nuances of the music—the pitch inflections, rhythmic features, expressive components.
3. Practice the music, learned from recordings, transcriptions, and writings about music, in order to be fully equipped to teach it.
4. Teach comparatively, in a "world music" manner, organizing specific concepts and elements that might appear in multiple world music cultures (such as meter, mode, or form).
5. Teach fewer cultures in greater depth, thus allowing opportunities for students to perform the music appropriately and to listen with comprehension.
6. Supply limited contextual information, since reference to its function provides further meaning to a music as it is experienced within its place of origin.
7. Contract traditional musicians living in local communities to perform and teach in schools, thus extending, enhancing, sometimes validating the curriculum.
8. Recognize that some musics cannot be taught, and should be left where they belong, in ceremonies, for rituals and religious occasions.
9. Know that traditions change, in that recordings may offer music that is no longer known by the people of a place, as other musical values and preferences have surpassed earlier ones.
10. When in doubt, don't be afraid to ask your local ethnomusicologist, as many are the go-to sources of information on performance practices and live and mediated sources. (Campbell, 1996b, pp. 70–71)

Even before the establishment of ethnomusicology as a bona fide discipline and field, textbook companies were offering a variety of folk songs in their collections. Ethnomusicologists came later, and were important in examining past material and recommending new repertoire that could be featured on recordings more than in print notation. Based on the broader repertoire to which teachers could have access, alongside clear indications that the nation and the world were forever changed by demographic shifts and efforts at globalization, instructional materials were diversified. American editions in the 1970s were presenting instrumental art music traditions from China and Japan and "rhythm complexes" of West African percussion ensembles. By the 1980s, musical expressions of African Americans, Latin Americans, and Native Americans were carefully selected for their authenticity and representation, and more recent editions have ensured that songs are contextualized according to their meaning within their cultures of origin (Campbell, 2002b; Volk, 1998). More than ever before, attention was given to the recordings that accompany the notated songs, so that artist-musicians were consulted in many cases and brought into the studio to be recorded singing and playing traditional instruments. Yet there were still many instances in which studio musicians were featured who were given notation for music from an unfamiliar tradition and requested to perform a piece on available instruments; thus, all recordings of Latin American music featured guitars, maracas, and a flute—and little in the way of rhythmic nuances (or instruments, or other musical traits) that differently characterize musical expressions from Argentina, Bolivia, and Brazil to Colombia, Cuba, Guatemala, and Mexico. Contributors to textbooks were often university faculty in music education, and occasionally ethnomusicologists were invited to contribute or review contributions; of the latter, those who were too demanding of culturally explicit details were dropped by publishing companies from the list of advisors. Particularly for classroom music studies in elementary and middle schools, songs from across the world were presented in standard staff notation, often with colorful yet stereotypical photos of musicians and dancers. Later editions feature recordings, sometimes capturing musicians and dancers in video excerpts for web-based learning. Music textbooks for use in K–8 music classes are documentation of the perception by publishers of the professional needs of the time and their interpretation of what teachers and their students would bear in the name of a diverse musical repertoire.

Collaborations of ethnomusicologists with educators for the publication of teaching resources came through various channels. Multicultural music specialist Judith Cook Tucker led an effort to provide books with recordings, beginning with her co-authored book, *Let Your Voice Be Heard* (Adzinyah, Maraire, & Tucker, 1986), of songs from Ghana and Zimbabwe. She established her publishing company, World Music Press, on a shoestring budget in her garage and has been an important force in the provision of further collaborations between teachers, ethnomusicologists, and culture bearers. Various books were published by her press, with particular focus on filling needs of elementary and middle school programs, and with recordings that featured artist-musicians from Cambodia, China, Ecuador, Italy, Native American cultures, Thailand, Vietnam, and other cultures; a set of choral octavos was developed as well for school and community choirs. Oxford University Press stepped into the realm of collaborative work, too, but with a focus on university-level books (with CD recordings). Beginning in 2004, the Global Music Series was developed to offer musical and cultural considerations for teaching and learning, through two framing volumes,

Thinking Musically (Wade, 2004) and *Teaching Music Globally* (Campbell, 2004), and a host of 26 music-culture case studies. Essential features of the music, musicians, and cultural contexts were provided by ethnomusicologists in print, with recordings and online instructional manuals prepared for introducing students (and their teachers) to the music of Bali, Brazil, Bulgaria, China, Japan, Korea, Mexico, North India, Turkey, and elsewhere.

Online materials are now available, and several websites are filling the needs of teachers for materials, thoughtful contextual content, and pedagogical flow. *Smithsonian Folkways Recordings* (www.folkways.si.edu) offers tens of thousands of recordings, liner notes, and 100 "music-culture curricular units," or theme-based lesson plans, on music from American folk traditions, children's music, and musical practices from across the world. Many ethnomusicologists, over several generations, have been involved in identifying, interviewing, and recording musicians, to the delight of music teachers who are designing instructional material. The music is embedded within the units, as are the occasional video-recordings, so that they can be brought to life in classrooms (see Chapter 6). The Association for Cultural Equity (n.d.) maintains an online collection of the archived recordings of Alan Lomax (www.culturalequity.org) and has recently introduced Global Jukebox as a means of further extending the reach of historic songs, dances and stories to scholars, students, teachers, and the public at large. Just as Lomax himself was committed to research of under-recognized music, dance, and oral traditions of American communities and cultural groups in the Caribbean and Europe, the collection is intended to preserve and disseminate these traditions and to reconnect people and communities with their creative heritage. A growing set of lessons is available at this site for use from preschool to post-college, and the music is embedded for the easy access and convenience of the teacher. Not all websites can claim collaborative work of ethnomusicologists with music educators, but these two are exemplary in their efforts to facilitate multicultural understanding through musical means.

SHARED CONCEPTS BETWEEN THE FIELDS

At the intersection of ethnomusicology and music education are terms and concepts that spring from one field into the other, or that find their way from use in society and schools into the lives of thinking and acting music educators and teaching musicians.

Multicultural and Other-cultural Aims

Various labels have been applied to societal movements and issues associated with multiculturalism, internationalism, and globalization, and some of these labels have made their way into the scholarly rhetoric and workaday world of music educators. Of the half dozen or so, "multicultural music education" is the longest-lived American referent, arising from 40 years of intersections between music education, ethnomusicology, and multicultural education. It is understood as encompassing the teaching of music in diverse cultures as well as the teaching of students from diverse cultural backgrounds. Suffice it to say that labels come and go; some have regional meanings, or are re-interpreted, while others emerge from a group or movement looking for a fresh phrase to denote what its members do. For example, intercultural is a preferred term in South Africa and has been applied by American music teachers in reference to the necessary growth by teachers in "intercultural competence." Of course, the literature in multicultural education discusses the teacher's necessary understanding of student-oriented communication styles and approaches (Grant & Portera, 2011), and subtle differences may appear in definitions of terms depending on the national and regional contexts of their use. A few terms are given pause, questioned, and sometimes laid aside for other labels. Within music education, multicultural sometimes is replaced with the term intercultural, in order to claim the importance of understandings and engagements across cultures. "World music education" is an all-encompassing label applied to the grand variety of global and local expressions, although it is sometimes erroneously interpreted as referring only to the music of far-away exotic islands, mountain villages, and bush cultures. (See Chapter 6 for discussion of *World Music Pedagogy*, a term that refers to a teaching-learning sequence of experience and study of music from global and local communities.)

Huib Schippers (2010) proposed a continuum of terms and positions ranging from "monoculturalism" to "multiculturalism," "interculturalism," and "transculturalism" as useful descriptors of least to greatest tolerance for musical practices and cultures. He suggested a means for developing from a single cultural referent, the monocultural focus on Western art music, to the ideal and thoroughgoing integration of experiences leading to a transcultural understanding of music as a pan-human expression. The in-between two positions are differentiated from each other by the extent to which cultures distinguish and separate themselves from other cultures (multicultural) or exchange and even occasionally fuse ideas and approaches (intercultural). This framework clarifies perspectives and approaches to curricular development and instructional practice, recognizing that there is likely to be fluidity between the positions—even in the work of a single music teacher, depending on the context of her teaching.

Bimusicality

In an effort to describe bimusicality, maverick ethnomusicologist Mantle Hood (1971/1982) imagined the challenges of musicians studying a musical practice outside their first and most familiar culture. "The initial challenge [of bimusicality] is the ability to hear" (p. 56), he observed, and suggested that the way to knowing a second (or third) musical culture is through repeated listening. Singing, too, but particularly careful listening, develops musical knowledge and skill, while musical analysis and theoretical studies have little place in one's becoming bimusical. Musical knowing of an instrument, a vocal practice, or genre, arises from fundamental aural perception in which listeners can note the rise and fall of pitches, the beat, its subdivisions and its rhythmic developments, the length of phrases, the extent of repetition, and contrast of material as the music progresses. Bimusicality emerges when a listener's attention to the music can lead to a full familiarity with the way the music "goes" and an awareness and understanding of the nuances and quite possibly the microtonal inflections of a genre. Notation is not the way forward to bimusicality, as many musical expressions are learned very well, and eventually are performed accurately and expressively by fine musicians, without the need for print. Bimusicality is an aim for some studies, especially by university-level students who choose to know another musical style (for example, Turkish *'ud*) beyond their study of Western art music, through intensive, even daily, practice. The key to becoming bimusical is the training of the ears, hands, and voice (and eyes for observing playing position and techniques) in order to be able to perform an instrument "like a native"—someone born to and highly experienced in performing a musical culture. As a goal for school music practice, bimusicality may not always be realistic, given the limited time (and the many musical cultures) of a curriculum. On the other hand, multimusicality has been suggested as a concept to strive for and has been defined as the capacity to perform capably in several different musical cultures (Campbell, 2004).

Authenticity

The issue of authenticity looms large among musicians and educators who are keen to perform music in a close match with the "original," to find the historic and true recordings to listen to, or to painstakingly find (or make) transcriptions that represent every minute detail of the singing voice, instrument, or ensemble. The concept may arise out of a sense of faithfulness to the group, which was explained in complicated details by Johann Herder, a Prussian preacher and philosopher in the late 18th century. In remarks on learning language, culture, customs, the arts, and music, Herder noted that the expression of a collective cultural spirit was key to distinguishing a group of people who claimed a community identity, and that being faithful to the nature of the group was a manifestation of authenticity. People ("das Volk") are the source of truth, he claimed, and of authentic wisdom, and so folk culture, folk arts, and folk music are demonstrations of the authentic essence of a community (Wade, 2004).

Musicians and music scholars involved in the documentation of folk music and musicians, including folklorists who collect songs, instruments, and tunes, strive to represent the music of the people as the unconscious yet pure sonic expressions that they may be. Some value tradition with such zeal as to maintain that despite recognition of the penchant of singers and players to interpret music in an individually expressive manner, music should continue to sound as it always sounded: unchanged. By holding to music as an object that can be frozen in time, continuity eclipses other factors associated with folk music, including the creative expression of the individual performer that so naturally flows from a deeply felt rendition of a musical selection. This restrictive view of authenticity prevents the possibility of creative expression, however, and ignores the concept of music as a living tradition in the hands of thinking musicians. For authentic-centric musicians and educators, orality (and aurality) is an unlikely route to the re-creation of the genuine sound, and preserving the music intact rather than venturing into creative expression seems essential. (See Chapter 5 for further discussion of the merits of orality and aurality.)

Matters of authenticity and compromise within music-educational practice stretch back many decades in efforts to multiculturalize the school music curriculum. Informally referred to as "the Big A," authenticity challenges teachers and learners alike to use their ears to be true and accurate to the music as it sounds in the origin culture. Those who hope for an authentic performance—whether of Guadalajara-styled mariachi, Korean *p'ung mul,* Georgian polyphonic song, Karnatic *kriti,* or Icelandic *rimur*—expend efforts to model the performance after live and recorded performances to which they have access. Matching-the-model is a musically challenging exercise, to be sure, and can be useful in tuning the ears as closely as possible to the nuances of the style. Yet it also can be discouraging, particularly if a teacher ventures bravely and boldly for the first time into unfamiliar musical territory, practices endlessly in mad pursuit of reproducing the sound (and bringing students to a reproduction), and then is told after a performance that the outcome by the group is musically inauthentic and contrived. (Ironically, the critique may come more from colleagues not associated with the musical culture than from a cultural insider!) Tales of an unnerving interaction spread quickly from teacher to teacher, often so distant from the source as to not know who experienced it, and thus many teachers become intimidated by "the Big A" and allay their fears of retaliation by keeping their distance from music outside that which they have studied.

Teachers are nervous about "being authentic." Yet concern about authenticity may be on the wane, led by ethnomusicologists and university-level music educators who recognize that a valuing of authenticity implies absolute values that are often nonexistent or unknown within historically long and culturally varied nations. Bell Yung observed that for much traditional music in China, it is difficult to prove in an objective manner the authenticity of genres that may be traced back many centuries and possibly even to earlier foreign influences (Campbell, 1996a). What then is the cutoff between authentic and pure music, and music in nearly every culture that has resulted from what is borrowed, adapted, and accepted by the people of the culture? Music travels through time and from place to place, and it is its dynamic character of change that makes it human, gives it life, and allows it to find its way from one musician to another. Further, authenticity may be an attempt to adhere to a model that may lack consensus within the cultural group itself, some of whose members may have versions and visions of their own as to how the music of a place, time, and genre should sound. True and original music is hard to find and may in fact be beside the point.

Context (and Recontextualization)

Ethnomusicologists study the contexts in which music is made, listened to, danced to, learned, and used in a myriad of ways by people of a culture. They question who makes the music, where and when it's made, how it's made vocally or on culture-specific or widely available instruments, what the music's history may be, its current incidence and embrace within a community, its uses and meanings, its significance to some but not all people within a place and time, its sustainability through teaching and learning processes, its presence in the media, and its support by societal agents. Since ethnomusicology is rooted in the study of music within cultures and communities, and attends to the manner in which music and musical instruments offer insights as to ways in which people think and behave, it is no wonder that context is at the core of the discipline. An understanding of music as sound, behavior, and idea is the wide compass that ethnomusicology offers, and thus music is viewed as its capacity to define individuals and groups, to understand people as social beings.

For generations of music teachers, context often goes unheeded. The longstanding meaning of music as a subject for study in schools is a sonic one, and thus greatest emphasis and time expenditure is given by teachers to the musical sound and not when, where, or why the music sounds. Regardless of the music—whether a children's song, a Bach chorale for choir, a Duke Ellington piece for jazz band, a percussion piece from the Ewe of Ghana or the Japanese *kodo* drumming practice, or a Mozart overture for chamber orchestra, music teachers with limited time on tight school schedules go directly to the sound. They warm up and tune up voices and instruments; deliver sequential sound-based experiences; evaluate, assess, and correct musical errors; and meanwhile keep the peace and respect among students in the group humming harmoniously along. Participation is the standard means of involving students in the music classroom. "Less talk/more music" is a slogan to adhere to, honed in pedagogy courses leading to music education degrees and jobs. Music's cultural meaning is not a priority, and most music teachers do not study music as bound up with identity, religion, politics, kinship, and economics—these being some of the ideals and interests of ethnomusicological study of a music culture.

Without contextual information, however, students imagine their own stories behind the music. No matter how much educators may value imagination and creativity, the made-up stories of children may be far from the truth and may in fact result in their own stereotyping of cultures. Some of the made-up stories may prove to be disrespectful to the musicians, perhaps overly simplistic, possibly belittling, and the lack of the true story-behind-the-music misses opportunities to allow music to serve as a window to understanding culture. Context gets at the bigger picture of music and its meaning in the lives of people who make it, and allows students to engage more deeply in music in a holistic manner. The histories and belief systems of the musicians who make the music, and of the audiences within the culture who value it, are critical to know.

Music in schools is typically out of context, and as a result music may seem to be no longer authentic in ways that cannot be helped. In featuring a Navajo social dance or an African American gospel song in a music classroom, everything about the school space is unique and distinctive from the source: lighting, room temperature and air flow, floor surfaces, furniture, and so much more. One might argue that education at large is often out of context, as students learn math as if they were engineers, or engage in a lab experiment as if they were chemists, or play in a concert band as if they were (professional) musicians (McAllester, 1996). Learning, then, is often decontextualized, and the use of nonindigenous instruments (for example, a Navajo melody performed on a silver orchestral flute rather than a hand-carved Navajo flute) is just another way in which a new context requires accommodation and modification. Such modification is very real, however, and must be accommodated by teachers.

Another way of viewing the shift of music's context from a traditional space to a classroom, is by way of accepting that a recontextualization quite naturally will occur on every occasion of teaching and learning music away from the source. By offering the context behind the music, sometimes through brief story-like nuggets that communicate meaningfully, teachers clarify for students the role and function of music in people's lives. Thus, the meaning of context in music education can tilt away from music as decontextualized and disconnected, to the realization that music is always recontextualized when taken from a different place or time, and can be made meaningful to students. With the provision of music's stories and backstories, and through the use of photos, videos, and other rich media resources, students can be guided to understand many aspects of the history and cultural context of the music. Campus visits by musicians and others from cultures that value particular musical expressions under study, and exchanges by Skype and online communication products can be extremely useful to students, who are then led to a discovery of why particular music sounds the way it does.

Essentializing, Representing, and Stereotyping

The extent to which a musical work represents a cultural group frequently is overlooked by teachers who are developing a multicultural repertoire, and many may struggle in coming to terms with the one selected piece that will stand for the entire national, regional, or ethnic culture. Yet no music ever can fulfill such a tall order, because a musical selection stands for itself, rather than for the entirety of the culture. Musical choices within an ethnic culture vary, depending on the age, gender, socioeconomic class, religious affiliation, and geographic region of the subgroups within the culture. To suggest that Thailand's *phleng luk thung* (country music) or *likay* (popular street theater) music, rather than the *pi phat* classical court ensemble, reflects the Thai national culture is to commit a cultural faux pas extraordinaire. Likewise, Mexicans from the Gulf Coast of eastern Mexico may identify with *huapango* music played on violin, guitar, and the small *jarana*, while those from the Jalisco region prefer mariachi, thus making it unreasonable to select one genre over the others as the single music of all Mexican people. As for African American styles, some Black middle-class people have come to view certain aspects of Black culture— from acoustic blues to barbecued ribs—as remote from their own experience. Yet given the whirlwind tours of musical traditions that occur in minimal time slots allotted to music education in schools, often teachers mistakenly choose one genre and even a single song to represent a richly heterogeneous culture. Sensitivity is central in making decisions as to whose music should be featured and what might need to be said about it as backdrop or explanation.

In an attempt to be inclusive, there is often a danger of presenting sweeping stereotypes of people and their cultural practices. Not all Belgians or Bulgarians are alike, and there is the danger of believing that one stands for all. Erroneously, young people have been led to believe that Mexicans eat (only) burritos; that the Irish jig their time away to a fiddle tune; that Japanese drink green tea, fashion origami, and (women) still wear kimonos; and that Native Americans are still war-whooping on their tribal land. It is unfair to have a single cultural experience—via a Vietnamese folktale, a Polish egg-painting venture, or an Afro-Cuban percussion piece—and to take it as full representation of all people, for all times.

Tokenism is real and stereotypes happen, and teachers are driven to work hard in steering students to understanding that their own unique individuality is important and that they themselves have their own identity (or multiple identities) separate from the stereotype. Students can be encouraged, too, to participate actively in various cultural practices of a group, often through lengthier units of study that allow multiple experiences to develop their understanding of a group. A playlist of 30-second music bytes can open the ears of students to sounds beyond the single token selection, even as a collage of images can help to open minds to the wide variety of ways in which people live. Moving beyond generalities requires efforts to provide multiple illustrations and experiences of a people and place.

Paying My Dues*.* Some years ago, I was told by a senior scholar in ethnomusicology that I'd "paid my dues" and, with a vigorous handshake, he smiled, commended me, and proclaimed, "Congratulations: You're an ethnomusicologist!" For an instant, I was thrilled: I had arrived. All the teaching of world music courses, at three universities, had earned me this badge of identity, helped by the ethnographic study of children's musical cultures that was consuming me, and the years of performance experiences in the music of Bulgarian, Ewe, South Indian, Javanese, Pakistani, Thai, Turkish, Vietnamese, and Venezuelan cultures. I rode this new identity with a certain thrill, owning the sense of distinction that I perceived was associated with a coming of age in my life as a music scholar. A few years ago, while serving my time as chair of our university's long-standing ethnomusicology program, I reckoned with the truth: I am a teacher, and I've always been a teacher, and music education is the name of my game.

But about the "ethno-interests" and their impact on my work in multiculturalizing music education, how did they happen? And how have they helped? We were a stay-at-home Midwestern family with no travels to the wide world, no exposure to third-world countries, and I had never traveled further than the Jersey shore in my school days. But interests rise early, and some of us can trace our adult preoccupations—be it baseball, cycling, stamp-collecting, dolls— clear back to our early childhoods. For me, it was "folk music" that held my rapt attention, then as well as now. Were these my first steps into "world music" and the field of ethnomusicology? There were dance tunes playing on Sunday morning Cleveland radio in our kitchen—an hour each for German, Hungarian, Slovenian, and Polish polkas, waltzes, *czardas, kolos,* and *obereks.* There were hillbilly bluegrass tunes that would come wafting in on Saturday nights from WWVA in Wheeling, West Virginia, not but a few hours following the broadcasts from New York City of the Metropolitan Opera. We listened to it all! As a child, I never knew that there could be anything special in my grandfather's gathering of friends on Friday nights to play fiddle, flute, guitar, and an out-of-tune piano. Their tunes would become the stuff of a recording, *Irish Music from Cleveland,* and I loved the lilt and would jig my way around the dining room long before Riverdance upped the ante for what the dance should be. I found my way through my father's basement collection of 78 rpm recordings to more distant cultures in the music he'd brought out of his service experience in Borneo and the Philippines. Then, my piano teacher from Vilnius would offer me an earful of Lithuanian folk tunes at the piano, and other tunes from the Baltic countries, Finland, Russia and Poland, all played pianistically by him. In my weekly visits to the local public library, I found the Folkways Recordings of Woody Guthrie, Pete Seeger, and Lead Belly, and since they were "reference only," I would sit in a booth with headphones on, listening. Meanwhile, there was the Motown coming down from Detroit to Cleveland's east side, sounding out on my plasti-coated transistor radio; I was captivated by the dance routines that my East Cleveland friend Cheryl, Sandra and Mary Helen would show us in the gym to the sounds of the Shirelles, the Supremes, and Martha and the Vandellas. These were early experiences that piqued my curiosity of how musically varied the world seemed to be, and these sounds laid the foundation for my further obsession with "people's music" and with ethnomusicology.

What does one do with the experiences we live, and the knowledge they offer us? For me, sampling the music from early on led to studying the music, which led to teaching the music, which brought me to the current work with colleagues in ethnomusicology and music education to figure ways to join together in achieving multicultural aims through the teaching we do.

FUTURE INTERSECTIONS

It is through the work of several generations of music educators, some inspired by or working alongside ethnomusicologists, that a wholesale reform of music, education, and world cultures is developing and may, with continued intersecting moments, come to fruition. The separate fields of ethnomusicology and music education are buoyed by their long histories of concentrated effort in unique realms of research and practice. Those toiling in these two fields will do well to check in on one another and to reach out to specialists in multicultural education, as well as in related fields of anthropology, sociology, and social work, in building collaborations to benefit diverse populations of students. A crafting of ways to serve students both musically and multiculturally may be directly related to the extent of time and energy that is expended through the intersections of specialists.

CHAPTER 4

Multicultural Education and Social Justice in School Music Practice

This chapter is adapted from "Multiculturalism and Social Justice: Complementary Movements for Education in and Through Music," by J. C. Roberts and P. S. Campbell, in *The Oxford Handbook of Social Justice in Music Education,* edited by C. Benedict, P. Schmidt, G. Spruce, and P. Woolford, 2015, reproduced with permission of Oxford University Press (www.oup.com).

Music joins the many subjects of a multicultural school curriculum as a critical response to changing demographics within a society with social justice in mind. At a time of growing awareness of cultural diversity within national boundaries, and globally, music appears as a promising means for honoring the beauty and logic in every culture—including the culture of classrooms in which students socially bond through acts of musical involvement. As the scope of multicultural education embraces equity and fosters cross-cultural interactions and understandings for students across race, ethnicity, language, culture, gender, and exceptionality (Banks & Banks, 2004), music teachers are potential agents for change in the movement to open minds to a spectrum of beliefs, views, and values. From an opening consideration of the meaning of educational equity, this chapter seeks to discuss music in multicultural social action and social justice in music education. The chapter's lens is focused on levels of curricular reform through efforts in multicultural music education, and descriptions of applications, aims, and accomplishments by music teachers are offered to exemplify equitable practices in school music programs. The rise of social justice in schools, and within the field of music education, is discussed as running parallel to multicultural education's fully evolved culmination in social action, and the reach beyond repertoire is noted as necessary to the full-flowered aim of multicultural education in and through music.

Multi-culti Music Specialist. What's a White, middle-class, midwestern woman like me doing in the thick of efforts at cultural diversity in music education? There was a certain surprise on the face of one colleague who met me after my published works began to flow. "Oh, so you're the multi-culti music specialist?" she asked, barely concealing her astonishment, disappointment, possibly disillusionment, that I was White, aging but not quite worn-out or beat-up, and certainly not very exotic-appearing. But wouldn't all of us help to multiculturalize (and globalize) curriculum and instruction in K–12 schools and in university programs that prepare music teachers? Wouldn't we expect that a sense of social justice could be owned by anyone? And that teaching is a professional practice that requires the embrace of justice in terms of the fair distribution of opportunities and privileges across all students? A fair chance to study the musically beautiful, to find the deep sentiment and the social connections in the music we make? I would not want to dump the responsibility of shoring up music-educational equity into the hands of my colleagues of color alone, without doing some of the heavy lifting, without going it together.

As a "multi-culti specialist," I know this: that all children should get to have lunch, all children should get to study math, all children (youth) should get to read Mariama Ba's *So Long a Letter,* Yaa Gyasi's *Homegoing,* Yukio Mishima's *The Temple of the Golden Pavilion,* Sherman Alexie's *Absolutely True Diary of a Part-Time Indian;* all children should have a chance to sing, dance, and play—in their own individual ways, collectively, beautifully, and skillfully. Musical competence requires the presence of a music specialist teacher in the classroom, one who will bring musical knowledge and skill both broad and deep into curriculum and instruction, one who is committed to the cause of culturally responsive teaching, to a cultural democracy with a line drive to musical democracy, to a way of sharing the wider world of musical possibilities with students of every circumstance. Regardless of our identity, and of the privileges we may have accumulated, it would seem that, in the professional track of our choosing, we would take quite seriously the task of working to accomplish multicultural aims through music with social justice very much in mind.

SHARED TENETS

The move toward educational experiences that are characterized by social justice has gained traction in the past decade, in both the fields of education broadly and music education specifically, as articles, books, and scholarly conferences devoted to the topic grow more common. (See, for example, Richardson, 2007, and Allsup & Shieh, 2012). Yet music teachers are more attuned to the precepts of multicultural education than they are to the application of social justice to their work, quite possibly due to the longevity of the concept within the professional literature, curricular development, and teacher preparation courses. To be sure, they view multicultural music education primarily as the teaching of music of diverse cultures in classrooms and rehearsal halls, although they also have come to view culturally responsive teaching as another important consideration for multiculturalizing music programs (Anderson & Campbell, 2010; Lind & McKoy, 2016). The term social justice is a murky one, a concept that has been seen as ambiguous and unclearly defined (Cochran-Smith et al., 2009), and one that is a relatively recent arrival to music education practice. It is a term that appears rooted in the philosophical principles and practices of multicultural education (Banks & Banks, 2004), a movement with a history of a half-century (at least) and that is critically concerned with the complexities of race, ethnicity, and social class in the design and delivery of curriculum. Scholars who employ the term social justice overwhelmingly emphasize the issue of equity as it applies across a variety of contexts and situations, and incorporate action components in which one works to challenge existing inequities (Cochran-Smith et al., 2009; Sensoy & DiAngelo, 2017). But in the field of music education, more than a generation of advocacy for multiculturalizing programs and practices has yet to be fully heeded in the design, delivery, and facilitation of a culturally conscious curriculum with the capacity to serve all students.

Equity is a core construct of both social justice and multicultural education. In efforts by multiculturalists to reform schools, the goal is that students from diverse racial, ethnic, and social class groups will experience educational success and social mobility (Banks, 2013a; Banks & Banks, 2004). In a survey of conceptions of multiculturalism, Nieto (2009) notes that multicultural ideals include "advocating for equitable education for students of all backgrounds, and that it goes beyond the classroom walls to implicate societal change as a fundamental goal" (p. 82). This characterization of multiculturalism resembles Reilly Carlisle, Jackson, and George's (2006) definition of socially just education, a "conscious and reflexive blend of content and process intended to enhance equity across multiple social identity groups (e.g., race, class, gender, sexual orientation, ability), foster critical perspectives, and promote social action" (p. 57). While not identical, social justice and multiculturalism bear many commonalities that warrant exploration; further, "social action," undergirded by a sense of social justice, is the fifth of five dimensions of multicultural education (Banks, 2013b; see Figure 4.1, p. 75). From the application of equity in education emerges equity pedagogy, a curricular approach that seeks to provide the means for students from diverse populations to attain knowledge, skills, and attitudes that are needed to function effectively within a just, humane, and democratic society. Since equity pedagogy requires reflection and application, students need opportunities to grow their understandings beyond the limitations of the school building and the school schedule (Banks & Banks, 2004).

There are shared tenets emanating from multiculturalism and social justice, and a study of their complementarity is a worthwhile venture that brings forth the aims and practices of the two named educational movements as they parallel, overlap, and enrich each other in educational practice. There are confirmable connections between the philosophical principles of multiculturalism and social justice, and their presence in music education curricular practice justifies describing their explicit and implicit influences. The framework of pioneering educationist James Banks (2013a) offers multiple levels of curriculum reform as a lens through which to view the practical advantages of encouraging teachers, including music teachers, to move toward more equitable classroom environments (see Figure 4.2, p. 77). These advantages may be realized by creating curriculum in graduated steps that progress from contributive "material" to deep structural change.

Nieto (2009) claims that "an enduring dilemma in multicultural education has been the gulf between theories . . . and how those are realized in classroom practice" (p. 90), a concern that many teachers share. By drawing together the works of key scholars of multicultural education whose research provides theoretical foundations for social justice in music education, we then can direct attention toward exemplary practices in music at the elementary and secondary levels, as well as in music teacher education programs, that are intended to realize the goals of musical, educational, and cultural equity. These practices suggest a passage for teachers in K–12 and university music settings to confront issues of multiculturalism and social justice and to incorporate curricular events into their classes in ways that can penetrate and convert current thought and behavior to an Other-directed sensibility.

ENSURING EQUITY THROUGH MULTICULTURAL EDUCATION

Multicultural education is more than a social movement: It is a field of study that emerged out of sociocultural realities (Banks, 2013b) and whose intent is to foster equal learning opportunities for all students. It advocates the design and delivery of a comprehensive, equitable, and culturally responsive education from kindergarten through secondary school, with support for furthering education and training at the tertiary level as well (Banks, 2013b; Grant & Sleeter, 2013). Multiculturally attuned educators are intent on embracing the needs and interests of students from diverse racial, ethnic, social class, and cultural communities. Efforts are directed at the identification of students from these communities, and at facilitating their acquisition of knowledge, skills, and attitudes necessary for succeeding in a multicultural (and global) society. Consistent with the principles of a democratic society, multicultural education is aimed at facilitating and championing access for all, rather than merely the elite and advantaged few. It seeks to embrace the means for developing logic and intellectual acumen, humanistic understandings, and aesthetic experiences for learners of every social circumstance and need, drawing them in to the study of literature, the arts, math, the sciences, history, and the social sciences (Banks, 2013b).

The struggle for equal rights in the United States has been long and historic, and American schools have mirrored in policy and practice the overriding perspectives that have directed the societal movement toward greater equality for all citizens. Multicultural education rose out of the Civil Rights movement of the 1960s and 1970s and embraces changes in the curriculum, instructional delivery system, and teaching/learning textbooks, materials, and tests so as to meet the needs of learners from all communities. Compelling cases have been made by multiculturalists (Banks, 2013b), and schooling has been shaped, to attend to the integration of a wide array of cultural sensibilities and to develop experiences that lead to the validation and empowerment of students from every community. While African Americans led the movement for educational reform, and the works of James A. Banks, Geneva Gay, and Carl A. Grant are early and continuing influences on the development of theory and practice, the evolution of multicultural education also includes specialists in the learning processes of students of various races and ethnicities, such as Carlos E. Cortes, Jack D. Forbes, Eugene E. Garcia, K. Tsianina Lomawaima, Sonia Nieto, and Derald W. Sue (Banks & Banks, 2004).

In over five decades of attention to changes in school policy and practice, the field of multicultural education has helped to crack open the question of equity that leads to creating a more democratic society through schooling. Not without its ebbs and flows, it is a field fraught with the challenges of turning theoretical analysis and pronouncements of curriculum reform into full-fledged action, as teachers with every intent to be democratic, inclusive, and attuned to the individual needs of all students confront the daily realities of time, energy, and expertise necessary to meet the multicultural goals. Yet inroads have been made, and equity has been attained in full or in part, in many contexts.

AIMS AND ACCOMPLISHMENTS
OF MULTICULTURAL MUSIC EDUCATION

Alongside the Civil Rights movement in the United States and globally, rapid developments in communications and transportation brought an awareness of the musical expressions of local and global communities not previously featured in curricular programs in music. Many music teachers awakened to the prospects of teaching music from multicultural perspectives and then interpreted multiculturalism to fit the scope of their own education and training. Many more ignored the call for diversifying curricular work, for developing culturally sensitive pedagogy, and for considering deep change to the content and method of their classes, studio lessons, and performance programs.

Since the mid-20th century, the prevalence in the media of African American popular music forms, from blues to R&B to soul, provided a sonic blanket of music that seeped into the lives of young people, and then into school life, if not into the curricular content of music programs. In the early years of attempts to multiculturalize school music programs, teachers preferred delving into West African "roots" music and rhythmic complexes (Schippers & Campbell, 2012; Standifer & Lundquist, 1972). Particularly in urban areas, teachers were attempting to draw students of color into elective music classes through genres that might be viewed as relevant, and even familiar, to them (Lundquist, 1985) or that featured the irresistible groove in elemental listening experiences. A canonization of sorts occurred, as particular music cultures and genres were extolled, such as West African drumming that could be taught, learned, and performed at school assemblies and in festivals. Music teachers, particularly those responsible for vocal and choral programs in elementary and middle schools, became curious about "the musical other" and were willing to experiment with music out of Africa, the Caribbean, and the Americas (for example, Native American and Hawaiian genres). At the same time, instrumental ensembles continued the skill building that led to performances of bands and orchestras in schools, at contests, and at athletic events. Internationally, too, music educators were turning toward curricular content that was multicultural and intercultural;

they, too, were inspired by a rising awareness globally of diverse populations within national borders and by the contributions of resources by ethnomusicologists that could be featured in class sessions.

The tenor of music education shifted, so that in the 1990s it was not unusual for schools to celebrate multiculturalism in musical ways at evening PTA performances, at districtwide arts festivals, and in student-centered oral histories that encouraged students' own investigations of songs, stories, and musical instruments in their family histories. "Discoveries" were made by teachers of Balkan and Baltic choral music, and percussion music and lyrical songs from Cambodia, China, Japan, Vietnam, and other Asia-Pacific regional cultures. Some school music programs became more vibrant through the development of in-school or after-school African drumming ensembles, Afro-Caribbean percussion ensembles, Mexican-style mariachis, and marimba ensembles featuring Shona-style music out of Zimbabwe. "World music pedagogy" and "cultural diversity in music education" were emerging movements, even as the post-9/11 period triggered in U.S. populations a regression from the global musical expanse to a more insular view of music that was sounding in local communities (Schippers & Campbell, 2012).

Yet following decades of exploratory experiences in world music, "multicultural music education" was equivalent to a reach for "multicultural music materials," as teachers sought out notated arrangements of musical works for performances of their school groups: A South African freedom song for a choral group, an arrangement of a Korean or Japanese traditional song for band, or a set of songs from Brazil or Bulgaria, Puerto Rico, or Ghana for in-class singing and playing. Due to the restrictions of tight teaching schedules, teachers only rarely introduced thoroughgoing units of music and musicians that realized the potential for cultural understanding. The full extent of the tenets of multicultural education went untapped in music programs, in that goals of equity and social action were articulated philosophically and in policy documents by music educationists but were not at the forefront of the work of most music educators.

SOCIAL JUSTICE AND EDUCATION

Issues of equity and fairness stand at the center of most definitions and applications of social justice in education, particularly with regard to curriculum, pedagogical approaches, and community relationships (e.g., Reilly Carlisle et al., 2006). In a socially just society, economic, social, and political opportunities must be equally available to all members, regardless of class, gender, race, ethnicity, social status, disability, sexual orientation, religion, political affiliation, or other group membership status. Often calling on themes from Freire's liberatory pedagogy (e.g., Adams, 2007), literature on the subject assumes a distributive perception of justice (Cochran-Smith

Figure 4.1. Five Dimensions of Multicultural Education (James A. Banks)

Content integration	Using examples, data, and information from a variety of cultures and groups to illustrate key concepts, principles, generalizations, and theories
The knowledge construction process	The procedures by which social, behavioral, and natural scientists create knowledge in their disciplines. Teachers help students to understand how knowledge is created and how it is influenced by factors of race, ethnicity, gender, and social class.
Prejudice reduction	Focuses on the characteristics of children's racial attitudes and on strategies that can be used to help students develop more positive racial and ethnic attitudes
An equity pedagogy	Teachers facilitating the academic achievement of students from diverse racial and ethnic groups and from all social classes
An empowering school culture and social structure	Restructuring of the culture and organization of the school so that students from diverse racial, ethnic, and social class groups experience educational equality and a sense of empowerment

et al., 2009); inequalities such as the discrepant funding among schools and districts must be rectified. In educational contexts, social justice recognizes that the inequalities that exist—both in school situations and in society—should stand at the center of the educative enterprise (e.g., Cochran-Smith et al., 2009; Sensoy & DiAngelo, 2017). In school parlance, this translates into learning activities that explicitly address issues of injustice, asking students to critically engage to create and execute strategies to help resolve the injustices they identify. The curriculum also recognizes that knowledge is not absolute, but culturally defined and therefore specifically cognizant of the many peoples that constitute the world's community. The focus on naming and redressing inequities does not come at the expense of content-area knowledge, but supplements and deepens growth in specific subject areas (Cochran-Smith et al., 2009; Reilly Carlisle et al., 2006).

Pedagogically, educators teaching from a perspective of social justice recognize the importance of student voice, value multiple perspectives, and emphasize the importance of reflective practice on the part of teachers and students alike. Bell (2007) notes that the process of a socially just education includes interactions between teacher and students that are "democratic and participatory," in which the teacher perceives herself as one who holds "power with" the students, not "power over" them (p. 2). Collaboration between students is common, and student choice often characterizes learning experiences. Peer relationships are valued, with an emphasis on a democratic classroom climate that honors the differences between students' experiences and perspectives, while also striving to ensure that students work together harmoniously.

Listening to the perspectives of the community is central to many conceptions of social justice in education, particularly the families of students. Family involvement contributes to academic success, and facilitating families' involvement in schools contributes to a socially just experience. Community communication is particularly important when the student body and their parents represent diversities (such as class and ethnicity) that differ from those of the teaching staff and administration (Reilly Carlisle et al., 2006).

SOCIAL JUSTICE AND MUSIC EDUCATION

Three major themes permeate the scholarship of social justice in education (as well as of multicultural education) and are making their way into music education literature and practice: equity of resources, equity of pedagogical practices, and equity within the curriculum.

A distributive theory of social justice, in which resources are allocated proportionally, has arisen as an issue in music education. Music educators have condemned the disparity in arts funding, noting that resources have been found to be less prevalent for students of color and those with higher rates of poverty; such inequities in music and arts education have been observed for decades (Hicks, Standifer, & Carter, 1983). Such funding discrepancy manifests itself in the number of course offerings, which are likely to be fewer in large urban secondary schools than in suburban and rural schools, and in schools in which the majority of the student body is non-White. Similarly, music classes at the elementary level are taught in dedicated music rooms less often in schools where the student body is of lower socioeconomic status or comprises primarily students of color. Music educators also have noted that the expense of instruments privileges the financially able (Frierson-Campbell, 2007). In a variety of ways, then, issues of equity play out in terms of the resources that exist for various populations, and proponents of social justice (as well as multiculturalists) have not only recognized the inequities but also suggested means of adjusting these imbalances (Howard, Swanson, & Campbell, 2013).

At the classroom level, scholars also have addressed the power inequities that occur as a part of teacher–student relationships in which the instructors control the content and quality of delivery (Benedict & Schmidt, 2007). Interactive styles of pedagogy have been seen as more socially just (Mayhew & Fernández, 2007), and music educators have documented their efforts to divest themselves of power. For example, in higher education, Baxter (2007) provided an environment in which preservice students crafted

Figure 4.2. Four Levels of Curriculum Reform (James A. Banks)

Contributions	Focuses on heroes, holidays, and discrete cultural elements
Additive	Content, concepts, themes, and perspectives are added to curriculum without changing its structure.
Transformation	Enabling students to view concepts, issues, events, and themes from the perspectives of diverse ethnic and cultural groups
Social action	Students make decisions on important social issues and take actions to solve them.

their own definitions of social justice, then created units for K–12 students that incorporated their interpretations. Such democratization of student/teacher power relations has been seen as more challenging for traditional secondary ensembles such as band and choir, in which the power typically resides with the conductor (Frierson-Campbell, 2007; Richardson, 2007). However, improvisatory experiences, particularly those with minimal parameters, have been found to be one way in these ensembles to provide educational environments in which high school students' voices can be heard (Friesen, 2009). Compositional practices in which teachers cede to the children much of the control over the decisionmaking process also serve as meaningful examples of socially just practices (Campbell, 2004). Throughout, the focus is on increased equalization of power relations between the students and teacher, providing students with greater autonomy and choice.

Finally, and most central to the decades of efforts in the name of multicultural music education (Anderson, 1991; Campbell, 1994b, 2013; Volk, 1998), is the attention paid by proponents of social justice to specific curricular content (Grant & Sleeter, 2013). Scholars have advocated diversifying the musical content of the curriculum in the name of social justice, in order to more adequately represent the cultural composition of the nation and the world. Calls for more varied repertoire have been made repeatedly for university-level schools of music, for music eacher education programs, and in K–12 settings. For example, Bowman (2007) not only urged diversifying the array of musical traditions included in the canon at the university level, but also maintained that study of the sociopolitical dimensions of the music should be included along with attention to its musical qualities. Beyond diversifying the musical repertoire, curricular implications of social justice ideals in music education have led to units that target specific injustices named by students, such as middle school students singing protest songs at the site of an oil spill (Allsup & Shieh, 2012). To date, examples of such curricular units are rare in music education publications, while more attention has been paid to issues of repertoire.

CONNECTIONS BETWEEN MULTICULTURALISM AND SOCIAL JUSTICE

Multiculturalism at its simplest level sometimes is seen as limited solely to the curricular integration of content from a variety of races and ethnicities. However, most multicultural theorists today see the field more broadly (Banks, 2013b), with issues key to the social justice literature, such as power and equity, deemed to be central to multicultural education as well (Nieto, 2009). In addition, most multicultural education theorists today maintain that multicultural principles apply not only to race and ethnicity, but also to issues such as gender, class, exceptionality, religion, sexuality, and language (e.g., Banks & Banks, 2013). They acknowledge the complexities of individual students in terms of the varied experiences they bring to schools, and acknowledge that learning is complicated by many family- and community-based circumstances. They recognize that values of home and school are not always resonant with one another, and that sensitivity and respect are critical to the educational enterprise (but that biases are amenable to change, too). Those who espouse social justice in their multicultural approaches to schooling note that while school is the context in which equity pedagogy is practiced, an educational plan can be put into practice that is responsive to the restrictions of limited school schedules and that considers sites outside the school building and in the community as important places of learning. Moreover, the terms multicultural education and social justice often have been linked together: Grant and Sleeter (2013) describe "multicultural social justice education" as an approach that "deals . . . directly with oppression and social structural inequality based on race, social class, gender, and disability" (p. 50). The work at the Center for Multicultural Education at the University of Washington includes implementation of plans for the reform of citizenship education and social justice, all of which include critiques of injustice in the world, along with the formulation and employment in schools of action for change leading to a more democratic and just world (Banks, 2007).

FIVE DIMENSIONS OF MULTICULTURAL EDUCATION

For music educators concerned with social justice and with the overlapping of multicultural ideals into music classrooms at all levels, the theoretical dimensions of James Banks (2013b) are a particularly illuminating way toward a more equitable curriculum that also might lead to deepened levels of commitment and involvement. Five dimensions of multicultural education reflect social justice principles and offer an effective framework for understanding the issues (see Figure 4.1). The five dimensions consist of: content integration, knowledge construction, prejudice reduction, equity pedagogy, and an empowering school culture.

Content integration refers to "the extent to which teachers use examples and content from a variety of cultures and groups to illustrate key concepts, principles, generalizations, and theories in their subject area or discipline" (Banks, 2013b, p. 16). Traditionally, content across subjects is viewed through the lens of the European American experience (in the context of the United States), and the incorporation of examples from other cultures is one way to move toward a more multicultural curriculum.

The *knowledge construction* process describes the ways in which ideas and expectations are formed, noting that implicit cultural assumptions characterize interactions between (mostly White, middle-class) teachers and their students, regardless of race, ethnicity, or other group membership status. Banks points out that ideas about what constitutes knowledge always reflect ideology, human interests, values, and perspectives, and that teachers must recognize the vantage point from which they come. Students and educators should learn to "understand, investigate, and determine how the implicit cultural assumptions, frames of reference, perspectives, and biases within a discipline influence the ways in which knowledge is constructed" (Banks, 2013b, p. 19).

A third gradient of multicultural education consists of *prejudice reduction,* the lessons and activities that explicitly address issues of prejudice. Stereotypes about specific minority groups continue to characterize young learners (Banks, 2013b). Learning activities designed to recognize the prejudice that continues to exist in specific situations and work to lessen it are seen as essential parts of multiculturalism.

The fourth of five dimensions of multicultural education is *equity pedagogy.* Equity pedagogy refers to the process by which educators "modify their teaching in ways that will facilitate the academic achievement of students from diverse . . . groups" (p. 19). This consists of incorporating an understanding of the learning styles that characterize many members of particular ethnic, cultural, or social class groups, while not essentializing individual students into a manifestation of their group status; each student also is seen as an individual.

Finally, *creating an empowering school culture* that encompasses the entire community of students, teachers, and professional staff is the ultimate goal of multicultural education. To Banks, access to a variety of experiences within the school setting is important. The degrees to which the various groups in a school setting participate in a variety of school experiences, such as differently leveled classes, sports participation, club participation, and levels of academic achievement, should be investigated, with any disproportionality studied to determine the reasons behind it. In an empowered school culture, a student's group status has negligible impact on his or her ability to become involved or participate successfully in any academic or extracurricular activity.

FOUR LEVELS OF CURRICULUM REFORM

Taken together, the five theoretical dimensions, all of which have bearing on social justice aims, constitute a multicultural approach to educational systems. For teachers with minimal training in and experience with these concepts, the prospect of incorporating them into curriculum can seem overwhelming. In an attempt to demystify the process, Banks re-configured the dimensions into a specific, tiered system of educational application, which he named "levels of multicultural curriculum reform" (Banks, 2013a). These levels of educational application are meant as a sequential and manageable series of steps that can be taken to move multicultural principles into teaching/learning experiences. The levels clarify curricular design and instructional delivery, thereby rendering the achievement of the overall goals less daunting. In a word, practicing teachers view the levels as straightforward, and the stepwise progression conveys the sense of an ever-deepening resolve by teachers to design and deliver multicultural sensitivity and understanding through the designated subject matter and its standards.

The four levels, as articulated by Banks, consist of approaches referred to as (1) contributions, (2) additive, (3) transformation, and (4) social action. (See Figure 4.2.) These approaches have been applied to disciplines such as social studies, language, and science (see review by Oakes, Joseph, & Muir, 2004). Applications to music education practices can be found in published literature that attests to these approaches but does not refer to these named levels (Howard et al., 2013; Schippers & Campbell, 2012). Notably, social action, as the final of the four levels, is seen as equivalent to the ideals of social justice, and for multicultural educators it is the full realization of multicultural ideals, which are sequentially developed as a result of implementation of the first three levels.

APPLICATIONS: MULTICULTURAL SOCIAL ACTION
AND SOCIAL JUSTICE IN MUSIC EDUCATION

Clarifications of the four levels of curriculum reform follow, including their manifestations in elementary, secondary, and tertiary music education practices. Relative to social justice in music education, these tiers of practice show increasing commitment across the four levels, from "contributions" to "social action," toward a conversion of music education to the achievement of goals in music and through music. In this way, all students may benefit from knowing music broadly and deeply as performance, listening analysis, creative composition, and improvisation, and from understanding the cultural meaning behind the music through various means of topical integration.

In the initial level of the *contributions approach,* the experiences of diverse groups are incorporated into learning experiences as a supplement to the typical, mainstream-centered curriculum. Sometimes referred to as the "heroes-and-holidays" approach, discrete aspects related to specific groups are incorporated at particular times during the year. The curriculum remains unchanged, with educational experiences serving as add-on experiences that often have little relation to the rest of the learning that occurs. Banks (2013a) notes that this can result in "the trivialization of ethnic cultures, the study of their strange and exotic characteristics, and the reinforcement of stereotypes and misconceptions" (p. 186), leading to a learning environment in which ethnic-cultural issues accessorize the dominant Eurocentric paradigm. For teachers with little knowledge or comfort level with teaching concepts of other cultures, lessons within the contributions level serve as an initial step into multicultural education, however limited it may be.

At the elementary music level, learning experiences in which children sing a song about the United States civil rights leader Martin Luther King in the days around the January holiday celebrating his birthday are a contributive activity. In a secondary band class, a learning experience with the mariachi tradition can be contributive, if a piece of music from the tradition is learned through a musical score employing conventional Western musical notation rather than the aural/oral model that is typical of mariachi music. Similarly, the activity is contributive when a choral class sings a South African freedom song and the music is learned from octavos, but without an opportunity to listen to the music repeatedly in order to process the aural model. (If the freedom song is learned aurally, and accompanied by culturally styled movement, experience with it might be seen as an exemplar of a move up a step on the curriculum reform continuum.) In a college music history survey course, students could hear a recording of *Machu Picchu Concerto for Kena and Orchestra,* by Nayo Ulloa, a piece of music that incorporates the *kena* (or *quena,* a traditional flute from the Andean mountains of Peru) along with a Western-style orchestra. If photo slides of the instrument are viewed, but with no further exploration of Peruvian musical culture, the experience stands as contributive. In all of these learning experiences, the music ornaments the traditional curriculum, providing a snapshot view of an alternative music that operates within the dominant musical standard of Western art music. Music educators often have employed this approach to teaching in the name of multiculturalism—one need only review the graded basal music textbook series of a few decades ago, or the volumes of college music history textbooks. While the contributive approach is an important first step (particularly for music educators whose comfort level or experience with world music cultures is limited), the educational outcomes are limited.

The second level of Banks's multicultural curriculum reform is the *additive approach.* Lessons at this level address issues in more depth than the contributions approach, with content, themes, and concepts incorporated into a variety of activities and understandings. The additional material is more extensive and allows a greater range of diverse material without changing the basic structure of the curriculum. While relatively easy for teachers to incorporate, cultural content is still viewed from a mainstream or privileged perspective. In addition, the learning related to the culture often stands as a separate entity, with connections between the minority group and the dominant one not made explicit. For example, a social studies class that studies the "Westward Ho movement" of American pioneers may learn about the experiences of a particular Native American group, but the entire unit is viewed through the experience of the White settlers. In addition, the complexities of interconnections between the dominant culture and the minority group are, at best, skimmed over.

In an elementary music classroom, a multi-session unit addressing music from Turkey would allow for more extensive learning experiences with an unfamiliar musical tradition, with the multiple experiences with the unfamiliar musical culture making it more extensive than a contributions lesson. Similarly, a secondary choral setting in which repertoire from multiple African American spirituals is used in the context of the established class structure—as critical listening experiences, sight-reading exercises, and a set of pieces in a performance—represents a multicultural learning experience in the additive realm. At the university level, a world music survey class is classified as an additive experience when the class structure resembles other music history classes, with drop-the-needle tests, lecture classes, and minimal music-making, classes in which connections between the new musical cultures and the dominant one remain minimal. The fact that the musical material is still viewed through a Western prism in these more extensive units renders them additive; for example, in a unit on music in Japan, students might be exposed to music traditionally performed on instruments common in Japan (e.g., the *shamisen,* a three-string plucked lute), but perform the music on available instruments (e.g., recorders, keyboard, other available instruments), with no attention paid to the difference in timbre. Music educators engage in these additive experiences with less regularity than contributive ones, for they take more organization and planning. For teachers intent on teaching with a multicultural focus, however, the lessons are a further step along the continuum.

The *transformation approach* takes an issue and views it from the perspective of different groups. An example from language arts involves a recognition of regional forms of expression, while other interaction styles, such as the language patterns of Ebonics and of European Americans from Appalachia, can provide students with alternative linguistic models to consider. Through these experiences, students begin to understand that knowledge is socially constructed, and they are able to recognize that diverse groups contribute in a variety of ways to a subject. In order to accomplish this, the typical curriculum often must be revised, which can be time-intensive.

In music education practice, transformation occurs as musical expressions are compared for their sonic structures, their uses and functions within cultures, their symbologies, and their cultural meaning and values. Examples of teaching with transformation in mind are found in Wade (2004) and Campbell (2004), who suggest that musical instruments, pitch, time, and structure can be explored across as many cultures as are available, "live" in person or through access to media and technology. Instruments can be examined for their cultural associations with gender, cultural status, and spirituality, for example, and for ways in which they are classified and organized into ensembles. Across cultures, pitch is variously treated, and every culture has made logical decisions as to how to refer to discrete pitches (by syllables, numbers, letters), what tunings to apply to a set of pitches, which pitches to gather into modes and scales, and whether pitches will be organized vertically into chords, clusters, polyphonic lines, or interlocking parts. Music's element of time can be studied by way of cultures that feature pulse or no-pulse expressions, and for how music is organized into meters and cycles, and into simultaneous layerings. As for the comparative study of formal structure, musical examples can be found in many cultures to address how the music begins and ends, whether it is fixed or freely improvised, and ways it is linked with ritual, worship, dance, theater, storytelling, and the visual arts.

For students in elementary music programs, the transformation approach can happen in a comparison of fiddles (or flutes, or other instruments) across multiple cultures. Different but equally logical ways can be examined of the construction of fiddles (body shapes, size of tuning pegs, number of strings), or of positioning them in the hands of a player, or of tuning the two, three, four, or more strings. Secondary school students can sing in choirs or play in bands or orchestras various cultural examples of music for weddings, or for funerals, for purposes of expressing cultural or national identity. University students can be led through an exploration of various solfege systems (in theory and musicianship classes), various Western and world events for which musical works were composed (in music history and culture classes), and various approaches to teaching and learning (in pedagogy and education methods classes). For students preparing for careers in music education, projects that encourage the design and delivery of lessons and lesson units on particular musical and cultural themes can lead to a way of conceiving of music instruction that allows school-aged students to develop an understanding of music from multiple perspectives.

Finally, the *social action approach* begins with learning experiences from a transformative background, but then requires students to "make decisions and take actions related to a concept, issue, or problem" that was studied in the unit (Banks, 2013a, p. 13). Not satisfied with solely identifying issues that exist within the status quo, teachers and students move to the level of social action as they make specific plans that will rectify inequities that they have identified within society. For example, a literature class may write a letter to the editor, or a blog piece, with suggestions for ways to demonstrate greater sensitivity and fair treatment within situations in which specific racial and ethnic communities are described (or neglected) in the media. This approach enables students to improve their critical thinking skills, articulate their values, and develop a sense that they are powerful, and empowers them to contribute to making the world a more equitable and culturally sensitive place. The unit may be more intensive than a typical in-school experience, as activities that transpire out in the community beyond school typically require not only time and energy but efforts to safeguard the off-campus safety of students as well as possibly a monetary commitment (for bus rental and meals or snacks).

Social action approaches are fairly rare in music education, in part due to the problems articulated above. Neither are all music teachers convinced of the need to go beyond repertoire and pedagogical processes within their classrooms in meeting the goals of multicultural education and social justice. To many who view a social action approach as an extra off-campus fieldtrip, the logistics are mind-boggling and the alternative of staying put in the classroom seems entirely within the realm of reason in meeting the call for teaching from a multicultural perspective and with social justice in mind. Still, there are exemplary social action approaches in evidence, where teachers work with students who prepare a repertoire of vocal and instrumental pieces for audiences in their school and at community festivals and competitions. Such performances can easily encompass wider audiences of senior citizens, disabled populations, and people from diverse neighborhoods, all of whom may be transported to the school or be visited by students bused to residential centers, churches, shopping centers, and community gathering places. Taking further steps forward, music teachers may facilitate possibilities for their students to visit with their audiences, to use music as an opening to conversations with them following performances, and to find ways of following up with customized notes and further visits, in order to develop meaningful relationships. Students might go so far in a social action approach as to invite an audience to join with them in singing or playing (for example, on hand drums), or even dancing to music, thus shifting a presentational music experience to a participatory one (Turino, 2008).

Occasionally, student ensembles may find themselves invited (or may invite themselves) to perform at civic rallies, political events, and assemblies connected to national holidays or local festivals on a theme. School bands march in parades for Memorial Day and the Fourth of July, and school choirs sing at events memorializing national figures (such as Martin

Luther King Jr.). While not always condoned by all parents, music teachers have organized students for participation as singers or players at community gatherings that call attention to supporting (or not supporting) fair trade, military service, gun control, or civil rights. Students become further attuned to the reasoning behind the issues and to an understanding of the democratic right to stake a claim on them, through their participation in these musical events; they may read of the issues in advance or following the event, and they may gain further insight through exchanges with others present.

At the university level, many possibilities exist for the involvement of students in social action. Music Alive! in the Yakima Valley (Soto, Lum, & Campbell, 2009) is one such program that has drawn music education students from their university campus to a Native American tribal school and to students of a school in a predominantly Mexican American community. (See Chapter 7 for an account of this project.) Over a series of field-visits and short-term residencies, students gain perspectives far removed from their urban campus life (and earlier suburban school experiences), as they sang, played, and danced to the music of their training as well as the music of the local students and their families, whom they came to know. With glimpses of life in these rural and remote low-income communities, each of which nonetheless proudly welcomed the university students into their homes and schools, those students accrued firsthand experiences in the meanings of cultural diversity in education. For some, this social action so enlightened them that they later sought (and found) positions in rural, remote, and impoverished communities across the state.

The impact of the Community Music movement has been felt in curricular reform involving music, multiculturalism, social action, and social justice in music education (Higgins, 2012). With a greater recognition of how music education can transpire in and out of school, Community Music has helped to bring about the linkages of universities with communities that surround them as well as those that may exist some distance apart. Opportunities have emerged for music-major students to become involved in community engagement activities—teaching music to young students in an after-school program, for example, or facilitating a song-writing experience for young people in a juvenile detention center. For course credit, for "service learning" requirements, or as internships that develop into employment opportunities, university music students are involved in social action projects that include working with children, youth, and adults in not only applied music lessons but also the development of drumming ensembles, singing groups, rock bands, song-writing classes, and social dance circumstances. In these ways, music educators are at the forefront of this fourth level of curricular reform, social action, and indeed of social justice as well, facilitating musical experiences for the communities that request them.

THE WAY FORWARD

The diversity of the United States continues to grow at an astonishing rate; 92% of the population growth between 2000 and 2010 comprised ethnic minorities (Banks & Banks, 2013), a trend that shows no sign of stopping. Given that our schools will hold children from an increasingly broad array of cultures, multicultural ideals must necessarily stand at the core of conceptions of social justice: An equitable musical curriculum must incorporate a range of musical cultures in meaningful and equitable fashion. The four levels of curriculum reform (Banks, 2013a) provide a useful road map for teachers and teacher educators searching for a framework within which curricular change can occur. From the earliest dipping-of-toes through a contributions lesson to an in-depth social action experience, the levels of curriculum reform offer a sequential means by which to guide music educators—even those with minimal experience in (and maximal anxiety about) issues of multiculturalism—and a means by which to alter their teaching to create fair-minded and equitable learning environments in which all students are seen, heard, and honored.

Building upon the thoughts and endeavors of earlier generations, the rise of social justice is deeply entwined within the aims and actions of nations and peoples earnestly committed to equitable treatment of citizens in society and its schools. The realization of social justice by thoughtful music educators is in step with the works of teachers devoted to the ideals of multicultural education who, as long ago as the time of the Civil Rights movement of the 1960s, were keen to reach all children and youth through school music programs, to offer relevant musical education that was resonant with their local community experiences, and to provide the means for students' success as citizens of a mainstream society. Situated at the nexus of the movements for multiculturalism and social justice, issues of equity and social action are impressively evident in schools, and these complementary movements are contributing to the education of students in music and through music, leading them toward the socially responsible citizens they will become.

CHAPTER 5

Transmission, Teaching, and Learning

Transmission and learning are topics of interest shared by ethnomusicologists and educators alike, and there are as many multicultural stances on music's teaching/learning interactions as there are musical expressions. On the other hand, there are also processes that operate cross-culturally as evidence of important matters of human learning to keep in mind when drawing music traditions into school music settings. The chapter is a medley of concepts related to the means and modes by which music is communicated, transmitted and acquired, taught and learned. The work explores the music teaching and learning interests of ethnomusicologists, the nature of orality (and aurality) and literacy relative to music transmission, and the array of formal, nonformal, and informal means of music learning. The realities of music's transmission processes are illustrated through a review of tools and techniques that operate in various cultural contexts of music learning, with a focus on musical enculturation and socialization in cases of learners of every age and experience level. The teacher's supportive role in transmitting musical knowledge and cultural heritage is addressed through attention to observation and imitation, strategies such as vocalization, and the nature of improvisation as it filters into music learning.

Drumming Without Notes. Weekly visits to Ramnad Raghavan brought me to the attention of not only his music but his way of learning, both brand-new experiences for me. As a master player of *mridangam* drum of the South Indian Karnatic tradition, Mr. Raghavan was staying with family in the basement of a small home on Cleveland's west side, and he was accepting students in the area to travel to him for lessons. He came from a family of musicians in Tamil Nadu and was widely known as both a performer and a teacher; he had taught for more than 30 years in American universities such as Wesleyan (Connecticut) and Kent State (Ohio). His move to the midwest did not prevent him from keeping a lively performance schedule in North America and India, and he would invite his key students to sing, play (on their instruments, including violin and clarinet), keep *tala*, or play the drone pitches on *tamboura* at concerts and festivals in the eastern United States and Canada. He developed a considerable corps of students and aspirant musicians, and built a community of avid listeners through the Cleveland Thyagaraja Aradhana festival he had established with T. Temple Tuttle.

The *mridangam* is an exquisite drum, albeit heavy, and I had to adjust to sitting in position on the floor, legs loosely crossed so as to allow the drum to rest on my right foot and ankle. Featured in Tamil literature and paintings, the *mridangam* is many centuries old and important to sacred and secular musical forms of the Karnatic musical culture of South India. It is made of a hollowed piece of jackfruit, and thick goatskin attached by leather straps constitutes the playing surfaces at either end. The center of the skin is covered with a sticky paste of rice flour and water, which functions to lower the pitch of the left membrane and give it a powerful resonating bass sound. As I organized my body into a proper playing position, I set a small tape recorder nearby to pick up any performances, demonstrations, or remarks by my teacher, and I opened my notebook and clicked my pen to await whatever hints and help I could jot down.

My Western way of learning was immediately dashed as Mr. Raghavan announced at the start of the first lesson that we would not be recording the sessions, nor would I be writing in my notebook. Further, he would not be distributing notation to work from. All these cues were prohibited, but he assured us that we indeed would learn by watching him, listening to him, imitating him, and receiving his immediate corrective feedback. Unlike in the many years of piano study I had known, I would have no audio reminders for later reference in practice, no handwritten notes by me or my teacher from the lesson, and no notation to decode. I came to understand that there were drum syllables to vocalize in a rhythmic manner, and that they represented the sound of the drumhead (and consequently signaled also which hand and what fingers would be utilized, in what ways—flat, cupped, near the edge of the drumhead, at its center—and whether one hand would be joined by the other hand).

My colleague, Alex Sidorowicz, and I had embarked on the journey to learn *mridangam* together. We spent an hour on the road each way, arriving at our guru's residence for a lesson that would range from 2 to 4 hours, at our teacher's choice. We assumed our playing positions in Mr. Raghavan's basement on an "Indian-style," maroon-colored carpet with a beige medallion center. We put our palms together and bowed to our teacher at the start of each lesson, and we learned to keep *tala* beats on our fingers while listening to our teacher play what we later would learn. We listened hard to the rhythms and imitated them immediately following the multiple repetitions of the phrases—first vocally and eventually on the drumheads. We learned to sing the melodies of selected *varnam* and *kriti* (vocal) pieces, which Alex eventually played on his clarinet at the request of Mr. Raghavan. We sat very still for the entirety of the lessons, folded up as we were for over 2 hours, and we learned the music by giving full listening focus to the tasks of acquiring technique and repertoire. Once we adjusted, we were able to gain tremendous insight into the music and its pedagogical way, and it suddenly dawned on me that I was learning more music, and about music, than many hours of lectures and theoretical readings could ever offer me.

To this day, I remember the music and I honor the pedagogical experience that took me down an extraordinary pathway that clarified the power of the listening ear as primary conduit of all the music I needed to know.

STUDIES IN TRANSMISSION

Music teachers and teaching musicians play important roles in the sustainability of music in culture. They preserve music by transmitting it to their students, and they sustain music through their efforts to foster not only the reproduction of musical works but also the inspiration to produce fresh interpretations and creative development of the music, especially in music cultures in which new interpretations and improvisations are expected and valued. Various techniques and methods are culturally maintained in the teaching/learning process, and like the features of the music so, too, are teaching/learning practices reflective of the culture. These techniques merit attention and can be honored in school experiences so that music can be understood not only for its sound but also for its behaviors and meanings within its origin cultures.

Western art music adheres to a system of notational literacy for preserving and passing on repertoire, and those who hope to perform the music of Mozart, Mahler, (David) Maslanka, and (Richard E.) McKee must master the capacity to decode symbols into sound. Outside this realm, music learning is chiefly tied to oral-aural transmission processes in which a keen listening sense must be cultivated in order to catch and keep the musical details. Some cultures employ one-to-one private lessons in which a teacher works with one student at a time to hone performance technique, while other cultures offer group instruction vocally and on instruments. Formally in educational institutions as well as informally in circles of players and singers, learning proceeds according to traditions that require the active employment of the ear, the eye (for note-reading or for watching every slight but significant maneuver of the master musician), the voice (regardless of whether the music is vocal or instrumental in nature), and the body. In adhering to the spectrum of music that can be taught in programs with multicultural outcomes in mind, attention by teachers to teaching/learning behaviors as well as the sound itself can be highly informative for students, who will learn, in addition to a song or an instrumental piece, how music reflects ways of being and cultural ideals.

Ethnomusicologists have studied the transmission of music in various cultures, both systematically and as a component of their field research. Alan P. Merriam's (1964) declaration of learning as basic to understanding music-as-culture was an early prompt to music scholars to look into who teaches and who learns, and how it is done. Bruno Nettl (1986) wrote of the importance of his consultants as teachers, including the Arapaho Indian Will Shakespeare, who sang a vast array of traditional melodies for him to learn and transcribe, and the Persian master Nour Ali-Bouromand, who taught him the *radif* collection of micromelodies that are core to improvisation. Dissertations and monographs, along with journal articles, have been important channels of information about who teaches and who learns music, in what contexts music is taught and learned, and how informal learning of music occurs through enculturation processes. Timothy Rice (2003b) described the incidence, within his examination of 85 book-length musical ethnographies, of those that referred to music learning and teaching to a greater or lesser extent: "About half of the 85 (43 to be exact) make at least a modest mention of the topic and thus provide useful data for cross-cultural surveys. . . . Ten of the 85 devote significant attention (a chapter or more) to the topic. An additional five of the 85 make music learning or teaching the central point of the monograph" (p. 167). Other issues have been given limited attention by ethnomusicologists, including the politics and economics of music learning. Through these investigations, not only are specific music cultures known more fully but a deeper understanding of the sociological features of music as human thought and behavior is developed.

Some scholars have discussed in fine detail the instructional transactions of learning to play an instrument, or to sing or dance, within societies that are open and eager to have the musical participation of all their members, while others have described music learning within the strictures of social class, gender, or ethnicity. John Blacking (1967) recalled the manner in which children learned the music of the Venda of South Africa by positioning themselves centrally in the midst of performances and practice sessions, so that they might develop as if by osmosis into their rightful role as participants in the music-making of their egalitarian society. For John Baily (2001), an ethnomusicologist with 30 years of study of *dutar* and *rubab*, two lutes of Afghanistan, learning to perform invites the practitioner into "the cognition of performance," the active movements and kinesthetic-spatial relationships, and the thinking processes of those at the center of musical life within a culture. Henry Kingsbury (1988) studied the training of musicians accepted into the conservatory system, that particular venue for the talented elite whose performance skill is judged to be of sufficient quality to reap the benefits of notation-based training, and Bruno Nettl (1996) wrote an incisive ethnographic account of the culture of midwestern American university schools of music as an institutionalized process that is dependent on (among other matters) notational literacy.

Ethnomusicologists have studied music learning in formal and informal settings, in conservatories, schools, private homes, and even out in the open air. They have examined the extent of verbal and nonverbal techniques, the use of vocalization and solmization, the extent of aural and oral techniques, the use of rehearsal strategies, and the pace of the instructional delivery from the teacher to the student (Campbell, 1991. Neuman's (1980) work discussed the disciplined practice (*riaz*) in the *gharanas* of North India, in which students are expected to put in long hours of rigorous working on their assigned drills on their instrument, and explained how the calluses on their hands and finger pads are evidence of the time spent. In the study of the Bulgarian *gaida* (bagpipe), Rice (1994) attended to the combination of aural, visual, and tactile means of learning the phrases that are connected to other phrases and later are recalled in improvisation. Likewise, Bakan (1999) focused on the critical importance of combined modalities that must work in a complementary manner to ensure that skills and repertoire develop, with students observing the hands of the master while they follow closely in imitation of them. In his study of jazz musicians, Paul Berliner (1994) found that many notable players transcribe entire solos from recordings but also use them for extracting and learning short phrases as vocabulary for improvisations to come. Rice returned to the sociology of music teaching and learning (2003a, 2017) to examine institutions and contexts for teaching and learning, including formal and informal settings, and to address through specific geographic and historic contexts what it means to be musical. These glimpses into culturally preferred ways of acquiring repertoire and technique are relevant to teachers keen to consider ways of instilling in students a more comprehensive sense of a musical culture, as well as to allow possible transfer of less familiar but potentially effective techniques into the teaching of other musical selections in their classes.

THE RANGE OF MUSIC LEARNING

There are constructs to consider in a discussion of culture-based practices of music learning, each of them definitive yet also somewhat overlapping and adding meaning to the others. A spectrum of learning practices is evident even in Western settings involving children and youth at home and in school, extending from the most formal means to the nonformal processes found beyond institutionalized settings, all the way to completely informal, indirect, and unintentional forms of learning. Learning may be defined through a differentiation of it as (a) formal, occurring through a teacher's intervention in highly structured settings such as school; (b) nonformal and only partly guided, occurring outside institutionalized settings through the prompting of nonconsecutive directives, frequently by expert musicians to novices; and (c) enculturative, occurring naturally, non-consciously, and without direct instructional activity (Campbell, 1998, 2010). Unplanned, resulting from daily life situations, this third category is known also as informal music learning, which may be conscious or not, and which develops as a result of interactions with peers and family, and even in self-teaching circumstances.

The formal realm of music learning is thoroughly linked to the standard processes evidenced in official and authorized institutions where teachers' selection, presentation, and rehearsal of students ensure that explicit knowledge and skills are learned. Examples of the nonformal process are a father's occasional coaching his daughter at home in the bar chords on a guitar, or a neighbor's intermittent modeling for a youngster of repertoire and techniques at the piano (Campbell, 2002a). In the last realm, enculturative learning, the psychic structure of a societal group is passed on through a cultural immersion process, so that a child develops an implicit understanding of the knowledge and values of a repertoire by nature of his or her membership and participation in that society. Enculturation naturally occurs across generations, as with the lullabies and bedtime songs a mother sings to her child, but can occur also from an older or more experienced child to another. Language and communications, including self-identity, gender roles, kinesthetics (body language), and daily rhythms are learned but not taught in an enculturative manner; they are acquired in ways that are automatic and outside children's own conscious awareness. These cultural patterns appear always to have been there as part of the ambience of a people's lifestyle, permeating the manner and style of their thought, expression, and behavior (Hall, 1992).

Various differentiations and descriptions of learning have been offered: apprenticeships and live-in private study with a teacher (as in the case of Thai *piphat* houses or Indian *gharanas*) outside of institutional settings, growth-oriented experiences that are arranged within a community (such as Suzuki violin instruction), and socialization, the process by which a group shares its beliefs and values in a learner- (rather than teacher-) constructed learning experience (Campbell, 1991; Jorgensen, 1997). There are further nuanced gradations of these instances, yet it is useful to consider them as degrees of formality in the means by which music is transmitted and acquired. These points of music learning, along with particular techniques of pedagogy and reception by children and other learners, are illustrated in the selected cultures described below.

Western art music is learned through formal lessons and in the formalized process of ensemble rehearsals. Meanwhile, folk, traditional, and popular music has long been learned through the oral tradition, informally and outside schools. As these oral music cultures have been drawn into schools, they also have been taught to students using formal procedures and techniques. When oral tradition styles such as klezmer, South African freedom songs, and Mexican mariachi are brought into schools, they are made to fit Western art music and school-based pedagogy that embraces notational literacy, "fixed" expressions (with no flexible interpretations), and a precise set of atomistic steps that break the larger musical experience into small segments. These steps are intended to bring every learner in the group along, assuming, sometimes incorrectly, that those who learn quickly and without need for every small step will wait for those who need more detail and processing time. While the employment of informal procedures for learning folk, traditional, and popular music would be a culturally preferred mode of music learning, in a school music class multiple musical expressions instead are treated as "materials" to be collected and squeezed into the formal processes of Western-fashioned institutions (thus depriving students of the opportunity to have a more culture-specific learning experience).

A consideration of formal versus informal learning brings up holistic and analytical issues. Following on the ethnomusicological observation that holistic learning is standard practice in learning music in cultures beyond Western art and school-based music (M. Hood, 1971/1982), Paul van den Bos (1995) charted distinctive teaching/learning practices in a comparison of holistic and analytical processes. Holistic learning is based on an interactive flow of teacher demonstration and student imitation (and sometimes just "doing it," i.e., the student's gradual immersion into the music as the teacher performs it repeatedly), while analytical learning involves the teacher as guide, breaking material into small steps, and in full control of the student's learning. The instructional procedures of holistic learning are concentric, nonsequential, and emanating from the music itself, while analytical learning involves a linear presentation of separate skills in a piecemeal manner as they are drawn out of the music. In holistic learning, the teacher is a performing musician, playing or singing but not involved in a sequential breakdown or buildup of minute components of the music, while analytical learning requires a teacher's active role in the method of learning, so much so that pedagogical knowledge surpasses the teacher's need for performance mastery. To get to the heart of the music, and to embrace it in order to make it, the holistic learner travels "beyond words" into the sound itself, inducing a nonverbal and non-notational journey through careful listening, watching, and doing. Holistic learning is not standard in school music classes and in fact may not fit the format of some Western curricular plans.

Building from earlier work and his own observations of music learning across diverse cultures, Huib Schippers (2010) furthered comparisons of music teaching and learning in a 12-point continuum that includes not only modes of transmission but also descriptions of context and interactions between teacher and student. He describes teaching–learning styles as spanning from atomistic–analytical to holistic, notation-based to aural, and tangible to intangible. Through visits to artist-teachers in their studios and classes, he illustrates transmission styles of specific musical genres and the master musicians who teach them. A West African percussionist, a musician of the Balinese gamelan (*gong kebyar*) practice, and a classical *bansuri* (flute) player from North India are studied to illustrate the manner in which traditional musicians teach. The nonverbal and strictly musical means of communicating music comes to the fore, as does the matter of tangible acquisition of musical knowledge and skills, even in the case of improvisatory styles that nonetheless require skill acquisition in order to attain the sublime expression. Not surprisingly, the learning process of many of the world's musical cultures maximizes orality over notational literacy. To be sure, music learning runs the gamut from "very formal" to hardly formal to quite informal processes, and a glance at this holistic–analytical spectrum across multiple cultures is a chance to recognize the tracks of human learning that are in operation. Clearly, the culture-specific transmission systems in play are linked to the music of particular peoples and places in the world.

ORALITY AND LITERACY IN MUSIC EDUCATION PRACTICE

Orality–literacy studies have long been of intrigue to music scholars. The groundbreaking work of Milman Parry and Albert Lord on epic song in Yugoslavia launched questions of orality pertinent to research in literature, anthropology, psychology, and education (Lord, 1960). From the analysis of Homeric poetry for the features resulting from its oral means of composition and transmission, Lord pursued, in *The Singer of Tales,* the study of modern Yugoslavian epic singing and brought to the fore questions of orality, memory, and the sometimes ancillary role that literacy plays in learning oral literature and lore, including music. Seminal works by scholars of music of the Middle Ages have highlighted the emergence of notation in oral performance and the interaction between literature and oral modes of communication of the time (Treitler, 2003). Jack Goody (1977) and Walter Ong (1982) have delved deeply into the development and impact of notational literacy in what once had been an entirely oral pursuit of learning music by ear. Notation may have evolved in the West to coincide with the concept of individual authorship of music by a single composer rather than the sense of a collective identity that develops among performers of music in many of the world's communities. Bruno Nettl's (1998) probing of improvisation "in the course of performance" drew together an array of scholars, many of whom were attentive to orality as a route for musicians to internalize music so as to amass a treasury of ideas from which to draw in the creative act.

Literacy is the gold-standard goal of school programs, and music curricular policies and guidelines pay tribute to it as central to the making of a well-trained musician. It is a prized technological invention renowned for its capacity to preserve and transmit music. For learning Western music, Western staff notation offers a detailed prescriptive way of communicating what a musician should play or sing (Wade, 2004). Even when it is acknowledged as an imperfect image, and only a pictographic sketch of the sound, it is hailed as useful and convenient. Despite his deep knowledge of oral-aural transmission (as in Korean *p'ung mul* percussion music), ethnomusicologist Keith Howard (1990) argued the commonsense use of notation in the teaching of oral traditions, noting that "even if we understand the way things used to be done (in oral cultures), we must be realistic: Rote learning takes time and time is increasingly lacking in our mad world" (p. 68). Indeed, notational literacy accelerates learning, once the system is learned and can be applied to all music that has been transcribed and notated. Transcriptions of musical sound to notation can serve well as an exercise in knowing the intricacies of the musical sound. Still, note-reading does not replace direct contact with the music, as musicians best become familiar with little-known music through the direct route: by listening. In some musical practices, for example, the Japanese *koto*, notation distracts from the learning process since both the ear and eye must take account of the sound and the subtleties of performance and execution of the sound. Traditional music of much of the world's cultures is learned aurally, whether it is Spanish flamenco guitar, Indian *sitar*, Bolivian *quena* (flute), Burmese *suang kauk* (harp), Irish fiddle, or the myriad of choral practices in Russia, Central Asia, South Africa, and the Pacific Islands.

Surprisingly, orality—or aurality, the quality of focused and attentive listening—is not a first consideration of many teachers, whether public school band directors, private vocal instructors, or university professors of piano or orchestral instruments. While none would deny that listening is a useful musical tool, few authors of elementary and secondary school curricular programs highlight the development of aural skills, including those who note the importance of learning the world's musical (and predominantly oral) cultures and aim for sensitivity to culture-specific behaviors and values. Teachers clamor for notation and scores, but are far less likely to request links to recordings of the pieces they will teach. Likewise, publishing companies provide scores for choirs, bands, and orchestras, but frequently leave aside the provision of listening samples. Yet listening serves its purpose in a notation-laden school music curriculum in which teachers who espouse sound-before-signs will initiate a lesson with aural exercises that lead to music's portrayal in standard staff notation. As well, there are still incidences of teacher-directed collective listening by classes of students to recordings of selected works, or recommendations by music teachers that students listen on their own to particular renditions of works under study.

CROSS-CULTURAL CASES OF MUSIC, TAUGHT AND LEARNED

Approaches to transmission, teaching, and learning come into view through brief descriptions of musical enculturation and education. In the sampling of cultural cases, aural learning is widely evident at home and away from school, and the presence of demonstration and imitation also is marked. Where music is mingled with movement and dance, the "visual" component appears for learners by way of watching the musician for gestures, subtle movements, and dance steps, postures, and patterns. An understanding of how music is taught and learned is revealed partly through these cases of the training of musicians in private studio lessons, in schools, and in everyday enculturative circumstances of children at play and in development.

In Japan

In Japan, where Westernization has been an integral part of the national identity since the late 19th century, schoolchildren have within their school music repertoire a set of Western orchestral and chamber works to perform and appreciate, and songs translated into Japanese from English, French, German, and other languages of the world. In after-school programs, many opt for experiences in wind band performance, where musical standards are high and competition can be fierce (Hebert & Kertz-Welzel, 2012). Their knowledge of their own Japanese musical traditions and song repertoire has been minimal, due to priorities set by the Ministry of Education to promote "basic musical skill" and "encourage children's love of music" through a Western-styled repertoire that has been a measure of excellence in musical education for nearly a century (Takizawa, 1997). Yet some path-breaking developments by Japanese educators and ethnomusicologists are redirecting materials and methods of teaching to musical genres, repertoire, and processes beyond the West, including Japan's own unique instrumental, musical theater, and *minyo* (folk song) traditions. Despite the enormous success of Western art music in Japanese schooling, a curricular shift is now in progress to raise young people to understand their Japanese musical identity as well as to know a broader and more global view of musical cultures.

When Americans first arrived in Japan in 1868 and for the following several decades of frequent exchanges between Japan and the West, a grand assortment of musical instruments, styles, and explicit pieces were introduced to children in Japanese schools. Japanese educator Seiji Izawa invited American educator Luther Whiting Mason to Japan for a period in the 1880s, and a curriculum was forged for elementary school music classes that was to bring Japanese schoolchildren the songs not only of their American peers but also of European traditions. The Japanese Ministry of Education developed *shoka,* a specific way of school singing in which Western song melodies were imbued with Japanese moral and patriotic texts. The aim of these curricular actions was to radically alter the culture by influencing the children and the women who would work with them, in music and through music (Manabe, 2013).

Yet even while *shoka* singing and Western songs were the musical mainstay in Japanese schools at the end of the 19th century, children continued a traditional repertoire of children's songs, singing games, and chants (called collectively *warabe-uta*) when off on their own and at play. By the 1920s, composers and poets were creating new songs of high artistic quality for children, with texts thought to be relevant to their needs and interests (Gottschewski, 1998). These songs merged Japanese and Western musical and textual sensibilities, which became the centerpiece of a school-based repertoire for much of the 20th century (Manabe, 2013). Yet when postwar Japan was in search of its own identity, *warabe-uta* were "rediscovered" and viewed as central to not only children's culture but also the Japanese spirit (Manes, 2012). These traditional children's songs were even seen as having been a musical foundation or inspiration for other genres such as the *nagauta* (the "long songs" of kabuki theater) and instrumental music for *koto, shamisen,* and *shakuhachi.* Traditional children's songs continue to be sung by Japanese children today, even in the midst of Western art music, Japanese traditional music, and the ubiquitous sounds of mediated popular music.

The study of traditional Japanese instruments by beginners of all ages typically transpires through highly stylized individual lessons beyond school, where the teacher's own musical competence is useful in modeling appropriate techniques (Campbell, 1991). Verbal explanations are rare, while demonstration and the physical interaction of teacher and student in clarifying finger and arm positions are common practices. Pieces for *koto,* as well as *shamisen* and *shakuhachi,* are learned through mnemonics— semantically meaningless aural cues that use pitched or rhythmic syllables to represent the music. Japanese teachers transmit phrases of melody and rhythm orally, singing or chanting them to the students, who immediately repeat them; teacher and students may sing and chant together before or during their performance of these phrases on the instrument. Even though notation is available, learning by rote or at least in a combination of rote and note is preferable, so that notation becomes a trigger for remembering what transpired in aural and kinesthetic terms within the lesson. The beauty of the physical execution of the music is a key aesthetic component in Japanese traditional music, and a teacher's modeling of posture and graceful movement is yet another component of the student's efforts at observation and imitation. Instrumental study in Japan typically commences in childhood, and while there is a steady stream of young people taking piano and violin lessons, a significant number are drawn also to the traditional instruments both for their sonic appeal and for the performance rituals that are embraced by the teacher and the culture at large.

Formal schooling in the traditional music of Japan typically emphasizes listening and appreciation. As in any music curriculum, there are some pieces and genres that are "fixed" and others that "go missing." The song "Sakura" is a constant among teaching materials in Japan, and a handful of *minyo* typically are spread through textbooks. *Koto* music commonly is featured, especially "Rokudan," a *shakuhachi* piece called "Shika No Tone," a *kabuki nagauta* selection, and the *gagaku* court ensemble piece "Entenraku." The musical canon in Japanese school texts does not feature, however, music of the 14th-century Noh theater, Buddhist *shomyo* chant, *biwa* lute music, or *gidayu* (the duo of musicians that perform in the *bunraku* puppet theater) (Takizawa, 1997). Where Japanese traditional music is taught in schools, the emphasis is frequently on understanding musical structure, cultural and historical context, and aesthetic values. Still rare in Japanese schools is the performance-based study by whole classes of students of traditional instruments or vocal music beyond select *minyo* and *warabe-uta*.

Among Native Americans

Among the people of the First Nations of North America, or Native Americans (including Canada and the United States), music is a communal event as well as a deeply personal phenomenon. Its transmission may be a matter of one's age, gender, and rank within a community, or it may be a result of a personal journey that leads to spiritual inspiration (Perea, 2013). Music is deeply embedded in ritual and social customs of the clan or tribe, in coming-of-age ceremonies, and in coming to terms with the supernatural, the ancestral spirits, and the spirits of nature and of living creatures. Some songs are group-owned and intended for all to know, while others are considered personal property, to be sung only by those whose songs they are or by permission given for their use. For many people of the First Nations, song is the equivalent of the Bible's Genesis and Leviticus in the moral lessons it holds, and those without knowledge of song are considered "poor," uneducated, or lacking an important piece of who they are.

For children growing up in Native American communities, music is a part of their personal and social identities. Concepts of traditional indigenous knowledge to be passed to the young allow for the music as a way of recounting history, predicting the future, passing on local wisdom, reflecting on meaningful places and contexts, and clarifying one's role within a nation and a clan (Diamond, 2008). Modern indigenous music and dance have emerged even as older layers are continued, so that a group of unaccompanied singers and dancers can still hold its own even as wired rock and country music bands perform their own blend of contemporary and indigenous expressions. Intertribal celebrations are raising new issues of ownership, borrowing, and sharing, as songs cross groups and become fused with different cultural expressions (Perea, 2013). Meanwhile, young people often are caught in the middle of the contemporary cultural revitalization that is occurring, trying to make sense of older layers of culture, including music, in their changing world.

Families are responsible for teaching songs and dances to family members in order to perpetuate their traditions. The Spokane and Coeur d'Alene tribes of the interior of the American northwest assert the primary place of song in their development as children. They remember it as the sound they awakened to, and to which they would go to sleep, when mothers, fathers, grandparents, and other family members sang alone and together. From birth to death, songs are there for points throughout the day and throughout their lives, from the morning song, the song for the birth of a child, for becoming a man or woman, for being in love, for marriage, for sickness and death. There are welcoming songs, songs for learning dances, for being a warrior, and for battle itself (Sijohn, 1999).

The Coast Salish groups who live along the Pacific Rim of the United States and Canada continue to pass on the lessons of their culture to young people through their songs. While stories are significant in that they contain metaphors, and important cultural knowledge about ancestors, family, animals, and plants, the elders believe that stories that are sung help retention. Singing often is reserved for the moral of the story, the bottom-line lessons to be learned, the story's most important turn of events. One account of song learning among the Snohomish people underscores the means of ensuring that the substance of stories and songs is learned. "My great-grandmother would sing the songs that went with the stories. Then somewhere during the story, my great-grandmother would stop and pretend to try to remember what came next (it was a test). One of the older children, who had heard the song many times before, would have to say, "Kaya [grandmother], this is what they did" (Miller, 1999, p. 30). A singer of the Makah Nation remembered the importance of repeated listening: "My dad . . . would make us sit down and listen to a new song 'til we were very tired of it! He'd just play the drum and sing the song, every day" (Goodman & Swan, 1999, p. 86). Although the oral method continues to be practiced by the Makah, children now learn songs via tape recordings given them by their elders. However, since children may no longer be "forced" to sit and listen repeatedly to their parents and grandparents, they do not practice regularly. The same is true of dance, where videotapes are available, but the viewing by First Nations children is sporadic when left to chance. With no one there to help them out physically and to correct their errors, children and youth know less of the traditional repertoire than they once did.

As in many First Nations cultures, Navajo children learn the songs of their culture by joining in as singing participants in the rituals and social functions in which adults play prominent roles. They also may sing the adult songs, or parts of them, away from adults, sometimes converting them into their own new expressions, adding interactive movements or combining them with games they know or invent. Among the Oglala Sioux of the Dakotas, the word for "compose" is *yatun*, literally "to give birth to a song," and yet the connotation of *tun* is "to give rise to something that has already existed in another form" (Powers, 1980, p. 33). Thus it appears that there may be an unconscious recycling of songs that occurs from person to person, with the singer uncertain of the song's evolution. Since country, rock, rap, gospel, and other popular forms have become embedded in the ambience of their communities, these styles are also influential in the music children make. There are, of course, traditional children's songs, too, and singing games, lullabies, and humorous songs, which are all part of the oral tradition passed on to them by adults (McAllester, 1996).

The traditional music continues, despite an attempt that was underway by the Bureau of Indian Education in the 19th century to "civilize" the children of First Nations communities. Indigenous people in Canada and the United States were banned from practicing their Native rituals, religious celebrations, and extended family gatherings; children and youth were sent to boarding schools where traditional practices, including heritage songs and dances, could be replaced by the curricular content of mainstream schools. By the 1890s, these schools were mandatory for all Native children, who were subjected to studies that were far afield from their tribal life and made to wear uniforms. Their hair was cut short, they were housed in barracks-styled halls, and they were fed a menu of foods foreign to them. Many schools were run like military academies, and wind and brass bands similar to those found in the military were established (Goodman & Swan, 1999). These actions were intended to bring assimilation to Native American children and to focus attention away from the culture they would have known at home, which would not serve to bring them into the mainstream of society. Yet in summer, when school was out and the children were back at home, the traditions, including the music, crept back into their lives. They serenaded one another, sang and danced with their families, and (depending upon the particular tribe) found drums to beat, rattles to shake, and flutes to play. People of the First Nations survived the boarding schools, and gradually the government-sponsored schools closed and children were returned to their families to be educated in their local schools, where curricular subjects today include Native American cultural studies and celebrations of music and dance, along with standard public school fare (Diamond, 2008; Sijohn, 1999).

In a Tanzanian Village

Holistic and fully embodied musical practice, referred to as *ngoma* by pro-Bantu linguistic-cultural groups, is a particular process of participatory musicking that invites all to join in a thoroughgoing expression of the human spirit. In Kiswahili, the lingua franca of Tanzania, Kenya, Uganda, Rwanda, Burundi, and parts of neighboring countries, *ngoma* literally means "drum, dance, and music" (Janzen, 1991 Mapana, 2007). Like the Greek mousike, the Blackfoot saapup, and the Wagnerian *Gesamtkunstwerk*, *ngoma* encompasses more than music alone. It is an enveloping experience that features three or more of these facets: drumming, singing, dancing, dramatic-interactive play, poetry, costuming, and pageantry. *Ngoma* is the syncretic blend of performative matter and functions in villages at public ceremonies, in private rituals, in celebrations, on religious and seasonal holidays, and even in competitive festivities. It does not so much signify a particular genre as it refers to a perspective on expression that honors multimodal, integrative, holistic, and communal characteristics (see www.borntogroove.org.).

While *ngoma* processes are found throughout much of the eastern, central, and southern African continent, it is within Wagogo culture that a "perfect *ngoma*" lives. As farmers and herders, the Wagogo are over a million in population, attentive to feeding their families, raising their children, carrying on their heritage, while also finding their way through the remnants of earlier colonial domination by Germany and Britain, modernization efforts (with more than a little help and influence from the United States, South Africa, and recently China), and the Swahili-ization of their nation (which requires their shift from the Cigogo mother tongue to the Swahili language that is widespread throughout Tanzania). Moreover, the Wagogo are singers, dancers, and players of a beautiful music that compels me to return again and again to Tanzania to hear it live, to dance to it and to sing it. Wagogo *ngoma* joins together song, dance, and musical instruments such as flute, a two-stringed bowed lute, a thumb piano of about 15 metal prongs called *ilimba*, and single-headed drums held between the knees and played while dancing. Sometimes dramatic episodes are enacted, and also sung, played, and danced. Song texts consist of poetic statements relevant to the health of villagers, the prevention of disease, the education of children, the perpetuation of Wagogo traditions, and various other contemporary topics of social significance (Mapana, Campbell, Roberts, & Mena, 2016).

The Wagogo value the integration of all the arts, which seems to happen naturally in the act of *ngoma*'s expressive practice and embraces the participation of many rather than singling out and raising to star status only the select and talented few. As the basis of a paradigm for encouraging all to know their fuller musical and artistic-expressive selves, *ngoma* is social music and collective musical experience. It is rich in polyrhythms and polyphonic voices, even as it allows individuals to shine solo in a dance maneuver or elaborate vocalized "call" before receding into the community of musicians. It is variously entertaining, therapeutic, and powerful enough to validate the importance of individuals to the social fabric of a community. *Ngoma* invites and envelops all, and while not everyone will sing, dance, and play every time, the Wagogo way is that the invitation is a standing one, open and accepting of individuals into the musicking experience at any time.

An experience in the Wagogo way of *ngoma* is reminiscent of children's propensity to sing, dance, and play. Although rarely articulated by children, this act of multiple musical participation is wholesome, healthy, and healing as a comprehensive expressive process. Music is threaded into the very beings of children as they play individually and collectively. In studies of children's musical cultures (Campbell & Wiggins, 2013), this penchant for integrative-artistic expression appears to rise out of children's playful interactions and exchanges, and in many circumstances and settings. Today's Wagogo children, and adults as well, embrace the music they themselves make live, sitting around after a meal, singing, picking up sticks to click, gourds to shake, an occasional *ilimba* or drum to play. Churches are alive with singing and dancing, as is the occasional café (in the larger villages where cafés are available), and there are hotspots of singing and "rhythmicking" (vocalized rhythms replete with dance movements) quite regularly just about anywhere in the village. Not only is the *ngoma* way of the Wagogo a fully embodied participatory experience, but it is learned by listening, watching, and doing. In an enculturative process, the music is present throughout a lifetime of daily work, play, celebration and mourning, devotional practice, and various rituals and routines.

In the Philippines

While continuing a long history of European- and American-styled systems of schooling in the Philippines that includes Western content and pedagogical processes, a movement was set in motion in the late 20th century for the rediscovery in curriculum and courses of indigenous musical expressions that constitute the unique identity of the Filipino people. The content of music within established conservatories and university departments of music, and the urban concert scene, is largely Western in flavor. Still, there are folk ensembles, vocal forms, and instrumental genres that reflect the indigenous, colonial, and immigrant groups that constitute the nation and that increasingly are becoming a presence in formal studies of Filipino music (Castro, 2011). The local Filipino music genres are often the first and continuing sounds that people know, and the local folk songs are now finding further validation through their inclusion in educational settings.

The Western tradition of established conservatories is tied to Western standard pedagogical methods, but within communities and schools, the *maystro* works to revive folk ensembles that have known a considerable history in the Philippines and continue to be important in rural areas and provincial towns. From the Spanish maestro (master or teacher) comes the *maystro* system, where individual musician-educators teach, arrange, and conduct music for school-aged members of *banda* (band) and *rondalla* (string) ensembles. The *maystro* prepares music arrangements in staff notation; many players are taught by rote. Every *banda* and *rondalla* player knows the melodic line by heart, and can sing it, and thus shares this identical aural and kinetic referent so that no one can get lost in the ensemble. Solfege frequently is utilized in learning melody and parts, so that a comprehensive musicianship develops in players that goes beyond keys and bowings (Trimillos, 1989).

The *maystro* system provides a template for social relationships in and through music. The *maystro* is coach and mentor of the students, and he typically takes on the person of a family member when he offers his home as the location of instructional sessions and rehearsals. Student players learn to help novice players and to seek out the advice and support of players more expert than themselves. In the case of improvisation, which is standard practice within the *rondalla* ensemble, young students learn the idiomatic ways of their instrument and a certain technical proficiency through the experience of playing the *maystro*'s arrangements and from listening to others. On cue from the *maystro*, adolescent and adult musicians are expected to take off from the arrangements, trying out new harmony parts and countermelodies (Atabug, 1984). The *maystro*, as authority figure and benefactor, provides encouragement and guidance and is viewed as the source of all early knowledge of the instruments and repertoire.

Within the Philippines is the large island of Mindanao, where the Maranao reside and retain their brilliant Muslim traditions. The Maranao have a signature vocal form, *bayok*, a love song of artistic merit sung by artists of either gender called *onor*. The *onor* must be prepared intellectually and artistically for the task of performing *bayok*, and so the cultivation begins in childhood when *onors* learn the Arabic language, Qur'anic recitation, Maranao social ethics, the principal Maranao epic, called "Darangen," performance techniques, and repertoire for the *kulintang* (set of knobbed gongs). The skill of a performing *onor* is measured by how well the *onor* delivers an improvised musical discourse with high literary value, using classical Maranao language, proverbs, humor, and poetic devices. The training requires long tutorial sessions filled with rote learning, with texts to be memorized in set melodic phrases. The Maranao *bayok* is highly specialized and thus requires rigorous lessons and practice sessions before a public performance is permitted (Santos, 1996).

The *kulintang* is by far the ultimate national musical symbol of the Philippines, exoticized by the renowned folkloric ensemble known as Bayanihan (Castro, 2011), and is fast becoming the instrument of choice for many young Filipinos living there and abroad. *Kulintang* is the name of both the ensemble and also a single instrument, which appears as an oblong wooden box with cords strung within it so as to support eight kettle-shaped embossed bronze gongs. Two long, light wood mallets, each with a small head of wrapped yarn and cloth, are used to play the gongs. The ensemble includes this instrument along with several hanging gongs and a single-headed barrel drum, and plays a percussive melody along with punctuating rhythms that drive the sound forward and motivate listeners to dance. The transmission of Filipino *kulintang* music occurs through an oral/aural process where demonstration and imitation are prominently featured, and singing the melody line may spontaneously occur while attempting to play it. The visual–kinesthetic channels of information are critical to learning, too, so that young players watch as much as listen to other players perform at high speed and then reproduce the gestures of the hands as they fly across the gongs. In early listening and performing attempts, student players "catch" the motifs and partial phrases and realize the general ideas of melodic contour, but it may take many trials before they can fill in the details that replicate the music as it is meant to be played (Campbell, 2001). *Kulintang* music is rhythmically sophisticated, and the ensemble of instruments sounds in interlocking fashion where one rhythm fits in between or surrounds another one to create a complex musical groove that is immensely appealing to Filipino youth.

Among Children

An "ethnomusicology of children" has emerged through the work of a generation of educators and ethnomusicologists who have shifted beyond the folkloric collection of children's songs to seek out children's meaning-making of music they create, re-create, and listen to in myriad ways, across many cultures (Campbell & Wiggins, 2013). Early studies of musical culture assumed that children passively received the artistic and linguistic expressions from adults, participating in the song and dance that came "from above to below." Children were left out of descriptions of a musical culture, as they were viewed by ethnomusicologists as incomplete in their representation of adult expressive practices. Diffusionist scholars, mostly active as folklorists (if not anthropologists at the edge of ethnomusicology), collected children's songs to examine as the source of understanding not just the concept of "child as primitive" but also the "primitive as child." A study of their songs was considered a way of knowing children at early stages of human development, and thus a means of examining theories of sociocultural evolution. Cross-cultural comparisons of children's musical expressions surfaced occasionally in ethnomusicology, if only to seek a more homogenous child culture that transcended specific music cultures (Brăiloiu, 1984; Herzog, 1950). Socialization of music-cultural norms has been of interest to scholars who contribute to an enculturative paradigm, where adult-to-child sociocultural education is examined for its influences in raising (musical) citizens within communities (Blacking, 1967; Waterman, 1956).

In the past two decades, however, border crossings by music educators employing an ethnomusicological method have brought attention to children's musical expressions as a means of studying their patterns of thought and social behavior (Bickford, 2017; Campbell, 1998, 2001; Marsh, 2008; Minks, 2013a). Dawn Corso (2003) focused her attention on informal contexts by which African American girls acquire a repertoire of music and dance. Her fieldwork captivated her attention to how they live and learn songs and singing qualities, how they develop their "groove," how they develop their lavish routines for the repertoire they acquire, and how they pass it on to others. Likewise, Kyra Gaunt (2007) studied the singing games of African American children through the lens of adult women flashing back to their musical childhoods in reminiscence of their sociomusical involvement and its meaning to them. Marsh and Young (2006) describe children's involvement in singing games, where along with copying in order to learn each task, "skills are also gained within a holistic framework and never fragmented or taught in isolation from the game as a whole" (p. 301). Harwood (1998) and Marsh (2008) similarly have observed that playground learning shows children as joining in and progressively acquiring skills necessary to participate in a game. Playground learning leads to engaged practice, and if teachers study the way children learn holistically, they can understand and adapt the method to the classroom. For children, "music is about stuff you do," as they prefer action to passivity—singing, dancing, and playing just as soon as they are able. Their participation and repeated attempts to acquire the tunes, rhythms, and words is their standard way of learning the music (Campbell, 1998, 2010).

Without immediate stimulation or direction by adults, the culture of children's ecological environment—their social networks—comes forward. Children sing, chant, and musically babble some of the linguistic, melodic, and rhythmic phonemes and phrases to which they have grown accustomed. As they bounce across the kitchen floor, "animate" their toys, and even play with their food, their music resembles the music of their surroundings. While it may be that children find unique and individual meanings in their very own personal music, which is evident in portrayals by Crafts, Cavicchi, and Keil (1993) and Campbell (1998, 2010), the sonic features of a Vietnamese American children's singing game are easily distinguished from those of a Mexican American children's singing game. Likewise, when Arab American toddlers engage in expressions that hover between speech and song, theirs are distinctive from the sounds of Native American toddlers by virtue of the separate musical environments in which they live. Children, in particular very young children on the brink of learning their language and musical language, quite naturally express the nuances of the motherese (or parentese), that infant-directed musical speech of their caretakers, which they have known as a constant stream of sound projected at them since birth (Fernald, 1990). Their expressive music, then, is related to the music they have received.

It has been persuasively argued, however, that families are not in complete control of their children's cultural experiences, and that home culture (and the musical culture within the family) is no longer exclusively the upfront and personal encounter of child and parent that it once was (Cannella & Kincheloe, 2002; Lury, 2002). Bronfenbrenner's (1996) theory is testimony to this, in that he conceptualizes the media and governmental policy as an "exosystem," a potentially powerful orbit of influence on children's interests and values. (In fact, governmental policy dictates the nature of programming on publicly funded TV and, to an extent, on commercial channels as well.) The barrage of visual and sonic information, components of Appadurai's (1996) mediascape, conveys information and attitudes to children that emerge in the style of their speech, movement, and song. Their musical play, in particular some of their collectively composed songs, singing games, and parodies of familiar songs, is laden with the music they have come to know on TV shows, movies, the Internet, and video games. Mediated music encompasses the songs of Disney's Little Einsteins and music by pop stars Beyoncé, Bruno Mars, and Ed Sheeran for singing along with and moving and grooving to. By the time children reach school age, as 5-year-olds, their child-produced activities fall within the realm of the media's influence. While the media radiates its messages to children in the home and within the family, it is generated from the outside the home and is thus fairly separate from live music-making in the traditional sense of home and parental influence. Traditional conceptions of childhood as a time of adult dependency thus are altered by children's access to mediated pop culture (Lum & Campbell, 2007).

Children will continue to be musically enculturated and to be active participants in the music socialization process that wraps itself around them every day, even as the "scapes" of their environment are impacted—even transformed—by technology, the media, and the circumstances of their families. The characteristics of their ethnicities, the economic status of their families, the child-rearing practices that are passed down from generation to generation are all influences on the songs they will know, the dancing they will do, the music they will make. Their musical education, the directed learning of music that happens in schools, will transpire even as the unplanned and informal music streams into their lives at home. The world of children at home, in their local communities, and even as it is constructed at school, is a complex auditory ecosystem that deserves attention and continued study by those who concern themselves with children's learning and development in music, including the web of social processes that are rich with musical content that helps to shape children's expressive selves.

THROUGH LISTENING TO LEARNING

Transmission is a cultural marker, and teaching and learning are practices that evolve over time within the particular circumstances of a culture. In featuring music in schools with attention to its cultural meaning, teachers do well to come to terms with the culture-specific techniques and procedures that are aligned with the music they will give prominence to in a lesson or rehearsal session. Deeper learning develops from new ways of experiencing music, including the processes by which it is sustained and maintained.

Without question, listening is vital to music learning across multiple cultures, sometimes simply to familiarize the learner with the components but often as the principal or even singular pathway to learning the music. In learning to sing a song or play an instrument, listening is central to the process by which young and old "get" the pitches and rhythms (and text). Some teachers will provide this listening by their own adherence to regular demonstration of music to be learned, possibly through a tightly arranged sequence of steps and stages, while others merely will assume that listening is operative in circumstances where learners acquire skills and repertoire. Thoroughgoing observation may require direction by a teacher to learners to watch as well as to listen in order to develop a sense of playing position, the execution of particular techniques, and the possibility of movements, including dance, that may be aligned with the music.

The precept of learning-by-doing is operant in the music-learning process, so that listening must give way—sooner or later—to making the music. Errors may turn up in early attempts to sing and play what is not entirely clear to the learner, but they can be corrected verbally or by demonstration of the correct sound. The literature on music transmission, and the experiences of children in their own efforts to transmit and learn the music and oral lore of their culture, points to the importance of orality (and aurality) over literacy. In keeping with music and its transmission as a cultural marker, teachers do well to facilitate learning in schools that is sensitive to informal processes, is attentive to music that is acquired through enculturation, and provides for experiences that are not solely analytical but holistic as well.

CHAPTER 6

World Music Pedagogy as Learning Pathway

This chapter addresses a development unfolding in music education called World Music Pedagogy (WMP) and programmatic frameworks that support and facilitate the WMP process. It considers pedagogical components that contribute to learning musical cultures through listening, including

This chapter includes components from "World Music Pedagogy: Where Music Meets Culture in Classroom Practice," by P. S. Campbell, in *Teaching General Music: Approaches, Issues, and Viewpoints*, edited by C. R. Abril and B. M. Gault, 2016, reproduced with permission of Oxford University Press (www.oup.com).

participatory musicking, performance, creative composition and improvisation, and the integration of cultural understandings relevant to the musical selection. Influenced by a recognition of music's essence as aural expression, the prevalence of orality in music-learning processes globally, and the sensitive adherence to a multicultural approach to music and its transmission, world music pedagogy is described for its practical contributions to questions of what and how music of cultural communities can be taught in elementary and secondary school programs. World Music Pedagogy concerns itself with the role of music within its culture of origin, how it functions, for whom, and for what reasons. Models of lessons are introduced and a discussion is offered of the place of WMP in the inservice education of teachers who seek to facilitate multicultural understanding through experiences with diverse musical expressions.

Listening as Core. "The cultivation of attentive listening and creative expression is a central aim in the education of student musicians." This was my way into *Lessons from the World* (1991), in which I stuck out my neck early on in asserting to teachers of notation-based music classes and courses that listening is essential to musical growth and that learners develop sensitivity to musical sound as a result of learning to listen. In peeling through historical layers of Western art music, and then examining a diversity of music cultures through my field observations and a long literature on music transmission, I implored my fellow music teachers to consider that listening is the key ingredient to developing students' musical insight, full comprehension, and ultimate expression. Interestingly, the book draft was pilloried in a preprint review by a senior member of the American music education profession, who denounced the view that music should be learned "by rote." Books have met their demise by far less force than the 10-page, single-spaced damning appraisal that had come forward to me, and I realized that I had truly touched a nerve within American school music culture in generating such a fierce review. Was I proposing that listening was so vital throughout history and across cultures that it even eclipsed notation in its centrality? I was, and I hold steady on the position to this day. The book was published, following my 10-page, single-spaced reprisal to the reviewer, in which I even more passionately defended the oral-aural channels of deeper learning through extensive listening. (I think that *Lessons from the World* was never read by many Americans, although it has been cited by an unexpected spread of international colleagues. One colleague recently implied that it was radical for the time, and suggested that it may have been a forerunner to another once-radical notion in the field: informal learning, a method that transpires "by ear" and has since become a carefully considered realm of musical discovery and skill development. See Green, 2008.)

I revel at the manner in which popular music the world over is learned by ear, and how a jazz sax player can run circles around a head melody in taking it far afield from the band's opening statement and bringing it back after the improvisation has been offered, and how Irish, and Cajun, and Cape Breton fiddlers "pick up the tunes" through immersion with musicians (and recordings), and how African American singers provide exquisite and elaborate filigrees of melodic beauty in their gospel solos over the choir's sound. Such musical power is not about reading notes, but is in the thick of musicians who are listening well in order to digest and assimilate the straightforward and subtle features of the music they make.

If the case for listening was not already persuasive, the *Songs in Their Heads* project (Campbell, 1998, 2010) confirmed for me, through children's astonishing capacity to learn music by ear, that listening is truly core to learning. Regardless of their familial upbringing and cultural identity, children's fondness for music shows a certain universal human wiring that quite naturally draws them to melodies and rhythms. This musical romance knows no bounds, and children often amass a grand diversity of songs, chants, rhymes, riddles, and other oral lore without visual assistance in print or on screen. Further, children who struggle with (music) reading seem to have no problem with learning (music) orally. Children's commentaries were solid evidence, too, of the import of learning by listening: "I listen and figure it out" (a response to a question to an 8-year-old as to how he learns the music he loves), and "Do too many notes get in the way of the music?" (the question of a 12-year-old, a polite articulation of his confusion and frustration over reading too much notation in school music classes, too fast). Yet notation, rather than listening, continues to be the end-all and be-all of music lessons and sessions for children, and listening dangles out there as an appendage and a footnote to teaching techniques. While I acknowledge that notation is a useful aid for enhancing memory and (sometimes) accelerating learning, it cannot replace the power of listening.

Enter World Music Pedagogy, an attempt to bring listening to the fore of a teaching/learning process. I wanted to pay homage to listening as so valued a way of learning. In *Teaching Music Globally* (2004)—which is paired with another volume, Bonnie C. Wade's *Thinking Musically* (2004), containing 59 listening tracks—my intent was to draw listening into a foundational base of other experiences: of musical participation, performance, creative composition, and improvisation. Even "integration" could be seen as linked to listening, so that various musical experiences could be wrapped up with excursions into music's cultural meanings. By listening to music, all matters of music as sound, behavior, and values esteemed by a culture could be known. World music pedagogy seems to make sense as a learning pathway to understanding music and people, and the results so far seem to be effecting positive change.[1]

MUSIC IN A MULTICULTURAL WAY

The power of music is in its palpable capacity to build bridges between people, to build social connections, to grow a genuine curiosity for "the Other," and to advance a veritable respect for the people whose music it is—both the music-makers and all those who identify with it. Such musical power comes through an involvement in the music in any number of ways, the first and foremost of which is listening, from which all sorts of further musical and cultural discoveries flow. For children as well as their teachers, their parents, and other adults, listening to music at school, at home, and in the car brings about an aural channeling and internalization of musical sounds that become more greatly valued over time. Listening, and all other means of musical involvement, leads to a recognition of the beauty of cultural diversity as well as the common features of our musical humanity.

Music is a formidable means of multiculturalizing the curriculum, as it provides entry points to beautiful heart-and-soul expressions of nations and cultures. Because people everywhere in the world make music meaningful and useful in their lives (Wade, 2004), the study of the world's music is a direct pathway to knowing people in ways that are compelling and enticing. Questions abound on the expressions of both local communities and distant music cultures, and study of "this thing called music" provides opportunities to understand beauty and logic in their various dimensions and contexts. Then, through a process of further layers of involvement, of taking part in music through participation and performance, and creating it and listening to it, music becomes us, simmering inside or buoying us up (Small, 1998). As we are musically involved in one way or another, so that we are sonically surrounded by it, music can stir us emotionally in transformative ways. People think musically, and in deeply human ways, as they do music. As they proceed to piece together a mosaic of relevant ideas about the music—who makes it, when, where, why, and how it is made—people grow a meta-view of music's reach into their lives.

An education that pays tribute to the splendors of musical and cultural diversity is as necessary as it is potentially metamorphic. The results of a many-splendored curricular program in music, of course, rest in the hands of capable teachers who draw from the wide variety of musical expressions that are out there "live" in their very vicinity and easily available in mediated forms. Music teachers put democracy and inclusion into practice as they give their attention to diversity in drawing up their blueprint of learning pathways. With a multicultural perspective in mind, their conscious selection of a diverse repertoire of recordings is only a step away from the design and delivery of a full-fledged instructional process. This proactive sequence can have a significant impact on the development of their students' knowledge, skills, and attitudes that then reflect both musical and multicultural perspectives. Such acts of planning and implementation readily can take culture into account in multiple ways, including the culture of school classrooms, of the communities that surround them, and of the people whose music is featured in lessons and various learning experiences.

The phenomenon of World Music Pedagogy arises from the intersection of ethnomusicological principles and dimensions of multicultural education, keeping in mind multicultural, cross-cultural, and pan-human aims for the in-school instructional process of musically educating children. Musical goals are enhanced rather than compromised by constructing listening and learning experiences that are fully multicultural in nature and extent, and the outcome of an overlay of WMP with other longstanding pedagogical approaches serves to complement and balance both. The essence of musical study as a means of knowing music and musicians comes clear, and a recognition by students of music for its social and cultural meanings parallels and undergirds the sonic substance.

DEFINING WORLD MUSIC PEDAGOGY

In its embrace of music, education, and culture at an historic moment in the education of students of all ages and levels of experience, WMP necessitates the efforts of music specialist teachers who go it alone in their classes, drawing students into multicultural understanding through musical involvement. Their work through five realms of experience, discussed below, can be successfully accomplished over the course of a single lesson, or stretched (and deepened) over multiple sessions. Teachers may work through the WMP dimensions with colleagues in an interdisciplinary way so that the music experience may further complement students' cultural knowledge, or vice versa. Their work may be enhanced through the contributions of artist-musicians or culture bearers who are invited to perform the music live, to contextualize music through the stories they can tell, to join in dialogue with students in sating their curiosity about the music and its cultural surrounds, and to provide students with a glimpse of the culture-specific substance of a selection or style. World music pedagogy grew from the interactions of music educators with ethnomusicologists, and they, too, may contribute insights through co-teaching, although such collaboration is unusual and not requisite for the dimensions to play out in ways that motivate or ensure learning.

World music pedagogy aims at the global expansion of perspectives on music and culture, and reaches beyond queries of "why (world music)?" and "what (music, from which culture)?" to questions of "what (meaning does the music hold within the culture?)" and "how (can the music best fit into systems and situations of musical education and training)?" WMP concerns itself, then, with the role of music within its culture of origin, how it functions, for whom, and for what reasons. It presses on the manner in which music is taught/transmitted and learned/received within cultures, and how the processes that are included in significant ways within these cultures can best be preserved or at least partially retained in classrooms and rehearsal halls. It assumes the expansion of possibilities for repertoire—"materials," in the language of teachers—as it also takes into account those culture-specific instructional techniques with which the repertoire is associated. Importantly, WMP pays tribute to the critical importance of learning by listening and of repeated listening in increasingly active and interactive ways. It underscores the logic of making sense of music as an aural art, a channel of creative practice, and a means of personal and communal human expression.

Those who have worked to develop this pedagogy, including the seasoned teachers who have shaped a flourishing summer course (see "World Music Pedagogy with Smithsonian Folkways Recordings," below), have studied with traditional artist-musicians and thus proceed with sensitivity to blend the expertise of active musicians into a pedagogical system that is responsive to contextual meanings of music and transmission systems within the culture. While they are enthusiastic about the impact of knowing the music through firsthand experiences, they are also realistic that opportunities may not always be easily available to teachers. These multicultural music educators, WMP dimensions in hand, are conscious of and pay tribute in their teaching to oral/aural techniques, improvisatory methods that may be integral to a style, notational systems (or their inapplicability), and even what customary behaviors precede and immediately follow instruction. They accept that less is more, that every step forward is closer to the goal of knowing music, musicians, and culture, and that an understanding of even a single musical piece through deep and continued listening, participatory, performance, and creative experiences (and the study of its cultural context and meaning) can impact the musical education of students. WMP proponents greatly value opportunities to feature culture bearers and artist-teachers from various cultures in their lessons and sessions, and to co-teach with them when possible. They also accept that in the end, the responsibility for teaching music as a pan-human and cross-cultural experience rests with them, so that in the end they themselves are obligated to teach the world's musical cultures (when additional expenditures for culture bearers may not be available to them). Within the WMP process is the necessary sensitivity to "old" (as in the original culture of the music) and "new" (the culture of the students and instructional setting), while the "how" of world music pedagogy requires bridging the two.

PHASES OF WORLD MUSIC PEDAGOGY

While there are various means of "teaching world music," central to the WMP process is listening, at ever-deepening levels (see Figure 6.1). Three learn-to-listen phases are linked to instructional processes for knowing music from any of the world's cultures: (1) *Attentive Listening,* directed to and focused on musical elements and structures, and guided by specific points

Figure 6.1. Five Dimensions of World Music Pedagogy

---

1. Attentive Listening

Multiple directed listening experiences focused on structures

2. Engaged Listening

Active participation while listening

3. Enactive Listening

Continued listening to performance level

4. Creating World Music

Invention of extensions, improvisations, compositions

5. Integrating World Music

Connection of music to life (and curriculum)

Source: Campbell, *Teaching Music Globally* (2004).

of attention; (2) *Engaged Listening,* the active participation by a listener in some extent of music-making (by singing a melody, patting a rhythm, playing a percussion part, moving to a dance pattern); and (3) *Enactive Listening,* the performance of a work in which, through intensive listening to every musical nuance, the music is re-created in as stylistically accurate a way as possible. These listening phases may occur as separate entities within a class session, or they may be linked in a sequence in which attentive listening leads to participation (engaged listening) and performance (enactive listening). To these three phases are added (4) *Creating World Music,* the invention by students of new music in the style of a musical model through composition, improvisation, song-writing, and even the act of extending a piece "just a bit" beyond what is represented on a recording; and (5) *Integrating World Music,* the examination of music as it connects to culture and as it illuminates a prism-like view of subjects as varied as history, geography, language and literature, the sciences, and the visual and performing arts. Altogether, these five WMP ways of knowing can feature in a teacher's facilitation for her students of music as sound, behavior, and values. The phases do not preclude the possibilities for co-teaching with culture bearers or with teachers of other subject areas (especially language arts or the social sciences), but as assembled they do suggest that a thoroughgoing understanding of music cultures can happen through the course of these phases. The five dimensions are examined and illustrated below.

For first exposure to a musical culture, genre, or particular work, *attentive listening* is the ear-opening experience that teachers facilitate for students. It is the gateway to ever-deepening listening experiences, the initiation into the music, the first occasion for connecting to sonic structures while also wondering about questions of who performs the music, when, where, why, and how the music sounds the way it does. The technique is intended to lead students to "big picture" items such as timbre (instruments and voices, and their nuances), texture, and the melodic and rhythmic components of the music. Students may be directed to listen while following a graph that maps the sound, or to listen while reading iconic or symbolic notation—standard staff or any other system—or they may be challenged through questions to listen for instruments, the metric pulse of the piece, a particular rhythm, a melodic segment, or the number of times a musical motif repeats itself. In the case of directing student attention through questioning, the placement of the question first allows students to narrow their focus to an important feature of the music that will lead them toward later phases of participation; multiple questions, one for each of three, or five, or seven listenings in a row (of as little as a 40-second excerpt) build an understanding of what is aurally there in the music. All music of any style is open territory for experiencing through attentive listening, from the most familiar to the truly "exotic," distant, or remote music. It is through a carefully constructed experience that encourages fine-tuned and discrete listening that an understanding of a wider spectrum of music's possibilities can be acquired.

Students of every age, from the very young to the more seasoned and sophisticated, are drawn to possibilities for interactive engagement with music, and thus *engaged listening* is a pedagogical technique of consequence. Students quite naturally may be drawn to an involvement with the music they listen to: moving to the pulse, humming the melody, adding a harmony, beating out a repeated rhythmic phrase, playing a melodic phrase, or dancing to personify the rhythm, form, and expressive features of the music. Students may find themselves learning (best) while doing, so that sometimes without provocation they sing, or play an instrument, or move in subtle or elaborate ways as they listen. Engaged listening is a process of participatory musicking, in which students are drawn into some extent of involvement in music-making while the live or recorded music is sounding. When students are intentionally invited by the teacher to an active encounter with the music, they attain a participatory consciousness in which they gain hold of the sonic features through careful and conscious listening that is far beyond the passive, armchair style. The benefits of musical participation are musical understanding and a more profound resonance with the culture from which the music derives—as well as with those in the group with whom one participates. Through multiple listenings, the musical engagement advances a musical understanding that is at once aural, analytical, and holistic (particularly if the ear inspires embodied or kinesthetic involvement that leads to thoughtful analysis).

In tribute to the oral/aural tradition so central in many cultures to the process of learning music for the intent of performing it, *enactive listening* requires a continuous commitment to multiple experiences of concentrated listening. It quite naturally follows attentive and engaged listening experiences, and by virtue of learning the musical nuances in order to sing or play the selection, it is long and involved. The teacher's role is to direct students to listening, then to matching what they hear, to listening again and then correcting, until the live sound is attuned to the model and students are in musical sync with the recording that sets the tone, time, texture, tempo, and every other feature. Performance is the goal of this phase, or minimally an earnest effort to participate fully in recreating the music in accordance with the recorded model. It is inarguably challenging for students to fully learn by ear complex examples of styles that were previously unfamiliar to them, particularly those beyond a singular rhythmic line or monophonic melody, and listening is certainly a time-consuming pathway to learning the music all the way to performance level. At times, partial staff (or other graphic) notation may prove a useful aid in guiding the re-creation of the essence of the music, and participants' own transcription may be meaningful. Then again, a continual revisiting of the recording (and video-recording) within the group, and individually, provides an aural immersion into the nuances of the style. The result of concentrated and continuous listening is a rendering of the music in performance such that it features the salient features of the style in ways that notation alone could never provide.

In *creating world music,* the dual aims of listening and a thoroughgoing internalization of sonic structures are achieved and demonstrated through the creation of new musical expressions. Composition, improvisation, song-writing, and even the act of extending a piece beyond what is represented on a recording are avenues of creative expression that are informed by attentive, engaged, and enactive levels of music listening. Creating world music is a solid measure of musical understanding, a high-water mark of the process of musically educating students. In the process of creating world music, students are learning the concept of people making music meaningful and useful in their lives by (1) extending the music beyond what's already there, or (2) making music in the style of what they are learning, or (3) applying compositional techniques from particular styles and forms in new ways. An example of the first of these techniques is students' own rendering of a continuation of a polyrhythmic selection from listening to the layered percussion instruments, playing along with the recorded performers and then silencing the recording and continuing in the very same spirit and style (and meter, mode, and such). The second of these techniques is illustrated through the manner in which continued listening fortifies students in knowing the nuances (and form) of an Irish jig, or a Venezuelan *gaita* (song), or Chinese *luogu* (drum-and-gong) piece, and then to be charged with creating these forms through a balancing of stylistic features of the genres with choices by an individual student or collectively as a student group of the pitch set of a melody, or the topic and verses, or selected instruments to be featured. The third approach offers students license to play with compositional techniques derived from recordings, such as to compose or improvise with focus on the interlocking parts of the music as is done in

parts of sub-Saharan Africa, or the call-and-response form of Afro-Caribbean musical forms, or the drones of Bulgaria, or a rhythmic cycle as found
in India's *tala* structures or within Indonesian gamelan performance. All the
earlier extensive listening, analysis, and performance of the music provide
ideas that lead to the making of new expressions, as students in a sense are
placed inside the music and its sonic structures, and are supported in efforts
to make the music truly their own.

The last of the WMP phases is *integrating world music,* which underscores the critical connection of music to culture, to understanding how
the music is meaningful to the people who make it, and to ensuring that an
interdisciplinary presence is evident in the design and delivery of the music
within curricular structures. Since music lies at the intersection of cultural,
historical, social, and linguistic studies, it quite naturally is a springboard
for developing these realms of knowledge. To know music is to know also
about music, to study it close up for understanding how it is transmitted
and learned, interpreted, and changed over the course of time and place.
Music does not exist in a vacuum, and thus study of it extends to knowing
something of the musicians who perform it, compose it, listen to it, and
value it. The biographies of the musicians are important information for
students, including knowledge of where their musical involvement began
and how they became increasingly committed to it. Contextual information
covering the function of a song for particular occasions, or the symbolism
of an instrument to a group of people, adds multiple dimensions to musical
(and cultural) understanding. In a way that resembles a prism of colored
hues, students wonder about musical beginnings (Who created the music?
Who first performed it?), musical continuities (Who performs it now? Does
it always sound the same way, or is it a genre with variability and a flexible nature?), and musical meanings (Are there particular social or cultural
themes to the music?). For music specialist teachers in schools, the integration of music into other subject areas is enriching, and classroom teachers of
all subjects have been found receptive to ways in which musical styles and
cultures flow into the study of language arts, social studies, and social skill
building. This integration can happen sooner rather than later, too; context
and questions about the music do not need to be left until last but rather
can be interspersed within opportunities along the way for experiencing the
music through listening, participating, performing, and creating. (See Figure
6.2 for an unfolding of the WMP dimensions that can be applied in various
contexts where music is taught and learned.)

WMP EXEMPLAR SEQUENCES

The five dimensions of world music pedagogy are outlined below, each with
its own explicit stepwise sequence of possible teaching/learning interactions.

Figure 6.2. World Music Pedagogy, Exemplified

Following the selection of a recording of a musical style (Puerto Rican salsa, Northumberland (English) hornpipe, Navajo social song, Trinidadian *soca*, Japanese *gagaku*, Brazilian *samba*, Turkish *maqam*, African American blues, Balinese *ketjak*, Argentinian *tango*, North Indian Hindustani *khyal*, for example), teachers can advance to pedagogical experiences for their students in thinking and doing music cultures.

1. *Attentive Listening.* Play a short segment of the recording (about one minute in length) at least three times—or as many times as there are questions to ask, with a directed question preceding each listening. Concrete questions may include, "Is the music energetic or restful?" "How many instruments (voices) do you hear?" "Which instrument (or word) sounds the highest pitch?" "Are there any repeated phrases?" "Can you find the pulse, both accented and not?" "What is/are the unifying element(s) in this passage?" More-reflective questions include the following: "What might be the function of this music?" "Who do you think performs this music (gender, age, geographic-cultural region, lifestyle, religious affiliation)?" "What mixed cultural influences (acculturative properties) do you hear?"

2. *Engaged Listening.* Play the same brief segment of the recording (thus extending from the first phase), with the invitation to students to participate in the music as it sounds, by singing the melody, playing an instrumental part on available instruments, or moving in lines or circles to the pulse (and even changing directions on the phrase changes). Pat/clap a distinctive rhythm phrase on available surfaces prior to playing on an instrument, or hum the melody prior to singing it full-voiced aloud and with certainty. Over the course of multiple listenings, become familiar with the music, practicing it and developing increasing skill and confidence in participatory engagement.

3. *Enactive Listening.* Learn by listening to the whole song or selection (or segment), with emphasis on the sonic features that can be performed vocally or on available instruments, repeating a cycle of listen–perform–listen checks and comparisons until the music can be performed in a reasonably close approximation of its recorded sound. Perform with the recording; imitate short segments of the recording (listening and then singing/playing). Repeat as necessary within a session and across sessions until the recording is no longer necessary.

4. *Creating World Music.* Listen to a familiar phrase or section of a piece, turn off the recording, and invite spontaneous performance of a second phrase or section in the style of the first—vocally or on instruments. (Students can be told in advance the key, at least, for playing or singing the newly invented segment.) With sufficient familiarity, create an entire piece in ways that are similar to and distinctive from the model but still resembles the style. Cull the compositional features of a style (AABB form, hocketing technique, melodic ornamentation) and create something new with available instruments.

5. *Integrating World Music.* Provide information on context and function of the music: Who performs it? Why? When? Where? How? How is this music historically and culturally important to the musicians and listening audience? What can be known through the music (or separately but informative of the music) about religion and ritual, the social hierarchy or political system of a culture, the gender roles, the cross-border influences?

They read like scripted lessons, replete with the sort of questions or comments a teacher might offer to stimulate student involvement. They are presented as illustrations only and may be quite literally a bit more or less than what may be necessary to foster learning. The clean linear line of the stimulus–response interaction is a model that may not meet the realities of learners who may require additional repetitions, a teacher's demonstration or "for instance-ing," and a branching out into additional strategies. The entirety of the five dimensions may run the course of many sessions, over many weeks or even months, with other music-educational activities appearing in the same session as the WMP experience, even as they also may fit within a single class meeting. Note that there are two five-part WMP lesson illustrations, both of them featuring working artist-musicians in performances of contemporary music rooted in longstanding cultural traditions.

"Fly Home—Fatima" is a musical impression of life in a war zone where Iraqis find joy in short bouts of temporary relief from noise, violence, and chaos, and yearn for yet another day without destruction. Rahim Alhaj, a virtuoso 'ud musician and composer, was born and raised in Baghdad, Iraq, and was a student from an early age of the revered 'ud player Munir Bashir. He studied composition and was awarded a degree in Arabic literature. He performs internationally, including in Europe, China, India, Russia, and the United States, and enjoys playing longstanding Iraqi repertoire and music that fuses with the styles of jazz guitarists, accordion players, sarodists, and indie-rock musicians. He strives to express the deep feelings of the struggles in Iraq that have continued for nearly a generation. Rahim Alhaj was twice nominated for a Grammy award and received the National Endowment for the Arts National Heritage Fellowship. The collection of pieces under the album title *Letters from Iraq* are abstract impressions of actual mailed letters describing the lives of those in war-torn Iraq. The inspiration for "Fly Home" is never directly explained, but one might reflect upon the artist's description of the sense of the Iraqi people living at home and abroad, that "normalcy and hope will certainly return" one day to their lives. The second part of the title, "Fatima," is a common Arab name (and also designating the daughter of the Prophet Muhammad).

Letters from Iraq

Material

"Fly Home—Fatima," Rahim Alhaj, Smithsonian Folkways Recordings (www.folkways.si.edu/rahim-alhaj/letter-7-fly-home-fatima/music/track/smithsonian) (Oud, violins, viola, cello, bass, percussion)

Attentive Listening

1. "What instruments do you hear, and in what order?"
2. Play track.
3. Discuss answers ('ud, violins, viola, cello, contrabass, percussion).
4. Play track so as to check answers.
5. "Can you 'pretend-play' one of the instruments?" (Explain that the object of the exercise is to identify an instrument while listening, and to pretend to play an imaginary instrument.)
6. Play track.
7. Respond to how the pretend-play appeared (rhythmically and with instruments in sync with one another).
8. "This song has no immediate story, but springs from a feeling that every moment of our daily lives is a precious gift. It is an expression of joy in being alive and well. Can you hear the joy?"
9. Play track.
10. Respond, noting the quick tempo and the ensemble sound of the instruments performing together.
11. "Given what you hear, where in the world might the musicians be living?" (Given the sound of 'ud and percussion rhythms, and possibly the minor mode, Iraq or somewhere else in the Middle East is a good choice.)

Engaged Listening

1. "Do you hear a rising melody or a falling melody? Show it with your hands."
2. Play track.
3. Point out that there are two falling melodic figures, one sounded on the 'ud and another on the violin. Direct attention to the first and more intricate one played by the 'ud. "How many times do you hear the 'ud melody?"
4. Play track so as to check answers.
5. Sing the second (slower) descending melody, "mi-re-do-ti-la," and invite students to sing it when it sounds on the recording.
6. Play track.
7. Tap eighth-note rhythms on lap or chest, challenging students to tap them out when they hear the percussion.
8. Play track.
9. Clarify that while there is no text or concrete meaning assigned by the composer or performers of this musical piece, they are playing in celebration of their safety, their very lives together, and the promise of peace and tranquility.

* *Repeat:* Play track again for opportunities to hum, show the 'ud's falling melody with their hands, sing the violin's (slower) falling melody, tap the rhythm of the percussion.

Enactive Listening

1. Sing the opening plucked pitch set, "la-mi," and ask students to sing it and show it with their hands as it sounds at the start of the track.
2. Play track.
   * Repeat.
3. "Sing the violin's "me-re-do-ti-la" falling melody with (and without) the recording."
4. Play track.
   * Repeat.
5. "Listen and hum along with the 'ud's fast falling melody."
6. Play track.
   * Repeat.
8. Using guitars, ukuleles, or other plucked instruments, slowly pick out the 'ud's melody, beginning on high "do," descending in thirds, and landing on low "do." (In a-minor, the starting and ending pitch is c-C.) Sing the part while learning to play it. Gradually increase the speed. (This will take some time.)
9. "Take hand drums or dombeks and tap the percussion rhythm."
10. Play track.
    * Repeat.
11. Using violins, or other available instruments (keyboard, flute, recorder), play the opening pitch set and the slower falling melody.
    * Repeat.
12. Combine all parts: (a) plucked opening pitch set and slower falling melody (violin or other instruments), (b) fast falling melody ('ud, guitars, ukuleles, other instruments), and (c) percussion rhythm.
    * Repeat.
13. "Sing and play violins, guitars, and ukuleles with (and without) the recording."
14. Play track.
    * Repeat.

Creating World Music

1. Brainstorm some topics to express musically, inviting students to share with the question, "What's on your mind?" Write answers that may include single words (peace, pain, struggle, hope) or full phrases ("Peace is a promise," "Hope leads us to a time without violence," "Treasure every moment").

2. Together or in small groups, with instruments in hand, create two melodies (A and B) that can be played on available instruments. Set parameters: 4/4 meter, minor key, one-measure (or two-measure) melody. Experiment with skips and steps, and with melodic directions that rise, fall, or stay fairly static.

3. Request students to play the short melodies and invite comments.

4. Suggest that these short melodies might be repeated and put into a compositional form such as ABBA, ABAB, AABBAA. Consider featuring distinctive instruments on the two melodies.

5. Encourage students to create a short verse on a chosen topic (rhymed or unrhymed) to be spoken or sung. By speaking the verse aloud repeatedly, a melody can emerge from the rhythm and inflections; this may lead to a declaration at the start of the piece, a recurring rhythmic statement that is chanted here and there, or a sung melody that conveys the verse (or possibly a silently kept phrase that inspires a fully instrumental piece).

6. Stitch the instrumental composition together with the verse. Note that non-pitched percussion instruments (as well as pitched instruments) may be played to accentuate particular textual or musical ideas.

7. Perform the composed songs and discuss ways to enhance or further develop musical ideas so to pique the interest of listeners (and invite their participation).

Integrating World Music

---

1. Discuss the general sense of this music, the situation that inspired it, the feelings that are conveyed.

2. Clarify that this deeply personal expression is called program music, in which there are no lyrics and no story but rather emotional feelings of a longing for peace, a deep sadness for human loss in wartime, feelings of fear and helplessness and of relief in times of ceasefire or a discovery that someone believed lost has been saved.

3. Discuss the comment of Rahim Alhaj, 'ud player and composer, on "Fly Home—Fatima" and other selections in this collection called *Letters from Iraq*: "All my music, perhaps all human-made music, touches upon our shared humanity. Especially since arrived to the U.S., my music is about a part of all of us that is very hard to face, but feeling deeply for others matters. I must do what I can to bring deep feelings more into our world. That's what these pieces are about, giving account, report a story. How else to document this period in Iraq's history, from Saddam Hussein's capture in 2003 until now? How else can I, can we, acknowledge the pain of the people there? They had suffered so much, and are suffering again now in terrible ways. Has the Iraqi soul been settled in these years? Listen."

4. Challenge students to seek out musical responses to war, in the repertoire of singers in the United States and in far-flung places such as Japan and Germany, Korea, Vietnam, Cambodia, and Syria.
5. Search for information on Rahim Alhaj, his training, and his career as a master 'ud player and composer.
6. Discover more about the music in Iraq, including Iraqi classical, folk, fusion, and popular music, and music associated with populations living in Iraq (including Arabic, Assyrian, Kurdish, and Turkmen).

The suggested experiences for Rahim Alhaj's "Fly Home—Fatima" provide an introduction to music of a region that is rarely featured in American music education programs and that offers students a thoughtful consideration of Iraqis in a difficult time in their history. The expectations for musical involvement are progressively more rigorous, thus requiring considerable musicianship but also strengthening and expanding it. Contemporary musical expressions in the world are no longer stuck in the rustic folk style of a nation's historical past, as is proven by this case of the music of an Iraqi-trained classical oud player with a musical curiosity to venture forward in progressive ways. Rather, an amalgam of styles is possible in the hands of musicians who honor their elders and the traditions they represent, while also owning up to their place in a changing world of many cultural fusions. Old-style Iraqi classical music features sung poetry, the iconic plucked 'ud, various flutes (such as the ney), zithers that are plucked (*qanun*) and hammered (*santur*), and percussion instruments such as *riq* (tambourine) and *darbuka* (or *dombek*, a single-headed drum). Musicians typically perform in prescribed modes of the *maqam* system, some of which are of a minor quality. A new chamber music has arisen in Iraq as well as in neighboring nations such as Iran, Syria, Lebanon, Israel, Jordan, and Egypt, where Iraqi traditions mix with Western classical music features, as in the case of the 'ud playing alongside a string quartet of violins, viola, and cello (with the addition of a contrabass and percussion). Some music tells a story, while other music is intended to offer impressions, to delve into emotions without plot or character development, and to provide music for meditation and contemplation.

"Ya La" is a signature piece of Oumou Sangare, a singer-songwriter of the Wassoulou culture in an area of Mali south of the Niger River. As a singer from her childhood days, Sangare has worked with bands from her early teens and has developed a professional recording and touring career that spans three decades. She is referred to as "the Songbird of Wassoulou" and serves as an ambassador of the culture, her songs attracting attention for their statements on women's rights, their right to free choice on whom they will marry, and the end of polygamy. She prefers the role of an artist rather than to move into the political arena, as some have recommended, particularly due to her convictions regarding women's rights in Mali. She has used some of her considerable earnings to build a hotel in Mali that serves as a haven for musicians as well as a model for women to improve their lives through thoughtful decisionmaking and hard work. In 2011, Oumou Sangare received a Grammy for "Imagine" in the category of Best Pop Collaboration with Vocals, a record that featured herself in performance with notable musicians Herbie Hancock, Pink, India Arie, Jeff Beck, and Seal. She joins many musicians in Mali in efforts to preserve and transmit traditional music and culture while also adopting elements of Western popular music into an Afro-pop contemporary sound.

Mali

Material

"Ya La," Mali Lolo! Stars of Mali, Smithsonian Folkways Recordings (www.folkways.si.edu/mali-lolo-stars/islamica-world/music/album/smithsonian) (Guitar, bass guitar, percussion, winds/brass, djembe, vocals)

Attentive Listening

1. "What instruments do you hear, and in what order?"
2. Play track.
3. Discuss answers (guitar, tambourine, drums, winds/brass, vocals).
4. Play track so as to check answers.
5. "Can you pretend-play one of the instruments?"
6. Play track.
7. Respond to how the pretend-play appeared (rhythmically and with instruments in sync with one another).
8. "This is a song about travel, or wandering away from home. Listen for 'Ya La' (or 'ya la la-ah') and, raise your hand when you hear the phrase."
9. Play track.
10. Respond. Ask whether there is anything in the music that would support the theme of "wandering." Discuss the tempo and rhythmic feel of the music.
11. "Given what you hear, where in the world might the musicians be living?" (Given the language, the sound of the guitar, the rhythmic drive, the vocal "whoops," Mali or West Africa is a good choice.)

Engaged Listening

1. "Listen and show fingers for the number of times you hear the brief opening phrase on the guitar before the entrance of the singer."
2. Play track.
3. "Discuss the eight repetitions of the opening guitar phrase."

4. Play track so as to check answers.
5. "Tap the rhythm of the percussion."
6. Play track.
7. Demonstrate and discuss the continuing fast sixteenth-note rhythms, four taps per beat, by "playing" them by tapping two hands (or two fingers) alternately on desktops, laps, floor spaces.
8. "Hum along with the sung melody. Listen for sung phrase 'Ya La' (or 'ya la la-ah') and sing it as it comes up."
9. Play track.
10. Clarify the meaning of the text further, noting that the singer is saying something more about wandering, in that it can make for aimlessness and idle behavior, which is not very productive over the long term.
    * Repeat: Play track again for opportunities to hum, tap the quick rhythm, hear the various instruments and words.

Enactive Listening

1. "Hum the brief opening phrase played by the guitar." In a minor key, the melody includes just three pitches: l, d, t (la-do-ti) or 6-1-7, in that order.
2. Play track.
3. "Sing the opening phrase with (and without) the recording."
   * Repeat.
4. "Take tambourines and hand drums, and tap the rhythm of the fast sixteenth-note rhythms." (Tap with the fingers, or with soft mallets or pencils with erasers.)
5. Play track.
   * Repeat.
6. "Sing the sung melody. Hum it, find the 'Ya La' (or 'ya la la-ah') phrase to sing and gradually slip in the phonemes for the hummed melody." (Learning the lyrics will take some time, but with listening and encouragement to form the phonemes that constitute the lyrics, they will come.)
   * Repeat.
7. "Take guitars and play the opening phrase (with and without the recording)."
   In c-minor, the phrase utilizes c (la), ♭ (doh), d (ti).
   In d-minor, the phrase utilizes d (la), f (doh), e (ti).
8. Play track.
   * Repeat.
9. "Add a simple bassline on guitars (or bass guitar, or keyboard) that dwells on i (c-minor), with a very quick hint of V (G-Major)."
10. "Sing and play guitar and rhythm with (and without) the recording."
11. Play track
    * Repeat.

Creating World Music

1. Brainstorm some topics to sing about, inviting students to share with the question, "What's on your mind?" Write answers that may include single words that relate to wandering (adventure, distance, loneliness) or full phrases ("Journey safely," "Open your eyes and ears to new sights and sounds," "Stay in touch with family and friends").

2. Together or in small groups, develop verses on a chosen topic (rhymed or unrhymed). Provide a metric scheme and a quantity of verses (2-3-4), and clarify whether a chorus section should be developed for insertion between the verses that might underscore the theme of the poem.

   * Challenge students to write all or part of their poem in a language other than English. (In Mali, people speak Bambara widely, and French. Have students seek out a phrase or two in these languages, for example.)

3. Share the verses through a rhythmic recitation that may appear as a group-performed "choral speech."

   * Repeat. (Note that with repetition, the rhythmic flow will improve. Listen for a melodic inflection that may emerge, too, and encourage prospects for converting the verse from chant to song.)

4. Add instruments. Suggest that not only guitar but also keyboard and a combination of other available instruments can be featured. For rhythms, try a drum set, a snare drum, cymbals, or high-hat.

   * Can the song be danced? Experiment with freestyle, footwork and step patterns, formations.

5. Perform the composed songs and discuss ways to enhance or further develop musical ideas so as to pique the interest of listeners (and invite their participation).

Integrating World Music

1. Discuss the meaning of the song and ponder the advisory to travel wisely (rather than aimlessly), to take precautions that keep one safe when far from home, and to avoid occasions that are potentially injurious.

2. Clarify that songs of wisdom and warning are present in many cultures. Challenge students to find examples of "advice songs," whether advising healthy habits of balanced diets and exercise, or warning of the dangers of places and people, in the wide span of repertoire.

3. Search for information on Oumou Sangare, Grammy Award–winning musician from Mali who was singing since childhood and a successful recording artist by her late teens with a number of notable

Afro-pop bands in Mali. Explore her songs of love, women's rights, and marriage choice.

4. Discover more about music in Mali, a large landlocked country in West Africa, economically poor but a musical hotbed and one of the roots of American blues, jazz, and rock (due to the pursuit of slaves from the West African interior who were transported to coastal cities and moved onto ships bound for America). Contemplate the elemental features of the American genres compared with Oumou Sangare's music and with Malian popular music. Explore the griot tradition of Mali, too, in which musicians tell tales as they sing to the sounds of their guitars and traditional 21-stringed harp known as *kora*.

For many good reasons, this set of experiences for "Ya La" is fitting and appropriate for learners. More than most of the African continent, Mali may well be the source of American musical genres, and its traditions may have influenced African American expressions such as the blues (and quite possibly jazz, rock, and folk styles). During the slave trade, Europeans and Americans captured men, women, and children from the interior of West Africa, going into landlocked Mali to transport people to the coastal ports, to be taken to the Americas. They brought with them their expressive culture, and the vocal and instrumental music of their homelands were not forgotten despite the tragic leaving of their homelands and their traumatic journeys to their new homes as enslaved people for the remainder of their lives. The longstanding Manding tradition of griots, musical storytellers who sang stories while playing accompaniments on *kora* (plucked harps), was continued by singers from Mali in the New World. At the end of a long day's work in the fields, they would sing their stories, sometimes finding materials to accompany themselves percussively or even remembering the *ngoni* as they fashioned a rustic banjo for plucking a melodic pattern. Some early rural African American blues melodies are not so far removed from melodies associated with Malian musicians. In a fascinating turn of events, the influence of blues on the development of popular music may well have landed in some of the Afro-pop music of contemporary Mali. From radio to the Internet, the global flow of music goes both ways, and the fusion of traditional ideas and instruments with Western-style electric guitar, bass, drum set, keyboards, and wind and brass instruments is very much in evidence. By listening, participating in, performing, and creating music of one Malian musician (and her band), and then framing it through interdisciplinary explanations of the music, a sequence based on this selection can enlighten students in music and through music about the people, their history, and their cultural identities.

MANY MUSIC-CULTURE SPLENDORS FOR CURRICULAR PRACTICE

It is evident that in the practice of music education at every level, the onus is on those who teach to configure learning in equitable ways that create an awareness of music as a cross-cultural, universal, and pan-human practice. Students deserve a rock-solid and relevant musical education, one that will let them know music with a capital "M," Music as it sounds and functions in varied communities.

Astonishing as it may seem, the precepts of listening work in performance-based band, choir, and orchestra programs, and the ideals of creating and integrating can be applied to all contexts. Very young children in preschool programs can develop bias-free impressions of music and musicians (and of people in cultures removed from their own) through the application of the elemental WMP features, as can learners in elementary and secondary school. Listening alone is not enough, but serves as an enticement to a host of experiences that are triggered from the early encounters. Each experience further illuminates the music and leads to evolving cultural connections. World Music Pedagogy offers a meaningful avenue to the broader development of musical knowledge, skills, and values, and as well as to the development of student sensitivities to the musicians and cultures in which the music is alive and very well indeed.

World Music Pedagogy with Smithsonian Folkways Recordings. When curator-director Daniel Sheehy invited me to the advisory board of Smithsonian Folkways Recordings, several ideas flashed forward on ways to share the sounds of the collection with listeners. A re-commitment of the label to education seemed a natural development, so that teachers in search of the means for meeting multicultural mandates in and through music might have resources and pedagogical frameworks to work into their curricular programs. WMP was already in place as a pedagogical sequence in my own music education methods courses, and since the Folkways recordings were readily available for public use, it seemed reasonable to join the pedagogy with the materials in a somewhat semiformal manner.

As the nonprofit record label of Smithsonian Institution, Folkways is dedicated to the documentation, preservation, and dissemination of "people's music" to the wider world, as proclaimed by founder Moses Asch. In fact, Asch set up the Folkways record label in a small walk-up office on 57th Street in New York City in 1948 and chronicled music and spoken word through his recordings of adults as well as children who had songs to sing and instruments to play. He signed music legends Woody Guthrie, Lead Belly, and Pete Seeger to his label, and produced thousands of Americana recordings encompassing bluegrass, blues, children's music, gospel, jazz, and spirituals, while seeking also to document the music of world cultures on recordings. The Folkways collection was sold to the Smithsonian Institution in 1987, when the recordings were digitized and further expanded under the leadership of director-curators Anthony Seeger and Daniel Sheehy. With a mission statement to support cultural diversity and increase understanding among people through lively engagement with the world of sound, Smithsonian Folkways Recordings was a rich resource to draw from for the development of learning experiences that could be both musical and multicultural.

Rita Klinger and I imagined a summer course that would utilize Folkways recordings for analytical listening experiences as a way into the study and experience of music of many cultures. We drew up a five-day intensive plan that might kick-start the effort when, in 2009, we launched a course in World Music Pedagogy at the University of Washington. Joined by Christopher Roberts and Amanda Soto, then doctoral students in music education; ethnomusicology colleagues Shannon Dudley and Marisol Berrios-Miranda; and Michiko Sakai as a remarkable administrative assistant, we fashioned experiences in listening, singing, playing, dancing, creating, and understanding cultural context. We invited traditional artists and culture bearers with impressive performance careers, some of whom were experienced visiting artists in schools—musicians whose performance and teaching expertise was as varied as Indian Hindustani *khyal* (vocal genre), Korean *p'ung mul* (gong and drum ensemble), Wolof drumming from Senegal, African American gospel song, Lushootseed storytelling, Wagogo choral music and dance of Tanzania, Afro-Caribbean percussion rhythms, Zimbabwean marimba music, and Trinidadian steel band.

The course has survived and thrived, and has found its way to ten sites in the United States and Mexico, including the annual June course at the University of Washington. It is a 40-hour intensive training in World Music Pedagogy, which serves primarily teachers of music in K–12 settings and tertiary-level teachers in community colleges and on university faculties of music. Others have joined the course, too, including teachers of language arts, Spanish, Mandarin, social studies, and the visual arts; elementary classroom teachers in all subjects; church choir directors; several school principals; and community musicians hoping to hone their teaching skills. For eight hours across each of five days, teachers meet to listen, discuss, and dissect recordings for their sonic substance, cultural meaning, and pedagogical relevance. They engage in collective listening, participation, and performance, and they create music and pedagogical sequences of their own. They learn stories and histories of the music through brief lectures by guest faculty and through exchanges in between the music-making and at break times. They are motivated to listen more and to peruse materials that will deepen their understanding of music and culture.

During a recent one-week course, dozens of spirited music teachers made music across a variety of cultural encounters. They sang and danced a *rucenitsa* from Bulgaria; sang-moved-played choral music of the Wagogo of Tanzania; danced to *cumbia*-styled *conjunto* music of south Texas; played rhythms on drums and gongs in a South Korean *p'ung mul* (*samulnori*) ensemble; performed (and moved to) polyrhythms of Trinidad and Puerto Rico on bottles as well as claves, congas, cowbells, and *guiros*; stepped the fundamental "café-con-pan" footwork rhythm for Mexican *son jarocho* music; engaged in a half-century of American children's singing games; sang and danced a graceful Turkish folk melody in five beats; kept *tala* for Hindustani classical music selections; added accompaniments on classroom xylophones to Tamil-Indian vocal melodies; played Senegalese sabar-drum style on classroom *djembes;* and adapted "El Cascabel" to a makeshift mariachi consisting of more than a dozen guitars, one flute, one violin, one trumpet, a *guitarron*, two piano parts, and a sousaphone. Teachers brought their expert pedagogical knowledge, honed through many years of classroom experience, in thinking through curricular content and instructional processes that were resonant with both the cultures of the music they were studying as well as the students whom they were teaching.

We fashioned a "certificate of accomplishment" to award to participants for their acquired knowledge and skills in teaching the world's musical cultures. With a decade of summer courses behind us, there are presently more than 500 teachers in possession of the certificate. This they earned through their development of "music-culture curricular units," inspired by the world music pedagogy sequence—many of which are available for review on the Smithsonian Folkways Recordings website—or tertiary-level lecture notes (for university-level teaching faculty), or annotated lists of readings, recordings, video-recordings, and online resources. Teachers report success in engaging their students in some of the musical experiences they themselves encountered in the course. Teachers also note their use of the WMP sequence in teaching all kinds of music, including selections of familiar Western art music that they had taught long before enrolling in the course. The course has steadily drawn participants together to accomplish educational aims relative to musical diversity and multicultural education, and I trust that the course will be continued through the collaborative efforts of music educators with ethnomusicologists and heritage musicians, and will receive the enthusiastic support of current curator-director Huib Schippers (and many fine teachers).

NOTE

1. A series of six volumes on the practicalities of World Music Pedagogy is scheduled for publication by Routledge in 2018, detailing teaching/learning strategies for application in early childhood education, elementary school, choral ensembles, instrumental ensembles, innovative secondary school music offerings, and school-to-community projects.

CHAPTER 7

Connections with Communities and Culture Bearers

Community is a key concept relative to music, education, and culture. Musical communities are collectives of singers, instrumentalists, dancers, or some combination thereof, and characterized as those who genuinely enjoy the music they make happen. A description of community, conceptualized, paves the way to the meaning of a musical community, and this then leads to brief excursions into selected musical communities for understanding how they define themselves for the behaviors and values they uphold. Reference to communities of practice melds into a consideration of learning communities and classroom cultures, which confirms the connections between schools and their local communities. As members of particular communities, the concept of culture-bearing musicians, or "culture bearers," is explored, with attention to their presence in short residencies in classrooms

131

and as contracted "visiting artists" in university programs responsible for educating musicians for school-teaching positions. Recent attention to Community Music (CM) and its place in music education practice warrants its attention here as a commitment by CM practitioners to the idea that all people have the right and ability to make, create, and enjoy their own music—styles and expressions that they prefer, that they grew up with, and that they are still growing to know. Relevant to CM, to music education, and to applied ethnomusicology is the concept of cultural democracy as a tool for empowerment; thus music-making in schools can be undertaken as a "bottom-up" rather than "top-down" approach to teaching/learning so that musical communities can rightfully own the music they make.

You Could Be Chicana. It was a dullish grey sky day when I first meandered over to El Centro de la Rasa in Seattle's central district to see about this thing they were calling a fandango. There were about 30 adults and children gathered in the dog-eared room of a run-down school building that had been converted to a community center for after-school enrichment, adult education classes, crisis advocacy, and various cultural events. The group grew through the afternoon to twice the size, as individuals, couples, and families with young children arrived to play, sing, dance, and be social. There were a dozen players of the small guitar-like instruments known as *jarana* and *requinto*, several singers holding in hand their books of makeshift collections of song lyrics, and my colleague, Shannon Dudley, sitting atop a large box-like bass plucking a set of metal prongs. All the musicians were stationed at the edge of a 10′ x 16′ wooden platform, about 6″ high, which was the centerpiece of the room and resonated with the sound of the hard soles of dancers feverishly stamping out their rhythms. People were engaged, including the children who came and went from the rim of the *tarima*. Probably ranging in age from toddling all the way to the cusp of adolescence, the boys and girls were watching and listening, clapping and stepping out the dance steps, and then dissolving into pairs and trios who laughed their way out of the room and down the dimly lit but reverberating hallways. There were several community tables of food, and with every additional arrival, there was yet another casserole dish of tacos, burritos, and tamales, joining the fresh salads, chips and dips, and cooler of juices and sodas that the firstcomers had contributed. The music was fairly nonstop, with the *jarana* players strumming and picking, and singers starting with specific lyrical texts and then venturing into their own improvisations on topics of women's rights, poverty, imprisonment without fair trial, inequities in the job market, and various other social justice issues. The language of conversation was Spanish, with occasional snatches of English. I found myself drawn to the singing, but gravitated also to some two-chord strumming patterns on a borrowed *jarana*, and was encouraged to join the fancy dancers on stage in a simple pattern of stamping to the "café-con-pan" rhythm. As I stepped off stage from a rather vigorous dance, one woman sidled up to me with a wide smile to say, "You could be Chicana, you know."

Later, over a burrito that we shared, she explained that to her, and to "them" (those within the fandango group), anyone who could join in the music was on the way to becoming a bona fide member of the community.

THE CONCEPT OF COMMUNITY

The idea of community has a warm and welcoming feel about it. The very sound of the word, with its "mmm" in the middle, has a convivial congeniality about it, and the word communicates a sense of belonging, a fellowship, a home-base, and a certain friendly alliance with people who share similar interests and perspectives. Similar to terms like *clan* and *tribe*, community points to a perceived kinship. At the very least, community refers to a social group that is aligned by shared ideals, a group of individuals who affect one another in their interactions, a self-organized network of people with common causes, and a collective of individuals who enjoy collaboration.

The concept of community seems to share some defining characteristics with other social units, especially culture and society. As community implies understanding among group members, it also carries with it the likelihood of shared language, tradition, and etiquette. There are overlaps and distinctions between society and community: A community refers to a group of individuals residing in a specific geographic location, while a society refers to a system of social relationships spanning a much larger population than a community. Members of a society typically do not share all manner of language and dialect, tradition, or beliefs, but they do understand and accept life as governed by legislation. As for community and culture, they are more closely related. If culture is the sum of customs and beliefs that are transmitted through language, ritual, institutions, objects, and artistic expressions, then community is a sharing group who often live in the same locality (although conceivably could be scattered but come together on occasion or could be joined "virtually"). It would be reasonable to say that the United States is the site of a centrally governed and legally bound American society, consisting of a population that preserves or fashions anew an overarching American-styled set of cultural practices—a conglomerate American culture—and that encompasses a large spectrum of communities with uniquely styled subcultural expressions.

There are many communities of like-minded people who work, play, or live together. They may be families, extended families, and even members of a tribe—a group of people united by kinship. More likely, modern communities are unrelated by blood, marriage, or common ancestry; rather, they share common perspective. A community may be a neighborhood, a collection of people who live "next door" to one another, geographically bounded by streets, parks, roads, or physical features of land and water. There are income-based communities, and communities can be segregated from one another, branded, and separated into poor, middle class, and affluent. Ethnic-cultural communities abound, too, where cultural identities are manifest in local shops and restaurants, in home décor and architectural styles of homes and apartments, in schools and places of worship—communities of African Americans, Ethiopians, Greeks, Haitians, Italians, Jews, Koreans, Mexicans, Puerto Ricans, Roma, Somali, Vietnamese (in the United States, each of them could be hyphenated, too, such that Ethiopians become Ethiopian-Americans, and so forth). Some communities may not feature people from the same locality; their communities may be characterized by religious affiliation and by sexual orientation, or may be based on professional identities such as teachers, nurses, chemists, attorneys, counselors, engineers, soccer players, journalists. There are also scientific communities and artistic communities, and communities in convents, in prisons, and on university campuses.

MUSICAL COMMUNITIES

Communities have musical identities, and musical communities form from the love of a musical practice and from the music that springs from a particular heritage. There are groups of people who participate in particular musical expressions and styles due to longstanding experience and training in the music, and sometimes because of their recent interest (or follow-through of unrequited love of a music they had not previously had the opportunity to spend engaged time with). The group members identify with a musical practice, genre, style, instrument, ensemble, and associated dance and dramatic forms. They are the communities of performer-participants in concert-style wind bands, church choirs, "old-time" and bluegrass groups, jazz combos, ukulele gatherings, local orchestras, barbershop quartets, and other groups with open memberships that comprise locals and other folks who, depending upon their earnest interest in a musical practice, may travel some distance by car and public transport to be a regular part of a musical community's rehearsals, concerts, and various social events. Members may be a mix of races, ethnicities, ages (and sometimes experience levels), and they may vary on other facets as well (religion, gender, and socioeconomic factors, for example). They may be professional or amateur, and they are bound to the community by the music they make.

The musical identities of many communities are tied to their cultural heritage, and to their race and ethnicity. While these communities may be open to all who wish to participate, and who do so with a musical commitment, there is history behind them that marks their identity as a longstanding musical practice that is forged from a shared history. Examples of these musical communities are the African American gospel choirs; the trios of Indian *sitar*, *tabla*, and *tamboura*; the Javanese and Balinese gamelans;

the Serbian ensembles of long-necked lutes known as *tamburitzas*; the salsa bands of Cuba and Puerto Rico; the South African *isicathamiya* choirs; the powwow groups of North American indigenous people; the ensembles of jig-playing Irish fiddlers and flutists; and the Chinese *luogu* of drums and gongs. These musical communities are associated with people of a place, and as the people migrate, so too does the music that is their identity marker. Often, music may be stronger in the new home of people than in their place of origin—as is the case of the Mexican mariachi's vitality in the United States whereas it is no longer performed regularly in much of Mexico (Campbell & Soto Flores, 2016). Musical communities change, too, even when they remain "home," as group members sustain and preserve some aspects but may be keen to modernize and fuse old ideas with new—for example, Tex-Mex *conjunto* music, which has mixed into its repertoire Colombia's rhythmically energetic *cumbia* form.

Ethnographic studies of musical communities have laid out considerable details of the manner in which music works as a centerpiece for a community, and reasons for music's powerful appeal to a group of people, its role as an identity marker, and the manner in which music defines place and people as a local (or not-so-local) collective. John Baily (1988) described in rich detail the community of professional musicians in the city of Herat, Afghanistan, while Anthony Seeger (1987) wrote of music within the Suya community of Amazonian people. Anna Schultz (2013) provided a close examination of a Marathi community of Hindu devotional singers in India, and Travis A. Jackson's (2012) work gave coverage to New York City's community of jazz musicians. Diasporic musical communities are described for the journeys of people and the sustainability of their music from one setting to another; for example, Theodore Levin's (1996) chronicling of Central Asian musicians at home and in Queens, New York, and Carol Silverman's (2012) profiling of Romani musicians in their travels beyond the Balkans. These and other studies are indicative of the extent to which the concept of musical communities is well developed and widely embraced by ethnomusicologists as central to their work.

The increase of online or virtual musical communities is a noteworthy development for the ways in which musicians tap into like-minded individuals to exchange information and opinions, to learn repertoire and techniques, and to discuss musical styles and artists. While fans for generations have shared their enthusiasm for the music and personalities of musicians, especially through fan clubs that meet in person and once communicated only by occasional newsletter (or through monthly fanzines), the Internet has opened up a world of possibilities for building virtual communities through social networking. For those living in remote areas, or in places far removed from the geographic source of a particular style or practice, digital social communities provide interactions across YouTube, other social media, and a network of fan sites. The growth of online performance, as in the case of the Virtual Choir of 185 singers that was launched by Eric Whitacre, is evidence of a phenomenon that reaches beyond talk about music and right to the core of drawing together a musical community whose singers perform with fervor, all together, in an effective and compelling manner.

COMMUNITIES OF MUSIC-EDUCATIONAL PRACTICE

If there are musical communities, surely there are music-educational communities. They are communities of practice (Wenger, 1998), so called to describe people who share a profession or career track. In their work on situated learning, Jean Lave and Etienne Wenger (1991) examined how professional teaching skills are acquired and suggested that all learning is situated and occurs in the context of its particular social practice. Of course, music learning is situated, occurring in formal contexts of school classes and ensembles, and in private lessons, as well as informally when old Uncle Jim teaches his nephew some Stevie Ray Vaughn riffs or Jessica and her friends get together to sing (and learn) songs of their favorite artists over YouTube. The act of learning as more than an isolated cognitive process but a kind of co-participation in which teacher and learners engage socially. This co-construction of learning encompasses also the transmission style and teaching strategies that set up and support social contexts, and even physical spaces that encourage learning. From a conceptualization of communities of practice have come the pedagogical strategies for various curricular subjects across a spectrum of settings. Music education has benefited from the thinking behind the concept of communities of practice, beginning with the theoretical framework and featuring elements worthy of application.

Music education is its own community of practice (or even multiple communities of practice). From one angle, it appears as a splinter group of the larger community of educators who toil in every subject and at all levels to facilitate learning by their students. Yet from another perspective, music education is many communities—band; choir; orchestra; "general music" classes; children's music (sometimes, music classes for young children and their parents, as in the case of *Kindermusik*); elementary school music (vocal, instrumental, and general); middle school music; high school music; classes of jazz, keyboard, guitar, popular music, song-writing, mariachi, and music tech; Advanced Placement instruction; and more. These communities meet in some of the same physical spaces, or at least in the same vicinity of the school building. Certainly, the processes, strategies, and outcomes vary to some degree according to the nature of the curricular offering, as a community of guitar students operates differently from a community of choristers. When taking into account the interests and needs of students enrolled in particular classes and ensembles, every school band or orchestra becomes a unique community of practice as shaped by its constituents.

A school's music-educational practices, within the music space and steered by a music curriculum, are the core of a school's musical community. Of course, musical activity also occurs informally in the singing games on the playground, in the freestyle sustained pitched and rhythmic interactions in the hallways, in PE classes when folk dances are brought into play, and in the language arts and math lessons when teachers employ rhythm, rhythmic movement, body percussion, and even an occasional song as learning strategies for their students. Still, communities of music-educational practice are built upon the selection of music repertoire and the choice of which specialized classes and ensembles to offer as required and optional study by students, and they are enriched when situated learning (or authentic learning) is given full consideration. Music teachers have sway in these programmatic choices, and they are most successful when they work with sensitivity to the students, their families, the teaching faculty, and the overall mission of the school and school district. Communities of music-educational practice are more relevant and successful when they connect to other facets of the wider school and neighborhood communities. The sociocultural contexts of communities of musical practice, including the rules, roles, and identities of the members, are in evidence in educational settings of every kind (Kenny, 2016).

GROWING UP IN FOUR MUSICAL COMMUNITIES

The importance of community involvement in schools is undeniable, as the health, well-being, and learning of students are directly related to the extent of engagement by their parents, families, and the wider community. When families, schools, and community institutions collectively agree upon their goals, everyone benefits. Thus, music teachers do well to reach beyond the systemic curricular patterns of school to the musical communities beyond school in order to understand the musical surrounds of the school and the valued musical practices that exist in the neighborhoods. Communities can provide teachers with music (and musicians) that can complement the standard musical repertoire and music learning pathways practiced in schools. Parents and families can furnish teachers with music that is already familiar to the students, and this helps to bridge the gaping divide that frequently exists between school music and music of "the real world" beyond the school day. Familiarity with a musical style may mean only that children have heard the music often enough and can identify it, but perhaps they've not had the opportunity to learn to make this music—in which case the school music program can provide the means for learning the instruments and the vocal styles. Or perhaps children know the music of their family but not of the families down the street or around the block, so that the flow of music from multiple cultures can help the music teacher to develop a music program that honors the many locally valued expressive practices. Of course, the curricular addition of one musical experience, of one culture, can begin the journey to a truly multicultural and musically valid curriculum that can go intercultural and global, too, in its content.

Knowing the everyday lived experiences of students can be challenging, however, as some cannot or choose not to articulate details of their language and dialect, customs and traditions. Yet brief excursions into the probable or plausible musical surrounds of four sample cultural groups can provide a beginning backdrop for understanding something of children's musical communities. Although not to be construed as fully representing members of these cultures, these descriptions illustrate the nature of expressive practices within an assortment of American families and communities. As always, going to the individuals within these cultural communities, inviting their perspectives, and joining with them at public events, school gatherings, and in common interests are the best ways of knowing them and their musical cultures.

Mexican American Comunidad

In considering "comunidad," or the concept of community, among Mexican Americans, it's noteworthy that (1) Mexican culture is distinctive from the cultural beliefs and practices of Argentinians, Cubans, Peruvians, Puerto Ricans, and other groups classified as Hispanic Americans, and (2) 60% of Hispanic Americans are of Mexican heritage, many of whom are from families with many decades as U.S. citizens, as well as a significant influx of Mexicans who have arrived since the 1990s. The importance of familial solidarity is characteristic of Mexican Americans, and families often live near relatives and have frequent interactions with them, thus shaping *comunidad*. Basic religious beliefs and values of Mexican American culture are preserved through traditional ceremonies and celebrations, including Cinco de Mayo, Dia de los Muertos, Navidad (Christmas), Quinceanera (the coming-of-age festivity of 15-year-old girls), and church holidays and selected feast days of the saints. Even for those families who appear to have quietly erased their associations with Mexico, holidays are meaningful times for instilling in children the meaning of Mexican American identity (Telles, 2010).

The music of special events and holidays varies and is dependent upon family preferences, the extent of the family's removal from (or connection to) Mexico, and the community in which the family lives. Children grow up in neighborhoods surrounded by standard holiday songs and family favorites, their homes veritable walls of Mexican-flavored music surrounding them from radio, CDs, TV, and various other media. Although its popularity is waning in Mexico, mariachi is "identity music" for U.S.-based Mexican Americans (Campbell & Soto Flores, 2016), while the Afro-Mestizo musical tradition known as *son jarocho* is bringing Mexican American families together on a regular, even weekly, basis. Families of Mexican American Texans, or Tejanos, typically prefer *conjunto* music over genres such as *mariachi*, *cancion ranchera*, *banda*, and *son jarocho* music as background or for dance entertainment.

West coast Mexican Americans who are drawn to pop-rock genres may prefer the sounds of Ozomatli or Los Lobos over the music of Mariachi Cobre (or Los Texmaniacs *conjunto* group). The rhythms, textures, and instrumentation of music in Mexican American communities are differentiated by the genres and artists, but connecting them all is a penchant for diatonic major- and minor-keyed melodies, tonic and dominant chordal harmonies, and strophic poems in the Spanish language (Sheehy, 2006). Children may learn to play some of the instruments of the various ensembles, including mariachi-style trumpet or violin; *bajo sexto*, *vihuela*, or accordion of *conjunto* music; and the omnipresent guitar. They learn the techniques and repertoire by osmosis, "by ear," in the informal ways of oral transmission by family members who play for the enjoyment of it (Sheehy, 2006). Moreover, because singing is so common a part of these repertoires, children grow up with a rich selection of Spanish-language songs to sing for affirming their identities as Mexican Americans (Loza, 1996). For Mexican Americans, theirs is a very musical comunidad.

Black Community

African Americans are justifiably devoted to the heritage, history, and current practices of the Black community they have created and sustained. Many African Americans traditionally have formed family communities that include parents, grandparents, aunts, and uncles. Grandparents often become the primary parents for young children, particularly in the case of one-parent families (usually mothers) who are working one or more jobs; middle-class families, more than those of lower socioeconomic levels, tend toward intact two-parent families (Conger, Conger, & Martin, 2010; Moynihan, Smeeding, & Rainwater, 2004). African American families, and all members of the Black community, cherish self-sufficiency, a strong work ethic, perseverance, respect for the mother's role in the family, and the good fortune of an extended family and thoughtful neighbors.

The church is a nucleus for many members of the Black community and a prime location for musical expression. Whether Baptist, Methodist, or another denomination, the church has been one of the special strengths of the Black community, where not only reinforcement of positive social values but also solace, relief, and support can be found. It is there that children are most likely to encounter the live music of gospel, as well as elements of the genres that have influenced it: blues, rhythm-and-blues, and jazz (Jones, 2015). From infancy onward, children may be exposed on a weekly basis (twice weekly, if they accompany their parent(s) to Sunday church and the midweek rehearsal) to the toe-tapping, hand-clapping, head-nodding grooves of powerhouse choirs and the instrumental combos that accompany them. They are immersed in the blues-flavored melodies and syncopated rhythms of this music, and are embraced by congregations that take seriously the participatory and improvisatory nature of African American music. Because they are surrounded by pews of churchgoers who sing and respond through movement to gospel song, they are enculturated into a valuing of music as something that people regularly do as a component of their African American identity.

The popular styles of mass-mediated music in the United States have long been associated with, or derived from, the musical sensibilities of the Black community. From 19th-century spirituals and the blues and ragtime music of the early 20th century, to gospel, a wide assortment of jazz styles, rhythm-and-blues, early rock-and-roll, soul, and hip-hop, these styles are rooted in the sliding tones of blues scales, syncopations and multi-textured cross-rhythms, vocal inflections situated between speech and song, and texts that tell the stories of hard times, oppression, and the challenges of life on the streets and in societies where the vision of equality is still more rhetoric than real. All children, including African American children, are likely repositories for the sounds of Jay Z and Beyoncé, and it is common for community radio dials and iPhones of African American children to be tuned to the sounds of other reigning dynamos of hip-hop. These sounds evidence themselves in the creative expressions of young African American children, whose playground songs and singing games are typically more numerous, more syncopated, and more integrated with vigorous physical gestures and movements than those of Euro-American, Asian, or Latino children (Corso, 2003; Gaunt, 2007). While most American schoolchildren—especially girls—enjoy a repertoire of singing games in the elementary grades, much of it can be traced to the styles and characteristics of African American music.

Community (*Phobail*) Among Irish Americans

Then—from their surge as part of a widely documented flight from famine beginning in the mid-19th century—and now in the comparative trickling of new arrivals, the Irish community, called *phobail* in Gaelic, has become nearly 20% of the population in America. They define this identity variously, by their "wearing of the green" on St. Patrick's Day, their listening preferences for Irish traditional music, and their genealogical expeditions back to Ireland in search of family roots. Children in conservative Catholic Irish American homes, especially among recent émigrés, tend to have firm and moralistic mothers who are kind and consistent in their care. Keeping a stable and harmonious household is important to young families in the

Irish American community, so that children will grow up feeling loved and responsive to the needs of others (Dolan, 2008).

One of Ireland's chief exports is its traditional music, much of it coming into the American recording market and through live performances on concert stages, in community centers, and in clubs and bars (Hillhouse, 2013). The musical identity of Irish Americans, for those who seek it out, is associated with learning traditional Irish dance, including both hard- and soft-shoe styles. In Irish American families that are keen to keep the heritage, young girls (more than boys), typically between the ages of 5 and 15, are transported to weekly lessons and learn the steps and geometric pathways of an ensemble of dancers to the recordings of standard jigs, hornpipes, and reels. Some families arrange for their children to pursue musical training in *sean-nos* singing, on fiddle, flute, and concertina, and more rarely the uilleann pipes and Celtic harp.

The organization called *Comhaltas Ceoltoiri Eireann* (or just Comhaltas), established in Ireland in 1951 to promote the transmission of Irish-heritage music, dance, and language to children and youth, has gone international, and branches of the organization have sprung up in American cities (Hast & Scott, 2004). At week-long festivities celebrating St. Patrick's Day, performances of traditional music and dance feature children on indoor and outdoor platforms and in parades through city streets. In addition, competitions on all major traditional instruments, "lilting" (singing vocables to dance tunes), *sean-nos* singing, and dance are sponsored throughout the year by the Comhaltas branches for children and youth of all ages (Campbell, 2015). For Irish Americans who hope to maintain or build back the links to their old-world culture, participation by their children in the community's traditional dance and its music is a valued means of attaining this goal.

Americanized Vietnamese Community (*Công Đông*)

When Vietnamese families fled their homeland in the 1960s and 1970s during what they referred to as "the American war," many learned how to negotiate their new American location through a daily diet of television that beamed into the tiny apartments in *công đông* (community) neighborhoods. As they sought economic stability through the jobs they could find, newly Americanizing Vietnamese parents were often too busy working to have the time to teach their children all the subtleties of traditional Vietnamese culture. Yet there was the *công đông* community of extended families and neighbors who naturally influenced children's acquisition of language, selected folktales, songs, and traditional values such as a strong work ethic and respect for one's elders. In the 1990s and beyond, many children (and their elders as well) still stood teetering at the edge of two cultures in the process of their Americanization, balancing the traditions of the world they left behind in Hanoi, Hoi An, Hue, and Saigon (Ho Chi Minh City) with the images and experiences they were acquiring through the media, in their new surroundings, and in their American schools. Two types of traditional Vietnamese families, the scholar family and the peasant family, co-existed in the homeland and in their adopted American setting, so there was the tendency to expect children either to excel at school (the scholar family) or to learn farming, fishing, household maintenance, and such American economic enterprises as restaurant work, dry-cleaning, and housekeeping (the peasant family) (Nguyen & Campbell, 1991). It was also not unusual, during this transitional time in the new American *công đồng* neighborhoods, for Vietnamese American children to live up to the expectations of both study and work (Zhou & Bankston, 1998).

More than instrumental music, it is the Vietnamese songs—traditional folk songs and popular songs—that have had staying power with Vietnamese American children and youth, even as they grow into adulthood (Reyes, 1999). The children of the resettlement period are now raising their own children (and grandchildren, even) who know Vietnam only through the memories shared with them by their parents and grandparents. Today's Vietnamese American children revisit the traditions of their elders on special occasions such as Tet (Vietnamese New Year) rather than as daily routine. During Tet, extended family meals are accented by recordings of Vietnamese music, and meal-time conversations that wax nostalgically for a while may break into songfests and karaoke contests of music-minus-one renditions (i.e., instrumental tracks that are intended as accompaniments for live singing) to newly arranged folk songs (Nguyen et. al., 1995). Families of moderate income may be able to afford lessons in the zithers known as *dan tranh* and *dan bau*, and traditional dance (for daughters more than sons), which result in performances in church and community venues, including local festivals that feature traditional and folk arts.

Contemporary Vietnamese American children, most of them two generations removed from Vietnam, have largely assimilated into the mainstream of American culture. They may recognize a few folk melodies due to their prominence in community performances and on recordings, such as "Co La" ("The Egret Is Flying"), "Ly Ngua O" ("Song of the Black Horse"), and an instrumental piece, "Vong Co" ("Longing for the Past") (Nguyen & Campbell, 1991). They may even show a mild interest in musicians and dancers with Vietnamese surnames who have "made it" in the musical and entertainment world (for example, Tyga, the hip-hop artist of Vietnamese and Jamaican ancestry, Cuong Vu, Grammy award–winning jazz trumpeter, Jabbawockeez, and Poreotics). Most Vietnamese Americans, however, are thoroughly Western in their musical involvement.

CULTURE BEARERS

The prospect of bringing culture bearers into the schools is tantalizing to many music teachers, so that a person who has consciously embodied a musical culture can make an appearance in person to transmit it to students. Musically speaking, culture bearers are often locally living artist-musicians who come into schools from their nearby communities to make their contributions as full-fledged performers; as demonstrators of musical genres, instruments, vocal styles, and dances; and as storytellers who give credence to the music by way of what they say about how the music functions or what it personally means to them and others within their communities. By their very presence, they can advance diversity mandates and inspire social consciousness. Culture bearers have been referred to also as tradition bearers, as visiting artists, and as heritage musicians, the last of which runs parallel to the manner in which linguists and language instructors refer to "heritage speakers" (Buchanan, 2017). They typically have been born into their community, either an international community (such as in Greece or Brazil) or a Greek American or Brazilian American community still connected to the cultural values of the "old country." The expectation among teachers is that culture bearers are competent in the musical practices of their culture, whether or not they possess formal and systematic training in these practices, with the assumption that culture bearers are keeping close ties with the culture of their ancestry. Culture bearers are valued for the musical knowledge and skills they bring, and for their capacity to frame their songs, tunes, and rhythms with a cultural perspective that only they can have.

Of course, everyone bears a culture, a tradition, and a heritage. But some are more "exotic" and thus have a certain appeal to teachers who know less about those cultures that are distant from their own. As special guests who are out of the ordinary routine and the standard model of music teacher, culture bearers fill gaps in knowledge and skills, and pique the curiosity of students. In great demand in schools are the West African dancers and drummers, Native American singers and storytellers, East Asian players of lutes and zithers of China, Japan, and Korea, Andean players of stringed and wind instruments, and Afro-Latin percussionists from across the Caribbean as well as Brazil and coastal areas of Central and South America. Instrumentalists and dancers are in greater demand as culture bearers than are singers, and teachers appreciate culture bearers who "dress the part" for what the apparel might say about culturally-preferred fabrics and visual designs. In addition, culture bearers tend to be male rather than female, almost as if to counterbalance the preponderance of women teachers on school faculties.

Culture bearers offer large assembly-style performances to schoolchildren in the cavernous school performance spaces that are available, from gyms to cafeterias (and the cafetorium, that school combination space of cafeteria and auditorium). They also come for a full day, moving from one classroom to another, enjoying closer contact with children in classes than is possible in full assemblies. They share their songs, stories, instrumental music, and dances, and orient students to languages, dialects, and customs of their home cultures. Often, their presence is the only experience students will have in meeting an individual from Cuba, Ethiopia, Korea, Mali, Peru, Samoa, or the Lakota Sioux Nation, and the aim of their visit is to open ears and minds to cultural ways of thinking and doing. Sometimes, the initial visit with the culture bearer piques the interest of students to know more, or may lead to a unit of study that a teacher will develop further. The benefits of a culture bearer flow also to the teacher, who learns along with the students and who observes the culture-specific pedagogy that is employed by the culture bearer. Teachers who learn the culture bearer's music without notation, for example, can then turn around and teach that musical selection in a similar oral-aural manner.

The manifold values of culture-bearing musicians in schools can be seen as musical, cultural, and pedagogical. Both students and teachers learn music they may never have known, led by musicians who know it very well, and thus musical understanding, performance skills, and cultural knowledge grow more diversified. They learn nuances through the verbal and nonverbal mannerisms of a communication style that has been shaped by the culture bearer's home and community environment. They develop an understanding of reasons for music sounding the way it does, due to issues of climate, geography, and economic, political, religious, and philosophical positions and principles. The songs point to people, their social relationships and historic figures, the treasured ideals and events of a place. Students absorb music and relevant cultural facets through interactions with the culture bearer, and the musical knowledge is tied to a transmission process, and a culturally relevant pedagogy, that is natural and commonplace within the culture of the music (and out of their own zone of teaching/learning practices). The benefits of culture bearers are worth every penny that must be eked out of a restrictive school budget to bring musicians on board, as even a single visit (and better, multiple visits or week-long residencies) provide a pathway to understanding music, culture, and community.

SOUND BITES AND VIDEO VIEWS OF COMMUNITY ARTISTS

Despite the very best of intentions, remote and rural schools, and schools with limited budgets, may not have the wherewithal to welcome culture bearers into the curriculum. Sometimes, Skyped visits can be arranged, so that artists can appear on large classroom screens to perform, to teach repertoire and techniques, to provide commentary on student performances, to be interviewed, and to interact with students. Music teachers also may bring the taste of a musical community into the curriculum through recordings and video-recordings of the work of artists, adding Internet interviews when possible but giving utmost attention to what is already available online. Descriptions of three heritage award winners follow, recognized as they are by the National Endowment for the Arts for their artistic excellence, their depth of cultural knowledge, and their passion in preserving musical heritage and culture through performance and teaching (Campbell & Lum, 2008). Their audio- and video-representations are accessible by teachers (www.arts.gov/honors/heritage) and provide a window to understanding the life and work of heritage musicians as an expression of both personal and collective ideals that reflect the communities from which they come. They each have worked in their own cultural communities, even as they also have reached beyond their communities to share their artistic vision and heritage with students, teachers, and the public at large.

Chum Ngek. In the wave of Cambodian refugees arriving in the United States in the early 1980s, the Khmer musician Chum Ngek arrived to begin his life as a musical and educational leader in the *pinpeat* ensemble music of Cambodia, locally (in Washington, DC) and across the nation. Chum Ngek is a master performer (and group organizer) of *pinpeat* (classical court music), *mohori* (entertainment music), and *phleng kar* (wedding music). Although he makes his living as a stockperson and a truck driver for a fabric store, he is especially well known as a master of the *roneat* (a 21-keyed xylophone) used in *pinpeat* and *mohori*. Chum Ngek remembers when he was a child, listening to his grandfather teaching music to students in Cambodia: "The first thing I learned was keeping the beat. My grandfather agreed to teach me the songs by having me sing the melodies without words. I just sang, 'nai, nai, nai, nai' before I started to play on the instruments. He had me start out humming the tunes like that. After that, he let me play the drums—the big drums—and he taught me to play easy patterns on them." The music of Cambodia is essentially an oral, aural, tactile, and spiritual tradition passed from teacher to student through the generations. Chum Ngek begins with the basics when he teaches music to his students, selecting simple songs but then rendering them in beautiful ways that stimulate the students as well as their eventual listening audience, and both the music and the responses of a grateful audience encourage them to continue their learning of Khmer music of Cambodia. While he serves his own Khmer community, Chum Ngek is also on hand as a culture-bearing musician who performs for and teaches many diverse audiences and student groups.

Gerald "Subiyay" Miller. A gifted singer, dancer, and storyteller, Gerald "Subiyay" Miller was also a carver in his time, a maker of masks and baskets, and a bearer of the traditions of the Skokomish people of Puget Sound in Washington State. Now deceased, he made it his aim to pay tribute the true value of Skokomish life and delighted in his work as a tribal scholar and *widadad,* or cultural teacher. He performed traditional songs, ceremonies, and rituals, and knew a repertoire of 120 traditional stories to tell, all learned orally from his elders. His work in reviving the First Salmon and First Elk ceremonies (once banned by the U.S. government) and in bringing back the winter ceremonies to his people is greatly celebrated. As one of 15 children in an extended household of parents, grandparents, a granduncle, and cousins, Miller's life mission was to make stories and language accessible to "anyone who's interested." He upheld the belief that the greatest means of preserving traditions of the Skokomish was to ensure that very young children spend time with their grandparents, learning in the group through oral means so that a lifelong interest and respect for these traditions could be seeded and nourished for growth. Miller was a role model as a cultural worker and a culture bearer, working inside and off the reservation with young people who would apprentice with him. As a community artist with expertise in visual and oral culture, Miller taught his students to weave and to make traditional reed baskets, even as he also wove the remembered stories and songs of the Skokomish people into their experience. Beyond his own tribal community, he was an important contributor to the development of curriculum in schools in his home state and in university programs.

Mavis Staples. A legend in gospel, blues, and soul music, Mavis Staples was lead singer for her father's group, the Staple Singers, on standard hits such as "I'll Take You There" and "Respect Yourself." She has been an important spiritual and musical voice for the Civil Rights movement from the mid-1960s onward and has collaborated with American popular artists from Bob Dylan to Prince, including Janis Joplin, Pink Floyd, Aretha Franklin, Santana, Los Lobos, and Tom Petty and the Heartbreakers. She is known for her big voice and riveting performances of protest and freedom songs, all of them with an elaborately expressive gospel flavor honed in her hometown in Mississippi. Referring to them as "message songs," Staples is eager to sing songs of inspiration to uplift people, to provide healing, calmness, and comfort, and to draw people into dancing and singing with her. Her contemporary performances continue to build on a family tradition of joining the gospel fervor with the shades of soul music and rhythm-and-blues, always singing from the heart and with integrity. She credits her father for her success, but her own musical brilliance impacts the Black community, the musical community, and all communities that attach an importance to an impassioned plea for and thoughtful reflection on freedom, peace, and justice.

VISITING ARTISTS IN UNIVERSITY–COMMUNITY COLLABORATION

University programs do well to serve as effective models of education that connects to local musical communities and culture bearers. Their students are watching, and many of them will graduate to school music teaching positions where they will "teach as they have been taught." At the University of Washington, the Visiting Artist in Ethnomusicology program was established as a means of bringing students into an interaction with artist-teachers from some of the world's great musical cultures from across Africa, Asia, and the Americas (Averill, 2004; Campbell, 2011b). For over 55 years, the Visiting Artist program has provided students with private lessons as well as ensemble experiences (depending upon the instrument and genre) by artist-musicians. Visiting artists have shared a broad array of traditions—Ashanti drumming, Balinese and Javanese gamelan, Chinese *guzheng*, Filipino *kulintang*, Indian *khyal*, *sitar*, and *tabla*, Irish *sean-nos*, Japanese *shakuhachi*, Korean *kayagum*, Lao *kaen* (and *mawlum* singing) Pakistani *qawwali*, Persian *ney*, Peruvian *siku*, Shona-style *mbira* from Zimbabwe, Sephardic Jewish folk music from Spain, Tex-Mex *conjunto*, Thai *jahke*, and Venezuelan *joropo*, to name just a few.

Among the criteria for selection for the Visiting Artist program is the expectation that these heritage musicians should have been raised in the tradition of their musical expertise. In this way, not only are culture-specific musical skills, knowledge, and repertoire transmitted to students, but also something of the fuller envelope and extent of music-as-culture. Artist-musicians function as cultural ambassadors, sharing ideas, within lessons, during ensemble rehearsals, and in various interactions at departmental events and social functions, and thus convey an understanding of people and culture along with music. These international visiting artists have also traveled off campus from the university to surrounding communities. This was especially true in the case of South Asian musicians who were welcomed and supported by Ragamala, their local community organization dedicated to music and the performing arts of South Asia (India, Pakistan, Bangladesh, Sri Lanka, and Afghanistan). African, Okinawan, and Filipino artists also are supported by representatives of local communities who attended university events and helped organize concerts or workshops for the visiting artists in local venues such as churches, temples, schools, or museums.

It is considered philosophically solid and financially feasible to tap the abundant talent present in Seattle's diverse communities in the development of community arts residencies. While international artists continue to be featured, the program is now tuned to support local artists from the community as well, while also finding ways for visiting artists from abroad to serve local populations of the cultures represented by the artists. Collaborations are fostered between university and community members so that students enrolled in a course with a visiting artist could learn not only from their intensive interactions with an individual artist but also from a community of other practitioners and culture bearers, and in spaces and social environments outside the university. Thus there have been town-and-gown performances and workshop engagements with communities of musicians and fans who identify as Mexican, Jewish, Irish, Indonesian, Puerto Rican, African American, (South Asian) Indian, Spanish Sephardic, and Guinean.

Community music residencies offer the opportunity for students to learn through participation in a larger community. If the original principle of the Visiting Artist program was to prepare ethnomusicology students for cultural immersion in "the field," the opportunity for students to participate in local communities of practice is an enhancement of this principle. Students must, of course, consider that people playing *son jarocho* or *bomba*, or performing Irish fiddling or Sephardic singing, inevitably will approach it differently than people in Veracruz, Puerto Rico, Ireland, or Spain, but the fact remains that engagement with music in community is engagement with music as culture. Working with local groups and artists also gives students the opportunity to continue learning after the university residency ends, and for those who will teach music, this connection to a local musical community is a precious find.

CAPITAL CM, AS IN COMMUNITY MUSIC

Switch the order and form of two words, musical community, to Community Music (CM), and a distinctive meaning emerges to describe a phenomenon that has drawn much enthusiasm in recent years. It is an influential movement that is relevant to all who are active in the engagement of people of any age and experience, in any context, in the music-making process. Multiple descriptors have been assigned to Community Music, such as "open," "flexible," "context-sensitive," and "breakthrough," yet it has remained elusive—particularly to those who have not had the experience of working as a community musician at the source of CM in the United Kingdom. Higgins (2012) cuts through the confusion of imprecise descriptions and conflicting definitions by incisively focusing on the participatory process of making music as central to Community Music. Linking it to cultural democracy, where "musicians who work within it are focused on the concerns of making and creating musical opportunities" (p. 7), he reflects the widely held view of CM practitioners who emphasize the importance of access to music for all and inclusion of anyone who wishes to be involved in any musical way. Community Music involves people, places, context, and diversity in a participatory ethos in which those who wish to make music are offered opportunities to do so. In its original conception, there is no teacher in a CM approach to music-making, but rather a socially conscious and group-sensitive leader to guide group members in their music-making ventures, to ensure that all voices are heard, and to guarantee a certain momentum in the engagement of individuals in their collective music-making ventures (Higgins, 2007).

As a dynamic and persuasive process, Community Music is enveloping and encompassing, active as well as reflective, often exuberant, and contagious. It is almost "a way of being" within the sociality of music-making, a model and a movement that has grown from its early life in the United Kingdom to the quite remarkable embrace it receives from professionals internationally in music education, music therapy, and community cultural development. Musical ideas come from the group members, and music is created and crafted by them together through negotiated give-and-take processes of improvisation and composition. Musical self-expression is encouraged, and creative rather than re-creative music-making is prominent and preferred among group members. All instruments and all styles of vocal production are welcome in the process, and certainly movement, from nods to grooves to all-out dance, joins well to the vocal and instrumental encounters of the group. CM practitioners facilitate musical activities in hospitals, places of worship, festivals, prisons, and after-school programs, and the sociomusical process of active participation leads to musical skill building, social bonding, and the development of a genuine sensitivity to sentiments, views, and values of individuals.

In Community Music, designated by capitalization of its initial letters, CM, in an effort to distinguish it from the meaning of musical communities, the community is the group that assembles to make music together. This community may consist of people familiar with one another, as in the case of after-schoolers who see one another in classes throughout the school day but then come together for the express purpose of making music. Or, the community may be a gathering of individuals who previously did not know one another, such as those who come together at a festival, or a workshop announced to the general public. They enjoy the prospects, realized in the community they become, of making music unshackled by curricular guides and other institutional standards, of contributing their parts to the music-making interactions that ensue. Many seek (and find) the satisfaction of belonging to a group and of making something beautiful, innovative, and socially binding. They appreciate the possibilities for developing friendships through music.

Community Music is an approach to active music-making that runs outside the realm of the formal, and yet it is also a democratic pedagogy whose ideals are finding a fit with some teachers in school music programs. The premise on which it is based, that "everybody has the right and ability to make, create, and enjoy their own music" (Higgins, 2012, p. 5), is well suited to the work of music teachers who are keen to welcome contributions from their diverse school-aged populations and the communities from which they come. Further statements of Community Music are fully resonant with the ideals of a multicultural and globally oriented musical education, including the emphasis that is given to musical diversity as a reflection of individuals within the group as well as the cultural life of the local community in which CM may transpire. It is also the desire of CM practitioners to respect music as the property of cultural owners of that music and to "do it justice" in new manifestations, and to foster intercultural acceptance and understanding through music. For these reasons, the educational potential of Community Music is ripe and ready for transfer to schools, and already is making tracks (Higgins & Willingham, 2017). CM coordinates well with pedagogical approaches such as culturally responsive pedagogy, authentic learning, and situated learning, and with the general shift in education and schooling from teaching to learning, and from teacher to learner.

At the Nexus. As fields dovetail and missions overlap, we see ourselves in the cracks between the fields. How do we describe what we do, without noting these multiple streams of influence? My experience is as a music teacher, applied ethnomusicologist, and CM practitioner, involved within the realm of preparing students for teaching (and facilitating) music in settings of considerable diversity—both in schools and in universities, and also in community projects and programs. My colleagues and I provide our university students with experiences in knowing diverse music practices (via listening and cultural analysis projects, performance and participatory experiences, and person-to-person exchanges). We balance the study of music in culture and as culture, and as it lives locally and across the globe. We aim to advance our students' understanding of music and its meaning through work with artist-musicians as short- and long-term visiting faculty for courses in ethnomusicology, music education, and world music performance. I work at the seams of programs that give steady attention to ways in which we can honor cultural diversity, including race, gender, religion, and socioeconomic status, allowing music to be the gateway to a developing cultural understanding of people close and far from "home." The music education students who will become state-certified music teachers and the ethnomusicology students who will find jobs in media, museums, archives, concert management, and community schools—and the PhD students in these fields who will land positions in higher education—will, I hope, be engaged in, receptive to, and supportive of a great diversity of musical cultures, expressions, and practices of the world's peoples. My shift toward Community Music coincided with my growing awareness of the interstices of music education and ethnomusicology. There was a small opening between the fields, which, through the rise of Community Music practice (and theory), is now filled by our music/their music and the processes by which "my music" (or "their music") can become "our music."

APPLIED ETHNOMUSICOLOGY

When ethnomusicologists engage in the active practice of putting music to use outside the realm of the academic and performance work at the university, they have made the move into the realm of applied ethnomusicology. Off campuses and out into musical communities, applied ethnomusicology transpires in education, cultural policy, conflict resolution, medicine, arts programming, and media work. Based in the "give-back" principles of social responsibility, applied ethnomusicology launches from or is guided by scholarship to use music to benefit a community (Titon, 2015).

Social and political activism has long been important to many working ethnomusicologists, quite possibly in recognition of an earlier history of colonialist scholarship that acted to oppress the very cultures they study. They are sensitive to the rights of the marginalized and in support of the voiced interests of minorities. Even as they study the music of a family, or clan, community, or broader culture, they advocate for the needs of that group and strive to protect and preserve valued music as well as to foster musical expressions that depart from traditions and may require contemporary instruments, recording devices, and media support. Ethnomusicologists are advocates and activists for the music and musicians they have come to know, and for other concerns beyond music that are meaningful to communities and cultures.

Applied ethnomusicology is music-centered as well as people-centered, and is sensitive to issues of human rights and cultural equity. Similar to the distinctions between pure science and applied science, ethnomusicology is more theoretical than it is practical (beyond the practice of teaching in academic settings), while applied ethnomusicology draws from theory into a wider scope of practice. While ethnomusicology is a discipline, applied ethnomusicology is a field that is committed to intervention through music with the aim of producing social, cultural, economic, and musical outcomes.

As in ethnomusicology at large, applied ethnomusicology happens in various contexts and through various efforts and skill sets. Those who are involved in cultural policy interventions work in applied ethnomusicology, wrapping themselves into efforts involving minority, immigrant, underserved populations, and indigenous peoples across the world. The sustainability of endangered or threatened musics fits into this category (Schippers & Grant, 2016), as do projects produced or otherwise supported by national and state arts and humanities councils (including the National Endowment for the Arts), especially in the domain of folk arts and community arts. Notable projects within the realm of applied ethnomusicology are the annual Smithsonian Folklife Festival (now a half-century in duration, in Washington, DC) and Northwest Folklife Festival (over 40 years running, in Seattle); the UNESCO programs for the preservation of intangible cultural heritage through concerts, tours, and recordings; and the national media programs on songs and stories of ordinary people (such as the radio broadcasts by Alan Lomax and the PBS programs on jazz and other American-heritage expressions). Applied ethnomusicologists are at work in the area of advocacy for music and musicians, including work in museums and archives, lobbying for arts spaces, and grant writing with community artists to sustain and celebrate their music in concerts, tours, recordings, and community education programs. They are involved in the music industry and in the management of artists for concerts, in libraries, in journalism, in peace and conflict resolution, and in medicine, therapy, and healing practices.

Applied ethnomusicology has a presence as well in fields that overlap with certified school music teachers and with community musicians, including CM practitioners as well as musicians from local cultural communities. In this realm, applied ethnomusicologists work to design and implement curriculum honoring diverse musical practices, facilitate visits of culture bearers and visiting artists in schools and on university campuses, and connect schools with community spaces where music is made. They have diversity and inclusion very much in mind in the work they do in education, giving attention to the fostering of musical performances by local artists and dialogues with musical communities, particularly those with particular ethnic-cultural identities. Along with diversity-minded music educators and CM practitioners, they work with cultural democracy in mind as a tool for empowerment. In this way, attention is geared to a bottom-up rather than a top-down approach to teaching and learning, allowing musical communities to rightfully own the music they make.

FIELDTRIP! EXCURSIONS TO A COMMUNITY

For the development of cultural sensitivity in students, firsthand interaction with culturally diverse populations has proven effective and often transformative. There are extraordinary benefits from visits by students to local communities, as experiences in context can be a powerful means for understanding music's cultural meaning and value. Such fieldtrips to musical communities are well worthy of the time and effort expended on arrangements, and yet considerable energy is involved in working through the complexities of scheduling an onsite visit, the transportation and meals (and sometimes overnight accommodations), and meeting the challenges of missed classes during students' time away. The evidence is strong that visits to musical communities open up ears, eyes, and minds to different but equally logical ways of conceiving of time and space, of thinking and doing, of musicking, music learning, and cultural transmission (Greene et al., 2014; Soto et al., 2009).

One such fieldtrip is the program called Music Alive! in the Yakima Valley (MAYV), 13 years in the making, whereby music students at the

University of Washington, most of them majoring in music education program with the intent of teaching music in schools, pack up for short excursions across the Cascade Mountains to the high plateau of the Yakama tribal lands. There in the rural towns of Toppenish, Harrah, and White Swan, students come to know the school-aged children and youth of Yakama and Mexican American families who live side by side on and at the edge of the Yakama reservation. The university students perform for the schoolchildren and youth, and they listen to and learn from performances by the children of unison songs and harmonized choral music, the school-style wind band selections, the rhythms of their African drumming ensembles, the social dance songs that Yakama children sing and play on homemade hand drums, and the Spanish-language popular songs, children's songs, and seasonal songs of Mexican American children. The outcomes of the MAYV program stream in two directions: to the Toppenish community and to the music majors. They include bridging the gap between privileged university music students and underserved school populations, providing a civic engagement of music majors with children and youth of poor and rural communities, performing for the Mexican American and Yakama children vocally and on instruments they have never heard or seen "live," and listening to and participating in the music made in these communities. With this last action, the aim is to validate a diversity of musical expressions that is beyond the standard university music-major repertoire.

The firsthand cultural interaction is a precious opportunity to know the people behind the music, as the musical communities of the Mexican Americans and the Yakama are distinguished by their location, their ethnic-cultural composition, and their socioeconomic circumstance. There in the Yakima Valley the music majors have opportunities to interact with students musically and socially in the comfort of the students' hometown, to feel the rhythm and pace of the people of the community, and to wonder about ways in which local values are reflected in the music of the *conjunto*, mariachi, and powwow events. There are day visits, overnights, and a week-long residency by University of Washington music majors in the Yakima Valley. The week-long residency transpires in January, and music majors enjoy homestays when they live in groups of three with families in town. This becomes an opportunity for music majors to quickly enter into the town's cultural environment, as they gain firsthand knowledge of what family life is like in this community so far from Seattle's city lights. Whether for the day or the week, homestays are filled with time to talk across the boundary that distinguishes rural from urban life, poor from privileged circumstances, and minority groups of Mexican Americans and Yakama Indians.

Questions emerge about the similarities and distinctions of music's role in culture, and the university students tick off myriad ways in which the people of the Yakima Valley think and do music. They find more commonalities than differences in the musical sound and in the ways in which music is transmitted, which shores up their belief in a shared human musicality. Without fail, the observation arises among students that all people are anchored in music, despite variations in sound, behavior, and values. Students find meaning in their excursions that they take back to their preparation in music education and to their work in school positions after graduation. There is the joy that we see on the faces of children who are visibly in awe of the university students' performances on violin, or saxophone, or guitar, their eyes wide open with astonishment in their reverie on the music. There is the positive energy that can be felt physically in the exchanges of university and high school students over instruments, repertoire, and the meaning of music. There is the way that university students return to classes, fired up and firm in their belief that they are destined to make a difference as musicians and music teachers in their lives ahead by reaching out to outlying communities (rural? poor? socioculturally distinctive?) they previously never connected to. There is their increased and genuine interest in "Other" musics and musicians. Finally, there have been more than a few students, over the years, who have taken the pathway to teaching jobs in places beyond their own familiar and safe suburban environments, to work with children and youth far from the mainstream who deserve highly skilled and sincerely dedicated musicians in their midst.

For some music majors, the program is a "startle experience," an "in-their-face" event that is mildly disorienting in the midst of their orderly university lives. After all, there is plenty of adjustment in going from the gentle flow of campus events to the sometimes raucous and riled-up activity of a group of schoolchildren (anywhere!), and they also must adjust from a warm room in the residence hall to a cot in a family's spare (and sometimes drafty) room. There is a certain distance, both literal and figurative, between university students and the children of a culturally distinctive rural community, a crevice that needs a bridge. For those who work with Music Alive! in the Yakima Valley, there is the continuing hope that they can help to lessen the distance, so that Seattle students and the people of the Yakima Valley might come to know "the other" through meaningful experiences in music.

COMMUNITY: BOTTOMS UP

Community is a concept with multiple interpretations, and a force to be reckoned with, and it offers many rewards. Teachers with diversity in mind are well served by tapping into the possibilities for connecting to musical communities, individual artists, culture bearers, and keepers of musical heritage. Visits to schools by musicians from the community, and by schools to musicians in their community locations, are enriching. As well, developing communities of musicians through authentic and situated learning in a Community Music pedagogical approach can be highly meritorious in achieving diversity goals. Neither university-trained musicians nor school music educators are the hub, source, or font of musical repertoire and skills to be experienced and studied in schools, although they can pull up their antennae to draw music and musicians of every style into educational contexts. By listening and talking with people in public spaces, at cultural festivals, in restaurants of various culinary tastes, in places of worship, in schools, and on the street, much can be learned about communities of musicians. This much needs to happen, if teachers are to live out their professional role of working musicians responsible for the musical education of their students in a contemporary society of considerable diversity.

Principles of Diversity in School Music Practice

Through descriptions of music teachers and their programs, evidence is provided of the pathways to musically educating children and youth, with diversity in mind. Documentation is offered of how the development of knowledge and skills in music goes hand in hand with realization of the dimensions of multicultural education. Points of practical wisdom are delineated, with attention to how music teachers may take into consideration the wisdom of ethnomusicologists and music education scholars in working through the realities of the teaching/learning act. Issues related to singing and playing "world music" are discussed, and contextualization is described as essentially the stories and cultural frameworks behind the music and musicians that make the connection to multicultural understanding, giving further weight and relevance to the music studied. The press of some musical experiences into standard teaching methods is examined, too, along with recommendations for adapting instructional practices to fit the music (rather than the other way around).

All We Need to Know. There was a time when a school music teacher thought that she should be the font of all musical knowledge, the keeper of facts, the epitome of a bottom-line veracity in her decisions and interpretations. She believed that teaching was about what she knew from her university music-major studies and what she would musically "give" to her students, that she should be the hub and heart of a community of young learners in her classes who could come to know the music as she knew it. Oh, and she really did know the music: She could sing many songs in French, German, and Italian, and play many instruments, as her studio studies in piano ensured technique and repertoire and her method courses attuned her to the fundamentals of band and orchestral instruments. She could make sense out of complex musical works and would lead students to perform and listen analytically so as to work out the meaning of the music and its importance to people of a particular time and place. Like the many-armed, multitasking Hindu god, Parvati, she was the source, calling attention to herself, reaching out and drawing students to the music that they should know.

True confessions: I was this music teacher. In the mid-1970s, in my first year of teaching, I thought I needed to know everything about music (that is, Western art music). I was fresh from my university degree in music education; the music we'd made was Western art music, and the music teaching that was modeled in methods classes and supervised teaching internships was monoculturally Western. Despite my curiosities and even engagements with other musical styles in my younger life, I hid those folk and popular music styles in a secret place in my past, far away from the focus of my professional work. Instead, I stormed through my studies of music of the Baroque, the Viennese classical period, and the 19th century, and was drawn into the experimental music compositions of the 20th century. In my first years of teaching, I stayed up late to fastidiously put lesson after lesson together, choosing scores, selecting recordings, studying the basal music textbook series of materials, and rehearsing—singing, playing, and conducting—the music that I would bring to the students the next day. I was weary from the preparations, but that was my professional task: to bring the music of the great Western way to the students.

People have moments of reckoning, thankfully. For me, it was one little girl's observation of my car collection of the recordings of James Brown, Nina Simone, and Stevie Wonder and her grilling me (I wrote her questions in my diary on that remarkable day in March 1975): "Why you got those cassettes but you never let us listen? You think we don't know James Brown or something? You know what his songs mean? How come you listen to Black music, anyway?"

That was the opening to my conversion, to coming through the sea change, from reckoning with what music I taught and how I taught it. Music branded as WEAM: Western (European) art music, music of my elite musical education and training, that I delivered to students without their input, that was fully notated, that was all about me and the line I'd fallen for hook, line, and sinker in my methods courses. "The rest is history," as they say, beginning with the unraveling of a false notion of what music education is all about. There came the start of listening to the students, mixing up the musical styles, pulling out the musical "secrets" I treasured, dipping into popular music, featuring a varied diet of musical possibilities, searching the music together for insights and perspectives on people and culture (and music), and having conversations about what music means to people of any time and any place in the world. It took a child to set me on track.

TEACHERS, TRAJECTORIES, AND BLUEPRINTS

As a theoretical web is woven of the intersections of music, education, and cultural diversity, and a history of the ebb and flow of attention to musical and cultural diversity in education is acknowledged, a set of principles comes to light that is germane to developing a multicultural consciousness through music. But principles are "word balloons," the little clouds of words that hover above the heads of cartoon characters, which, unless acted upon, will dissipate and be dispelled until the next round of "talking heads" takes another stab at it, gushing new verbiage, glad-handing at the close of another conference session of clever schemes and propositions. Without implementation, principles are mere platitudes. The professional literature is thick with policy statements, pretty words, and impressive theoretical models of what could be/should be done to multiculturalize the music curriculum. Yet in the end, it is left to the music teacher to determine just how to put the principles of diversity into school music practice. Skilled and state-certified music educators have great potential to convert ideals to realities. Guided by theories they learned in their university work, and by inservice demonstrations and discussions to launch their practice, they can power up to serving the causes of equity and justice, of diversity and inclusion for the benefit of the children with whom they work. They can collaborate with colleagues who teach various subjects, with culture bearers and heritage musicians who live in the community (or are accessible online and through the media), and with the broader collective of community members who may be awaiting an invitation to commit time and energy to the greater good of developing the multicultural consciousness of students.

Music teachers have made inroads in diversifying their music programs, often with too little time, sometimes myopic and inconsistent university training, and negligible financial support to assist them. While few teachers have run the full gamut in teaching music as a pan-human, global, and cross-cultural phenomenon, some have stepped up to the challenges and have shaped all-encompassing plans to do double duty in teaching music and culture, in mixing local and global expressions, and in meeting musical and multicultural aims. Their work has raised the bar for what is possible, and a synthesis of their efforts flows into three brief "trajectories," one for each of three music education settings in schools: elementary school (vocal/general/classroom) music—grades K–5, middle school music—grades 6–8 (or 9), and secondary school music—grades 9 (or 10)–12. Even as they appear as three individual case studies, the descriptions here are "conglomerates" of practice sewn together from my years of observations and conversations with a wide assortment of school music teachers in the United States, Canada, and abroad.

Trajectory 1: Music for All Seasons (Elementary School)

Change comes to a curriculum, and stabilizes, in the hands of a teacher who dedicates herself to a set of goals, to her children, and to the families and local communities that surround her. Anna is a veteran teacher of 14 years at the very same public elementary school where she began her career, located in a working-class neighborhood of predominantly White families but with a 40% mix of African American, Latin American (mostly Mexican), and Asian American (especially Vietnamese, Khmer, Lao, and Hmong) children. Her schedule provides for three weekly 35-minute classes with children in the earlier grades (K–2) and twice weekly 45-minute sessions with children in grades 3–5. In addition, children may elect to join hour-long weekly sessions in a choir, an in-school international dance club, and a "zimarimba" ensemble of Zimbabwean-style marimbas. Anna's schedule is unusual for its flexibility, in that she has daily prep periods to plan for classes, set up for the various classes and special group sessions, write emails to collaborating teachers and culture bearers, and make phone calls to parents. She has engendered a general understanding of her ultimate musical and multicultural goals in her classroom teacher colleagues, and many are supportive of, and even collaborative in, some of her program ventures. Some of them marvel at her endless energy, and her capacity to leap from one musical style to another and to work with a wide developmental span of children ranging from 5-year-old kindergarten children to 5th-grade students on the brink of adolescence.

From a music-educational perspective, Anna's program goals are spread across the six years, K–5, and appear aligned with the district (and national) standards: music (notational) literacy; aural skill proficiencies (listening and "inner hearing"); development of the singing voice; foundational competence on piano, ukulele, guitar, recorder, and various pitched and non-pitched percussion instruments; and creative skills at play in song-writing, composition, and improvisation. She is adamant about the integration of music with understandings of people and culture, and while some teachers work with her in extending the musical experiences to their geography, history, and language arts studies, Anna knows that she needs to bring some of the extramusical matter into the experiences she designs in the music program. She has taken her specialized training in Orff, a music–movement–speech pedagogy, and Kodály, a vocally based program intent on developing music literacy through singing.

Anna is a world music pioneer, continually in motion to fit one new musical discovery after the next into her graded lessons. She teaches comparatively, organizing lesson content in cross-cultural ways so that children can listen to, sing, play, and dance to wedding music from Greece, Japan, Kenya, and the Philippines, and likewise experience music of work and worship, of lullabies and love, and of five-tone pentatonic scales and triple meter through multiple engagements with cross-cultural selections. She integrates folktales, photos, and stories from large-size picture books (regardless of the age of the children), and searches the web for best examples of music and musicians that can provide children with images they can hear and see. Anna thinks that listening is an underestimated and often overlooked activity, and so she ensures that there is at least one choice piece in every class for her students to focus on. One thing leads to another, too, so that in having her children listen to a selection by the Kronos Quartet, or Homayun Sakhi, Toumani Diabate, Beyoncé, Altan, Mariachi Vargas, Te Vaka, Son de Madera, Oumou Sangare, Jake Shimabukuro, Anoushka Shankar, or Rhiannon Giddens, she will expect them to eventually be able to sing it, dance to it, or play it. Her energy is up with the children, and she leads through a rapid-pace questioning technique to pique their attention to listen for instruments, melodic and rhythmic components, formal structures, lyrics, and possible functions of the music. She wants them to know the music through repeated listening, the stories of the musicians, and the reasons why the music sounds the way it does.

There are expectations for performances (or at least participatory music events) by Anna's students in the periodic public programs for parents, families, and the whole community at her school, and she's ready for it. She prepares the children to celebrate the seasons through welcome songs at school orientation (September), the Festival of Lights (December), Black History Month (February), Spring Fest (late April), and graduation (June). There's plenty of vocal music, sung a cappella (as so much music is performed in that manner, without the need for piano or guitar) and "with heart" (and often with basic movement, gestures, and simple dance forms to accompany the songs). The Festival of Lights celebration brings on the choirs, the recorder consort, the grade-level class groups as singers and players of music in celebration of Divali, Hanukkah, Sankta Lucia, Christmas, and Kwanzaa. In February, the program consists of choral speech of addresses and poems by Martin Luther King, Maya Angelou, Langston Hughes, Rosa Parks, and Nelson Mandela; the obligatory African American anthem ("Lift

Every Voice and Sing"); selections such as "Follow the Drinking Gourd," "This Little Light of Mine," "Get on Board, Little Children," and children's songs of the African diaspora such as "Sansa Kroma" and "Kye Kye Kule"; and the vibrant sounds of their zimarimba ensemble. The Spring Fest in late April features a host of "music of many nations" and a guest artist from the community who will have had several weeks in residence with the children; past guests have included an Andean panpipe player, an African American blues guitarist, a player of Khmer/Cambodian xylophone, and a five-piece mariachi group of guitar, two violins, trumpet, and *guitarron*. Anna is flexible with the possibilities for the graduation performance, which typically consists of an original play by the graduating 5th-grade students and songs they wish to sing and play (on recorders, zimarimbas, ukuleles, and various classroom percussion instruments). The performance concludes with the international dance club performing in line and circle formations, with an invitation to the audience to join in on the final selection. For Anna, the public performances are manifestations of the rich experiences that the children have through the multicultural curriculum she has fashioned.

Trajectory 2: Rhythm in Our Bones (Middle School)

It's not unusual for a middle school of three grades, with a student population of over 800, to have on staff three certified music teachers. Particularly in states where music is a state-mandated subject for study through 8th grade, the music education staff works long days with large groups of students. Daryl is the third of three music teachers, hired most recently, and at almost two years into his position he's still working out the kinks and wrinkles so that he complements the specializations of his colleagues while also serving a population of students who claim no interest in school music studies. The school sits in the central district of a large metropolitan city, which has a peculiar mix of low-income housing right around the block from condominiums that are valued at nearly one million dollars. About a quarter of the children, mostly White and Asian American, enrolled in the school come from the condo families, while the remainder are largely African American, with a trace from Caribbean families. Daryl is a trumpet player, both jazz and straight, and had a dream of teaching instrumental music in an award-winning high school music program. But that job was not open, and so he landed in the middle school for what he hoped was only a temporary position before he would move on. His charge was to teach "all the rest" of the school population who were not the motivated or at least mildly curious students filling the seats in the band, choir, and orchestra classes. He was teaching the spillover kids in the nonspecified classes called "general music," and he could decide what that might mean.

The school had three working keyboards, a dozen recorders, four out-of-tune autoharps, and six acoustic guitars at the time Daryl was hired. He asked for a budget and received $150 for his first year—about the amount needed for new guitar strings for the six guitars—not enough, he realized, for his sizable "mass-classes" of students that would be meeting five days weekly; trading off instruments would hardly motivate learning for the 80% of the students who, without instruments in hand, would be sitting, listening, distracting, and simply not learning. Darryl would have 6 periods of these classes, each with a mix of 6th- , 7th- , and 8th-grade students. Frantically in search of a way forward, he remembered what had driven him to play trumpet when he was the age of his students (particularly in his effort to learn to play jazz, blues, funk, and groove) and recalled that there was something about the music's rhythm that had so captivated him. He recognized, too, that belonging to a band of motivated players—even in a school classroom, possibly even in making non-melodic but rhythmically cohesive music—could be a badge of identity, a genuine feeling of group membership, that could be important to young adolescents. So he took a chance, acting on a hunch that rhythm and "belonging" factors might create a genuine interest in students to learn music: Daryl spent the budget on 40 plastic garbage bins from the Dollar Store and had 40 pairs of foot-long wood dowels made for him at the hardware store.

In his first semester of teaching, Daryl taught "bucket band" to two classes, plus two more conventional general music appreciation classes, a "mixed instruments" class (utilizing the seriously skewed set of instruments), and a song-writing class. The concept of making rhythms on buckets was an immediate sensation, however, and by January he had converted two more classes to bucket-playing. The excitement was there, and a little Stomp and Bang-on-a-Can video-viewing was enough for the students to see how the music was valid on the world stage as well as highly stimulating to them in their everyday classroom activity. With his own money, Daryl added buckets of various sizes and materials—some of them plastic, others more with spongey rubberized consistency, and a few made of metal. He worked with the students on keeping the beat, dividing the beat, listening for different timbres, playing solo and together in call-and-response form, and simultaneously playing several rhythms at once for a polyrhythmic effect. When the sound of many drums became too much, he divided the students into two groups: players and "pantomimers," so that as one group played a rhythm the other group would put their sticks down and use their fingers to rhythmically pat their laps or gesture in the air. He allowed some invention time, too, when individuals would play solo an invented eight-beat pattern, followed with imitation by the group. Sometimes he added a bit of body percussion—claps, stamps, finger-snaps, and chest-slaps—as a break from the buckets, and occasionally he would offer vocalized rhythms on made-up phonemes or proverbs, rhythms, and student-created phrases.

In the spring of his first year of teaching, Daryl had a revelation. He'd gone to a music festival, and there he heard a band of musicians whose roots were in Ghana, who were drumming and dancing to traditional Ga rhythms. He made a connection with the master drummer and began weekly lessons with him. He learned *djembe* (drum), *nono* (metal bell), and *fao* (gourd rattle), and was soon joining in at rehearsals of his teacher's band just for practice and for a chance to truly absorb the rhythms, the playing techniques, the ways of ensemble playing, and the topics of the banter of drummers at the meals they'd sometimes share at the end of the evening. He learned to play *kpanlogo,* popular among young people in Ghana, and even grew into the quite natural manner in which players would dance while they drummed. He found recordings of Ga music and listened to various percussion styles from the region by the Akan, Ashanti, and Ewe musicians. He started watching videos of musicians from Ghana and read works by Ghanian authors (Amu Djoleto's *The Strange Man,* Francis Selormey's *Narrow Path,* and Nana Ekua Brew-Hammond's *Power Necklace*). Daryl was now immersed in the music and culture of Ghana, and realized that this was music and cultural understanding that he could bring to his students: real music on real drums by real musicians with real-life stories.

Daryl started his second year by linking the bucket band students to rhythms of Ghana and by December had been awarded a district grant to buy Ga-style drums, bells, and rattles, to bring in culture-bearing, Ga-heritage musicians for short residencies in the spring, and to pay service fees for downloads of recordings and video-recordings of Ga music. His enthusiasm boiled over to two of his colleagues who, in their language arts classes, are now featuring a section on West African authors to complement the music studies. Daryl switched musical gears and goals, and his student groups were developing musical performance "chops" and cultural insights. He claims to have much learning ahead of himself, because now he's interested in the African diaspora of rhythms in the Americas and has a plan to learn and then integrate Afro-Latin rhythms and cultures into the studies of his middle school students.

Trajectory 3: Traditions and Innovations (High School)

Most teachers of high school music programs would agree on the goals of music education, which reflect the influence of the National Core Art Standards (1994) as well as century-long values in the acquisition of musical knowledge, appreciation, and skills in music reading, performing, and note-reading. The musical knowledge they have in mind is exclusively Western or Western-oriented "music made for school ensembles." Some will argue that school band music is its own culture—and there is truth to this—and will claim this position as reason to support and continue this music. Official program statements may assert that participation by secondary school students in bands, choirs, and orchestras is a way of gaining insights into many cultures, but the evidence is still slim as to how this can happen when ensemble repertoire remains loyal and locked to Western art music styles (particularly in the case of bands and orchestras).

Alicia is the instrumental teacher at her high school, and she shares an office with her colleague who runs the choirs and two keyboard classes. Alicia claims proudly her identity as a musician first, a music educator a very close second, and a band director third. She's been teaching for six years, working to make kids more musical in a 9th-grade concert band, a symphonic band for grades 10–12, a beginning jazz band and a "senior jazz band," and an all-school orchestra. She gets teaching load credit, too, for running the marching band in fall and the pep band in winter/spring. Because she was educated in a strong school music program where students began instrumental study at age 9, she's been playing clarinet since 4th grade. She started study on alto sax and flute in high school and then returned with gusto to her principal study of clarinet in a performance degree program at a highly rated conservatory of music. She later tacked on a two-year teaching certificate for reasons that included her interest in working with young musicians and because she recognized her folly in not thinking through the job market for clarinet players. Alicia returned home when she landed the music job at a top-ranked public high school in a metropolitan area, a school located in a leafy suburb of middle-class families, most of them White, with a mix of Asian Americans of Korean, Chinese, and Vietnamese ancestry, African Americans, and Mexican Americans comprising 25%.

Alicia is a smart musician and a devoted teacher. She strives for the development of her students' musicianship alone and together, and wants them to meet their full musical capacity. She expects full-on notational literacy and features sight-reading exercises in all her classes. Most of her students are high achievers, and their music-booster parents are there to support them with private lessons, uniforms and concert outfits, and all the amenities of fieldtrips to festivals and competitions. Alicia wants the best literature (i.e., repertoire) for her students, and she is adamant that the symphonic band *will* play Vaughn Williams's *English Folk Song Suite* and Grainger's "Irish Tune from County Derry," just as she will toil until her orchestra students can play musical works like Beethoven's Symphony No. 6, Ives's "Variations on 'America,'" and Bizet's *L'Arlesienne Suite No. 2*. Likewise, her senior jazz band plays Billy Strayhorn's "Isfahan," Charlie Parker's "Yardbird Suite," Johnny Mercer's "Autumn Leaves," and Jack Taylor's arrangement of "Oye Como Va"—because they can, with Alicia's guidance.

A multicultural mandate drifted into her office mailbox at the beginning of the past school year, and Alicia took it to heart. In the course of her own musical life, she'd played Dixieland, swing, bebop, and cool jazz. She'd played in a klezmer band, a Balkan dance band, and an Israeli-styled wedding band. Just for fun, she'd played snare drum in a second line band while living briefly in New Orleans, and had an inside view of bluegrass due to a good friend's standing gig in a Thursday night bluegrass band at the local tavern. To Alicia, it seemed a no-brainer that she easily could move her students into a multicultural awareness through a little post-concert experience with music "off-the-grid" of their performance-based band, orchestra, and jazz programs of study. They could continue to be competitive in their performance "with excellence" of standard works, but they also could take post-concert time to renew and refresh by having a look/listen at these other musical worlds. They listen and then try learning by ear the melodies of Irish reels and jigs and bluegrass tunes (orchestra) and klezmer and Mexican *banda* pieces. Alicia sometimes features a snatch of diverse musical selections for listening at the start of her classes (just after the warm-up scales), or as a five-minute "break-out" between rehearsals of festival pieces, and she challenges students to listen with attention and to play what they can. She puts a playlist together of musical styles from the region, American music genres, and some world music features, and challenges students to listen-and-learn them at home. The grand surprise to Alicia (and she has reported this to her approving principal) is that students are meeting in practice rooms before school, playing their own renditions of klezmer and second line selections that they've been listening to, and are looking up the history and culture of these styles. Without losing her strong valuing of instrumental music, Alicia has (with a little incitement from the administration) begun a journey to multiculturalize and globalize her program.

Key Features of Three Trajectories

Three collage-cases of teachers, holding strong on their commitment to the musical development of students, depict some of the ways in which issues of diversity pertain to goals and strategies at play in school music education programs. The trajectories of these teachers are similar to those of others who, in similar placements as music teachers in elementary, middle, and high schools, face comparable challenges, tweaked for student age and school circumstance, in meeting standards in music and multicultural education. Knowingly or not, music teachers are joining with faculty of all subject areas in the team effort to broaden the scope of experiences that are leading to the cultural (and multicultural) understanding of their students. By and large, they're doing so with curiosity and even genuine interest, and through musical means.

Rather than having to brace themselves for a backlash from students on material far afield from their experience, music teachers are following what appears to be a natural course of development of experiences with intriguing new musical sounds and meanings. With regard to the five dimensions of multicultural education (Banks, 2007), they are in motion within these trajectories, albeit sometimes unbeknownst to practicing music teachers who are inventively "doing the best they can" and whose attempts sometimes have not fully developed into what they could become. The integration of local and global musical repertoire seems to be working like a charm. Subtly, knowledge construction is at work, particularly in the way in which Anna is proceeding in a comparative manner to view the treatment of musical features and functions from culture to culture, possibly helping students to understand reasons why the music is fashioned as it is by musicians from a place and time. Is there any hope of a reduction of prejudice when children study the musical works of people from various places in the world? Idealistically, of course there is, and it's useful to have musicians from these cultures visiting in person or online, in dialogue with students about music and cultural matters. It seems reasonable to expect that an equity pedagogy is in play, too, when music teachers consider pathways to understanding that include aural and kinesthetic means along with the visual, and that "visual" means notation (at times) as well as the observation by students of performers for how they position themselves, what sorts of gestures fall into place as they perform, and all the small behaviors—fingerings, embouchure, bowings, mouth position—that make the sound what it is. These teachers are working to empower the students through performance, and they are contributing to a healthy educational environment that can suit all students and teachers, and their families and friends, musically, socially, and in ways that stimulate their intellectual and artistic selves. (See Chapter 4 for further discussion of the five dimensions of multicultural education as espoused by James A. Banks.)

Consider music teachers like those described, the synthesized sketches of their work, the frameworks within which they work, and the set of strategies they offer for drawing students into the thick of the musical expressions and cultures they experience and study. Their trajectories operate as blueprints for others to take note of, as they are meeting multicultural aims through music and diversifying the meaning of music as it is differently defined from place to place and yet also finding the commonalities they share. They are connecting to local communities, even as they are looking outward to the world of musical possibilities. Honoring aspects of oral tradition, they are working with oral-aural processes at the edge of World Music Pedagogy's aim of learning by listening. They are providing cultural context by integrating understandings as the questions come up, popping in bits and pieces about the musicians themselves, responding to student curiosities by sharing online video bites. They are offering creative interventions in their classes, too, playing with the possibilities of new musical sonorities, making small contributions in expressive ways that fit the style. Regardless of the children they teach, the ages and previous experiences of their students, and the communities in which they work, their trajectories combine into a blueprint of features for realizing musical and multicultural goals.

POINTS OF PRACTICAL WISDOM

The act of teaching music from a multicultural perspective, and with inter-cultural and global aims in mind, requires a firm commitment to the ideals of a cultural democracy. Music educators who succeed in this act are willing to go the extra mile to listen to the needs and interests of their individual students, and to take into account the dovetailed fields of research that feed into suitable and insightful pedagogy. Late-breaking revelations in music, cultural behaviors and values, learning and development, childhood and adolescence, and community development are all relevant to the work of thoughtful music teachers. Their matching of scholarly perspectives in these spheres with curricular questions, instructional strategies, and understand-ings of layers of cultural complexities that operate within any population, including young learners, is the way forward to informed practice. The fol-lowing points of practical wisdom are intended to pave the way to success-ful teaching of music and realizing multicultural aims as well. Theory meets practice within these featured topics, and advisories are offered that are based in the successes of well-seasoned music teachers with their ears to the ground on matters of music, education, and culture.

Setting the Scene for Learning

Music teachers are forever setting the scene for music learning that will oc-cur in classrooms and rehearsal halls. When they are traveling from room to room with instruments on a cart, as in some elementary school programs, the scene-setting is minimal in the amount of time expended for set-up and maximal in the potential for having a negative impact on learning (due to the limited number of instruments that fit on a cart, the poor audio quality from necessarily small speakers, and the matter of students stuck in their same surrounds without travel to a well-equipped and acoustically tuned music space). When teachers have their own designated spaces for music education, there is plenty of set-up to do, as one class may feature xylophone-playing while the next one requires room to move for eurhythmics and dance exer-cises. At the secondary level, the same room may be used for bands as for orchestras and choirs, and sometimes for jazz bands, vocal groups, and jazz choirs (with the necessary array of mics and amps), steel bands, mariachis, and African drumming, thus entailing the set-up or removal of music stands, the placement of chairs in lines or circles, and the distribution of instruments to various places in the room. Further, if there are multiple spaces for syn-chronous classes and ensembles, as occurs at the high school level, there is the concern of "sound-bleed" so that teachers may be working to stuff up the doors to dampen the sound that comes into and goes from the room.

With multicultural aims in mind, both environment and set-up are important. Classrooms require space for movement, as in the case of learning music of the sub-Saharan African *ngoma* style in which music is sung and danced, and even sung, danced, and played. Since so much music of the world's cultures is embodied, when space is at a premium, desks and chairs can be set aside so that students may stand in order to move to the music they hear or make (and sit for rests between the participatory experiences or during lecture). With additional instruments, there is not only the matter of their placement for students' easy access during class but also questions of storage: Should guitars, and ukes, and drums, and gongs, and flutes of the world's cultures be shelved or stacked, mounted on the walls or hung from the ceiling? These instruments need to be readily available and readily removed so as to keep the space flexible. Lighting and proper ventilation (especially for singers, wind-players, and dancers) is important, too, in setting the scene for learning, and some equipment is a prerogative such as a wide display screen for viewing musicians in their cultural context, Skyping in performers or master teachers, and listening/watching videos of student and professional performances.

Some teachers go for the gold in setting up their classrooms. There are posters plastered to the walls of singing, playing, and dancing musicians from everywhere in the world, and maps of the world, or of city neighborhoods, of regions where blues and gospel, salsa, mariachi, bluegrass and country, powwow, and various Asian American styles can be heard. Photos of community performers can be enlarged and tacked up in celebration of the local. Unusual instruments, sometimes donated by community members or picked up at garage sales, are laid out on tables or in glass cases or attached to the wall. Learning spaces do not need to be dullish square and oblong areas with no identifying features, or throwbacks to "portraits of the great composers," but can be colorful places with images of the world's (musical) cultures. Creating conducive learning settings is about space, equipment, and visual images, and music teachers are wise in considering the scene-setting activity as an opportunity not only to open students' ears to musical possibilities but also to offer visible means of discovering further dimensions of music's diversity.

Fitting Pedagogical Acts

For a deeper understanding of music and its cultural meanings, teachers make forward strides when they consider how music is linked to music-learning behaviors, so that students who learn music the way it is transmitted and learned in a given culture are learning about the behaviors and values of people whose music it is. Indigenous pedagogy is bundled up with indigenous music, so that styles like Mexican *son jarocho* or Persian *ghazal* are best learned in schools and other formal contexts as they are learned within the culture: aurally-orally and without notation, holistically and through immersion rather than analytically, and with flexibility such that a measure of improvisatory freedom (or at least variation) is not only acceptable but expected. When the teaching/learning process is what is standard for the music's culture of origin, the musical experience reaches beyond the sound and well into the realm of an experience in the facets of cultural communication.

An early attempt at the development of a literature on aurality and the demonstration–imitation process of music transmission is found in *Lessons from the World* (Campbell, 1991), which was intended to distinguish formal Westernized pedagogical practices based in notation from the more informal processes by which art and traditional/folk music has been learned across the ages. Opportunities to learn via pedagogical methods that emphasize listening and viewing, rather than reading notation, are time-intensive and laborious, but they are worth their weight in gold in bringing student attention to the manner in which the music is passed on through the generations. The teaching/learning method is as culturally construed as is the musical sound itself, and thus the manner of musical acquisition (Do they chant the drum strokes before they play the drum? What solmization system is in play in learning a vocal composition? How are movement and dance mixed into the learning process?) offers insight into the musicians and their valued ways of transmission.

The multicultural flurry in music education was for many years a frenzied search for material, preferably melodies, rhythms, and multiple parts that were fully notated via standard Western staff notation. All music was fixed and meant to be performed vocally or on instruments, and little to no attention was given to personal interpretation—much less improvisation—since music education was aimed at the replication of the sound from notation. (Ironically, notation can never be precise, and Western notation does well with fixed pitch and rhythm but is ill-suited for communicating the expressive nuances of these elements or of timbre and articulation.) Since movement is not easily notated, and the notation systems available, such as Laban and Benesh, are not easily decoded, music of the world's cultures is learned largely as music without movement even when the two are intertwined in the culture of their origin. Thus, some of the world's musical cultures, such as the music of Akan drumming or Andean, have been taught in ways that match longstanding school-based styles, through staff notation, without any improvisatory "give," and in stand-still, stiff, and unmoving, person-to-person rows of singers and players. Through study with master musicians, or viewings of YouTube and video clips, pedagogical acts can be shaped for curricular experiences that reflect the ways of music learning, rehearsing, and performing.

Applying Familiar Techniques and Methods

Sensitivity by teachers to culture-specific pedagogy does not necessitate a sweeping away of carefully groomed teaching techniques that are effective in all sorts of music teaching and learning circumstances. A strong and in-tune singing voice is tantamount to effective music-making in elementary vocal/general programs and secondary school choral programs, and there's a payoff as well to having teachers with strong singing voices in instrumental classes so that they can sing phrases and vocalize rhythms for immediate imitation by students on their instruments. Performance of an instrument comes in handy, too, for modeling musical accuracy as well as musical expression, and the piano is a useful tool for reinforcing any instrumental or vocal lines that are not sounding out (or sounding accurately). Conducting is an artistic performance in itself and can be inspiring to watch, and it is a useful set of maneuvers for focusing the attention of performers and music learners alike to phrasing, expression, and the nuances of rhythm and pitch.

Teachers with particular pedagogical training in three classic methods, the Orff-Schulwerk of Bavarian Germany, the Hungarian approach inspired by Zoltan Kodály, and the eurhythmics method of Swiss musician-teacher Emile Jaques-Dalcroze, frequently find themselves refreshed in the repertoire that comes from various regions of the world. They also recognize that techniques such as aural learning (and oral teaching), speech rhythms, rhythmic syllables, solmization, improvisation, and movement/dance are common to many of the world's musical cultures and workable within the realm of their pedagogical approaches. The conversion of these European-based methods, or the particular techniques of these pedagogies, fits quite naturally the music from various places on the African continent, the Pacific Islands, parts of East, South, and Southeast Asia, Latin America (including the Caribbean, Central and South American, and Mexico), the old-style and mostly rural European traditions, and the many diverse communities of North America, creating pathways that complement and balance one another. The overlay of selections from the world's musical cultures onto well-established pedagogical approaches is not only an acceptable means of meeting musical and cultural aims, but may well infuse new energy into these methods.

Working with Songs and Singing Styles

For many teachers, especially of secondary school choirs and elementary school programs, singing is a significant means of musical engagement. Everyone has a voice, and as the adage goes, "if you can talk, you can sing." Singing is a skill that can be developed through vocal modeling (live by the teacher and on recordings), choice of voice- and age-appropriate repertoire, rigorous exercise and sustained practice, and a balanced diet of honest appraisal and encouragement. For schools with budgetary constraints, singing requires no purchase or rental of an instrument, as the voice is portable, readily accessible, and makes a most personal contribution to the collective of voices intent on sounding something beautiful together. Songs are vessels of cultural expression, as their texts themselves offer glances into poetry and verse, and the stories of people and places deemed important to a culture. One need only recall the power of a freedom song like "We Shall Overcome" to recognize that songs have the potential to fill minds and ears with a wealth of diverse views and visions, and multicultural understandings can be grown through a song-based curriculum.

The experience of singing a song in the language of a culture is rewarding culturally, as language and culture are deeply connected. The practice of translating of songs out of their original languages into English does a disservice to the culture and its music, and misses the opportunity for singers to enter more deeply into cultural understanding. Such translations typically alter the rhythm and rhythmic accents of the music to accommodate new words that do not precisely fit the musical flow. Singing songs in their original languages is not without its challenges, but musicians are fine-tuned to enable students to discriminate the fractional sound variations of language so that they readily learn songs in various languages in order to perform them and teach them. Songs like "Que Bonita Bandera," "Cielito Lindo," "Al Citron," "San Sereni," and "De Colores" (Spanish); "Somagwaza" and "Shoshaloza" (South African); "Einini" (Irish-Gaelic); "Obwisana" and "Sansa Kroma" (Ghanian); "Hotaru Koi" and "Kaeru no Uta" (Japanese); and "Erev Shel Shoshanim" and "Dodi Li" (Israeli) deserve to be sung in their original language.

Learning (and teaching) songs from the world's languages requires careful listening to live and recorded renditions of singers born into or trained in the original language of the song. Focused and attentive listening can occur over the course of multiple opportunities to "listen up," and the teacher's guidance of students to listen for details of the song is essential: the rise and fall of the melody from phrase to phrase, the starting or ending pitches of a phrase, particular melodic and rhythmic phrases (those that repeat as well as those that come up only once), and specific words or word phrases. Learning by immersion is straightforward, and a teacher's own repeated singing of a song will familiarize students with the song's components. As the teacher sings, students can be directed not only to listen for musical and textual components but also to play more active roles by joining in on expressive gestures that are aligned with the song's text, or conducting, or performing body percussion ostinatos. With increased listening opportunities, a song's language and melody begin to trip off the tongue of the singers. While it may be necessary to speak aloud the language of the song, sometimes with students imitating the rhythmically spoken phrases of their teacher one phrase after the next, it is by listening and doing (i.e., singing and sometimes dancing and/or adding simple harmonic or rhythmic accompaniment) that the songs become bridges to understanding people of many cultures.

Shoring Up Instrumental Music Potentials

As concrete physical objects, musical instruments are enticing cultural symbols. They are important representations of "music," and every culture in the world has its intriguing embodiments of musical culture, for example, the Japanese *koto* (plucked zither), the Bulgarian *gaida* (bagpipe), the Afghan *rebab* (plucked lute), the Burmese *saung kauk* (harp), the Thai *ranat* (xylophone), the Spanish guitar (and its variants through Latin America), the Indian *sitar* (plucked lute), the Shona *mbira* (thumb piano of Zimbabwe), the Native American indigenous wood flute, the Irish fiddle, the Andean *siku* (panpipes), and the Chinese *er hu* (bowed lute). Instruments have associations with gender (women do not play or sit near the Native American powwow drum), spiritual ideals (the Japanese *shakuhachi* flute connects sound with nature for Zen Buddhist meditation), cultural status (the highest status instrument in Korea is the court music zither, called *komungo*, played only by highest ranked musicians), and aesthetic value (the Senofo of Ivory Coast, West Africa, play xylophones whose buzzy tone from spider webs placed over the gourd resonators is prized) (Wade, 2004). An examination of instruments in the classroom, online, or in museums is a journey into cultural meaning and values.

As children are enticed by instruments to touch, to hold, and to play, it's a reasonable decision for teachers to want to have a sufficient supply of *djembes,* ukuleles, tin whistles, gongs, steel pans, and xylophones. With budgetary constraints and the whole world of music to experience and study, substitutions are necessary, so groups of students may play a Hindustani *raga* on guitar or keyboard rather than on *sitar*, or play Brazilian samba rhythms on a classroom mix of instruments that include sturdy school models of *djembes* and hand drums rather than *surdos, tamborims, caixas,* and *pandeiro*. Other objects substitute for instruments, too, such as plastic buckets turned upside-down as drums, dried gourds harvested from the garden that quite naturally become maracas and similar shake instruments, and even tin pie pans that make a metallic (if not quite a gong) sound. Classroom drums have been constructed from cylindrical oatmeal boxes, flutes have been fashioned from reeds in the field, and kazoos have been made from wax paper on combs. Of course, there is also the point at which the sound of a substitute object or homemade project is just too far afield from the real instrument, as in the case of a toilet paper tube not sounding like a horn, or a young child's multicolored toy xylophone that simply does make the sound of (nor does it have anywhere close to the feel of playing) marimba music from various parts of sub-Saharan Africa. Still, best efforts forward by teachers can produce stimulating possibilities for playing world music.

School bands and orchestras invite occasions for knowing a wide variety of musical cultures through the act of performance. Through the use of conventional wind, brass, string, and percussion instruments, all manner of music can be experienced. Notation is always possible, of course, with transcriptions of a recording developed by the teacher—or as an aural dictation exercise by students. A more direct way of learning is by listening, repeatedly, to a performance by, for instance, a Chinese orchestra, a Mexican mariachi, or a North Indian brass band. Following multiple sessions of hearing just the first 20 or 30 seconds of a work, looped repeatedly, students may be able to play by ear the melody, rhythm, and harmony or other textural component. A teacher may give the starting pitch (although some students will have the ear to figure it out), and away the students may sail, playing along with the recording, working it out, finding the part that fits. This kind of enactive listening gets at the core of the music, challenging students to go forward into the music with the instruments they have, learning by ear, repeatedly, without the need for notation. The end result of playing mariachi with clarinets, saxophones, cellos, and the like will not match the tone colors and textures of the Mexican genre, but it can offer students a participatory way into the music that builds musical comprehension and, with a little stretching into discussion of the music's function and cultural significance, a cultural understanding.

Furnishing Context and Telling Stories

In honoring the view of ethnomusicology that music is culture, and that music is sound and all else that surrounds the sound gives it fuller meaning, teachers furnish what has become known as "context." This is to say that a song is more than mere sound: It is a message carried by the lyrics, its history, its origins and evolutions as it travels through time and across place. Context is the backstory of the singer, why the song is sung, how a particular song has "spoken" to this singer. For instrumental music, it is understanding why particular instruments play it, what it takes to learn to play it, what sorts of interactions happen across players in a group of musicians performing it. Why sing a powwow song with no attention to why it is sung, where, by whom, and for what powerful purpose? Why play blues without revealing some of the hardships that this form evolved out of? Why play an Akan drumming piece (from Ghana, West Africa) without knowledge of who the Akan are, where they live, how music features in their lives, who the master drummers may be, and how the drums are constructed? Also relating to the Akan music, when the singing begins, who leads it and what is the song about? These are some of the very questions that students may ask, and they are windows of opportunity for featuring music as a launch to cultural study. The stories behind the music are important, and the musical sound may trigger explorations by the class or by individual students into the lives of performers and composers.

A thoroughgoing understanding of the music takes knowing its place in the life of a culture. For example, klezmer is vibrant music of clarinets, violins, trumpets, flutes, accordions, and drums, a form of music that sings, sighs, and draws listeners into a compulsion to dance. The music lilts, laughs and lifts up the mood, even as it also weeps; there is both joy and sorrow that emanates from the musical sound. Klezmer is also important music rising out of the Jewish Eastern European tradition, taken up by young Jewish American musicians to express a new-world ethnic identity that connects to Jewish roots, a blend of styles from Moldavian, Ukrainian, and Balkan sources. It reaches across a century of migration, stretching across regions and eras (Slobin, 1992). This cultural and historic contextualization adds shades of meaning to knowing klezmer, and the integration of information on European and American Jewish culture only deepens the knowledge of the music.

Stories and storybooks may link well to music of particular cultures, and make for worthy projects in the integration of literature, poetry, and music. *Ada's Violin: The Story of the Recycled Orchestra of Paraguay* (S. Hood, 2016) encourages listening to Paraguayan music for the violin and invites children to imagine and then hear the music in a small Paraguayan town where children play instruments made of recycled trash. *He's Got the Whole World in His Hands* (Nelson, 2005) offers a journey of discovery of this historic spiritual as precious African American expression of belief and values; the song really must be sung by children for the full impact. John Steptoe's rendition of *Mufaro's Beautiful Daughters* (2008) is a traditional African tale on the theme of good triumphing over evil and is effectively told over the sound of a recording of kora music. *The Rough-Face Girl,* by Rafe Martin (1998), is an Algonquin version of the age-old Cinderella tale and is effectively experienced with pauses here and there for children to play a brief melody to allow reflection time in the storytelling. The possibilities are rich for combining music with stories, thus offering a more thoroughgoing cultural excursion.

Collaborating with Culture Bearers

It's expected that teachers will teach their subject, and that music teachers (like teachers of math or language arts) will go it alone in their classrooms. They follow curricular manuals, utilize approved textbooks and instructional materials, and compare notes with other teachers, but in the end are seen as the main guide for their students' learning. However, the potential for collaborations is not only enticing; it is an effective mode of knowing music in the hands (and voices, and feet) of working musicians. Consider the gamut: a Chinese duo of *pipa* (lute) and *dizi* (flute) players; a small group of old-time Anglo-American folk musicians on guitar, banjo, and fiddle; a Persian player of *qanun* (plucked zither) and *sehtar* (plucked lute); a Native American storyteller and singer; a group of drummers and dancers from Haiti; a pair of singers of Spanish-language *plenas* from Puerto Rico. Since music teachers did not cover the world of music in their own university training, culture bearers and heritage musicians from the community are a godsend; they can share the songs, instruments, dances (and all the trimmings) they may have known all their lives.

The tendency for teachers to want to link to culture bearers is strong, and as fiscal resources allow for it, musicians, dancers, and storytellers successfully reinforce and extend the learning of a studied culture. They offer a personalization of the artistic-cultural experience, and they accentuate the musical and cultural qualities that teachers may feel they are not addressing adequately. Culture bearers arrive at schools, campuses, and community locations fully equipped with instruments and often wearing the traditional clothing of their home culture. They may offer a single performance or assembly presentation, or may be contracted for brief visits to various classes for demonstration and discussion. They may "workshop" a group of students, teaching songs, dances, and instrumental repertoire over the course of an hour, or are invited for residencies lasting one or more weeks, or a full academic term. They may be involved in all ways, spending the day or returning for a residency in the school for a week or more. Their presence can go so far as to build respectful relationships with students and to break down previous biases based upon fear of the unknown.

Teachers are in the thick of planning and facilitating the presence of culture bearers. It's useful for them to prepare students for a visiting musician through musical experiences, so that they might have some orientation to the musical essence—the instruments, singing styles, dance forms, language, and even cultural frameworks. This paves the way for the culture bearer's visit, and following the visit some time can be given to reviewing the music; recalling the meaning and function of the songs, dances, and instrumental pieces; and discussing the visitor's cultural wisdom. Teachers are responsible for selecting strong musicians from the community who possess the skill set to communicate well and in a developmentally appropriate rhythm, pace, and style. To maximize the success of a residency of a culture bearer, teachers make the arrangements relative to schedule and fee, and clarify in some detail their expectations for the visit. They do well, too, to clarify to the culture bearer preparations the students may have had in advance of the visit as well to offer a heads-up of any possible concerns regarding student needs, interests, and behaviors.

TACKLING TENACIOUS TOPICS

In converting principles to practice, there are "sticky wickets" that challenge teachers who aim for musical and multicultural outcomes. They have the interests and needs of their students very much in mind, keep abreast of the professional literature, and are active in their continuing professional development as musicians and teachers. Yet they wonder and worry about tenacious topics that simply do not go away. While they themselves are tireless in their capacity to problem solve every complication that emerges, these topics are notable as potential stumbling blocks to well-intended ideals.

In its musical sense, "diversity" refers to the musical expressions of as many cultures as people claim membership in. Music is classified in geographic categories or labeled for the nations in which it appears to belong, such as "music of Germany" or "music of India," when in fact there may be many more musical subcultures defined and claimed by people of a particular age, class, region, faith, gender or sexuality, and other lifestyle characteristics. Even style-wise, in every culture there are folk, traditional, art, and popular music, and it's useful for teachers to play with the various manifestations of musical diversity. Popular music of the world's multiple cultures is given less attention than it merits; teachers do well to share with their students *reggaeton* as well as Jamaican folk music, *bhangra* as well as classical Indian *khyal*, K-pop as well as Korean *pansori*, and *soca* as well as Trinidadian calypso.

Following on the realities of micromusical cultures, the potential for stereotyping a culture is strong when only a single musical example is selected for study. Teachers risk essentializing a culture when a single song or instrumental piece is learned, as if to represent the entire population. Not only are there multiple musical expressions within a place, but an individual musician also may be a compilation of layers of musical expression and interest. For example, a Chinese musician who performs on the two-string *er hu* fiddle may enjoy playing in a Chinese orchestra, as well as performing in an experimental new music ensemble or a popular music band.

Over the course of a year (or the full extent of an elementary or secondary school music curriculum), the choice of music for study and experience can be a balanced blend of local and global styles. To be sure, the study of locally living musical cultures is fascinating for knowing the neighborhood and celebrating the indigenous music of a place, and certainly the presence of heritage musicians in the school is an exciting human interest venture. At the same time, music teachers are responsible for providing understandings of the world beyond the neighborhood, and thus encounters with music from across the world lend a global perspective to people, issues, and interests.

The question of authenticity has driven many music teachers away from the inclusion of music with which they may be less familiar. Some fear that they may err in their own performance of the music, as well as in their facilitation of performative experiences for their students. Yet teachers also contend with the culture of the classroom, and of the students, and with the realities of how closely they can be expected to sound like the musicians of the far-distant culture of study. In fact, the challenge of authenticity is that there are two cultures involved in teaching the music of the world's cultures to children: the music's origin culture and the culture of the classroom. A reasonable response is to accept that the best-case scenario is a compromise between the cultures, with the music teacher pressing students to make headway into the musical culture, while also tempering expectations so to allow students to sound musical, even if their sound does not precisely match the culture.

TREASURING THE TEACHER

Of the extant research, there are several studies that point to the preparation of teachers to adequately teach music of the world's cultures. Many teachers appear to regard "multicultural music" as a priority of their school music programs, but feel generally underequipped to facilitate experiences in music outside their training (Butler, Lind, & McKoy, 2007). Not very long ago, a vast majority of music teachers reported no training in world music cultures within their undergraduate curriculum (Legette, 2003). Even as university programs are updating their programs to include world music–culture courses, many teachers are graduating without a strong sense of applying their academic study to pedagogical practice (Campbell, 2013). Music teachers in practice are attuned to the necessity of equity in the construction and delivery of a curriculum, so that students understand that there are many musical cultures worthy of a place in their study, their playlist of recordings, and their active participation. Music teachers require greater guidance, including pedagogical modeling, in configuring ways of meeting the goals of multicultural understanding in and through music.

It takes a teacher to convert ideas to actions, to turn theoretical thoughts into instructional actualities. Multicultural perspectives on musically educating children and youth have been espoused in print for decades, but the devil is in the details. Similar to celebrating people for their unique and distinctive qualities, a respect for diverse musical expressions does not come naturally but takes time and effort to achieve. Even with the availability of materials and techniques that are aimed at providing avenues for the recognition and enjoyment of a new or unfamiliar musical culture, the essential piece of the puzzle is a thoughtful, sensitive, earnest, and honest teacher who will translate, mediate, and facilitate student acquisition of knowledge and insight. The teacher is not the hub of classroom activity, or the star around which students orbit. Musical and multicultural understanding develops when there is ample humility on the part of the teacher, an openness to student ideas and interests, passion and compassion (for the music and the learners), and a willingness to learn from reputable sources—including students who frequently bring an astonishing extent of experience, intuition, and discernment to the learning process. Both music and multicultural education aims are well served by thoughtful teachers who are committed to the cause.

Diversifying Music Education

R-E-S-P-E-C-T. "The children shall lead us. In my school, I teach music—not civics, or science, or language arts. I teach children, and in the weeks and months to come, I will pull out every song I know that speaks of peace, friendship, helpfulness, respect for all our neighbors. And I will double up on social dances that require you to take a partner's hand and move in sync. Because that is what I do, that is who I am, and I'm committed to increasing our consciousness of one another, and of developing a 'culture of kindness' in these times."

These words tumbled forward from a teacher, as did many more messages of similar ilk, in the dark days of November that followed the 2016 American presidential election. While the global disbelief in the unprecedented outcome is widely known, the fears and concerns of teachers and their students also have been felt and shared, and merit a response and an action plan. Worries about the exposure of deep racial and cultural divisions, and the deportation of immigrants, are widespread, on the part of both children from immigrant families as well as their friends. For teachers, one of the greatest challenges is the fostering of respectful dialogue in classrooms, beyond tolerance, to compassion, genuine understanding, love. Music teachers are prioritizing expressive outlets, safe "zones" for students to convey their feelings through experiences in song-writing and composing in their own personal preferred styles. There's an uptick in music classes of performances of "Oh Freedom," "This Little Light of Mine," "Simple Gifts," "Shalom Chaverim," and "Guantanamera." Any number of experiences are circling round popular songs as anthems of peace, hope, and love: John Lennon's "Imagine," Izzy's (Israel Kamakawiwo'ole) rendition of "Somewhere over the Rainbow," Bob Marley's "One Love," and Aretha Franklin's "R-E-S-P-E-C-T." The last movement of Beethoven's 9th Symphony, "Ode to Joy," is a presence in schools, too, sung by choirs, played by full student orchestras, and given hearty melody-only renditions by 3rd-grade recorder players. To many teachers and their students, music is proving indispensable, a necessity for instilling and expressing courage, calm, humanism, and a sense of belonging together as a unified whole.

As in the case of the harpsichord cadenza at the end of the first movement of J. S. Bach's *Brandenburg Concerto No. 5,* these few pages constitute a cadenza of sorts that concludes the volume, offering several ideas in free flow, with ornamental flourishes. They are meant to underscore perspectives from the fields of music education, ethnomusicology, and multicultural education, and to rally around the urgency for musicians and educators to address a multicultural redesign of curricular content and pedagogical action for music education. With acknowledgment of present circumstances in American society and its schools, the onus is on all sectors to work through fear and suspicion, to confront what is something of a myopic sense of complacency, and to weave together ethnomusicologically inspired ideals for educating students musically and multiculturally. More than ever, music education must be multicultural, intercultural, and global, and with intent to feature musical diversity while facing the everyday realities of teaching children from a diversity of cultural communities.

Music is more than a nicety, an appendage, or a frill: It is an essential piece of a comprehensive education for children and youth, one that values their intellectual and social–emotional development. Music is recognized in culture after culture, across all ages and social circumstances, for its capacity to express joy, empathy, comfort, identity, and a sense of belonging. In unique ways, music can be directed toward spirituality and sociality, and school music can bring about experiences that are expressive of the self and of the group, and that build the bonds of human relationships that emerge through the process of participation in song and instrumental music (and in the spillover of music to dance and drama). Long overdue is the recognition by schools and society of music as central rather than peripheral to children's learning and development, and a key component to a balanced education.

DIVERSITY, EQUITY, AND INCLUSION

In school music programs at every level, diversity, equity and inclusion go hand in hand in attention to the content and process of curricular plans and individual lessons. A grand diversity of musical cultures is essential if a music program is to extend beyond the limited and exclusive scope of Europe's art music expressions (as well as European-influenced art music of standard school classes and ensembles). The selection of music by teachers, policymakers, and curriculum designers is a statement on valued cultures, as well as on the people of the cultures whose music is included in or excluded from experience and study. The dominance of Western art music is perpetuated by secondary school ensembles whose festival repertoire consists of approved competition pieces that are fully Western in nature, absent of any considered attempt to feature musical forms (if not instruments) from the world's cultures. It is maintained by elementary school programs where classroom (vocal or general) music studies are viewed as stepping stones to membership in school bands, choirs, and orchestras. It is prolonged by university-level, music-major programs that dismiss world music cultures as incidental, so that those students who follow the pathway of music education catch only a glimpse of all the rest of the world's music, typically in a single course. An honoring of diversity requires a commitment to a broad embrace of music, deeply and continuously.

Inclusion and equity can be defined in multiple ways that are vital to a more multicultural music education. Most apparent is a recognition of music as good for one and all, so that as a pan-human characteristic rather than a quality owned by the talented few, it deserves a place in every school schedule, for students of every hue. Music cannot be dismissed when budgets tighten, when musical study is seen as expendable and noncore, because if music fulfills so many intellectual and social–emotional needs, it cannot be viewed as superfluous and disposable. In the curriculum of elementary schools, kindergarten children should not be left out of formal music instruction, as they so frequently are, when they are ripe and ready for lessons in listening, vocal expression, coordinated instrumental participation, and creative music-making opportunities. Nor should state or district requirements for mandated music study be lifted or excused at the end of elementary school, checked off as "accomplished," leaving students a narrow selection of choices of ensembles and classes that may hold no interest to a significant segment of the student population. Inclusion means casting the net widely for a curriculum that appeals to students, which, by the time middle school students have opportunities to select courses, may include African drumming, song-writing, steel band, guitar, gospel choir, mariachi, music technology, popular music, and hip-hop courses designed to be experienced by listening and doing. Equity means the guarantee by educators that children who are drawn to music can study music of a grand variety, including those styles that extend far beyond the traditional offerings based in Western and conventional school music genres.

At least two further meanings of inclusion are directly related to the pedagogical process. The ethnomusicological definition of music as *sound, behavior*, and *values* is an all-inclusive interpretation that suggests to teachers that learning music for its elemental features—pitch, duration, timbre (instruments), and form—offers partial understanding of its meaning. To know music in an inclusive way is to study it for the human behaviors and values that are associated with its invention, performance, and consumption. Sound alone is an exciting but single inroad to music, while students may be just as intrigued and more fully served by knowing why a musical instrument sounds the way it does; when a musical work can be performed; how a song is inspired, composed, and improvised upon; who the members of a musical group may be; and where in the world music is performed in ritual practice, as a means of telling a story, or for audience participation. More than knowing the lives of composers whose works are performed, an ethnomusicologically inspired three-pronged approach to music provides students with an inclusive and equitable means of learning any music from any place in the world.

Inclusion refers also to another three-point concept, the goals of a curricular program in music. School-based music education offers elementary and secondary school students experiences that lead to the development of musical *knowledge, skills*, and *values*. Through adventures in listening to music, as well as through participation, performance, and creative-inventive experiences, students make progress in the accumulation of knowledge in music and about music. They develop an assortment of musical skills that are transferable to other music-making endeavors, both in and out of school, immediately and for a lifetime. Their musical education leads to their treasuring and valuing the artistic qualities that constitute music as coherent, logical, and communicative of a range of sentiments that include beauty, joy, sadness, and the sublime. Music education that features diverse practices provides students with the bases for knowing music as a pan-human phenomenon, for developing a palette of possibilities for the pleasure of their current and future performing, inventing, or listening, and for discovering the world through a cultural practice that is meaningful to the music-makers themselves. Diversity lives in the music that is available locally and globally, and the curricular inclusion of many styles, experienced in many ways, studied from multiple perspectives, will lead to the realization of goals that are both musical and multicultural.

PATHWAYS OF PROGRESS

Much effort has been expended in diversifying music education, and successes and challenges abound. There is great joy in the land when a group of children have devoted their best efforts to performing a Samoan *sasa* song and dance, seated onstage, radiating their amusement, singing and gesturing in a collective rhythm. They are recreating a Samoan village activity, singing as they move to make the gestures of a group of paddlers in a large canoe, or flying birds across the sky, or fish swimming in the sea. They have worked for weeks with their music teacher—and their classroom teacher has provided extra rehearsal time, too—to learn to sing like the Samoans, listening to recordings, watching videos, repeating melodies in a distant and unfamiliar language, coming to terms with why they do what they do. The visit of a culture bearer to their school was helpful, too, as was the fieldtrip they took to the Asia Pacific Cultural Center to interact with artists, teachers, and community leaders. Samoan musical culture was exotic to these 5th-graders, but they grew into the song, the dance, bits of Samoan language, history, and culture, until it began to feel familiar. To the delight of their families and friends, they performed an encore of the *sasa* song and dance, inviting their proud parents and excited siblings to join them in imitation of the gestures they had honed.

Likewise, the winter concert at the high school featured the band and choir in performance of music that pressed beyond the graded repertoire of standard school ensembles. In their most genuine manner, with all their earnest attention directed to the best musicianship they could muster, the instrumentalists and choristers performed a truly mixed bag of musical selections, aimed at offering something for everyone, including parents, siblings, a few grandparents, friends, and peers at neighboring high schools. The program included the Irish hymn, "Be Thou My Vision," John Rutter's "A Distant Land" and "The Gift of Love," a dramatic version of "Battle Hymn of the Republic," and Jay Bocook's composition, "As All the Heavens Were a Bell," which had premiered just following the 9/11 terrorist attack. They went further, though, in collective agreement that they could and they would learn music by ear—so long as a heritage artist could be called on to guide them through learning the language (and getting the musical nuances). Without notation and through the creative invention of several motivated instrumentalists, they prepared their own arrangements of a South African freedom song, "Siyahamba," for their voices and instruments, a Jewish song in Hebrew ("Bashana Haba'a"), and two Spanish-language songs, the Bolivian "Carnavalito" and the Mexican "Cielito Lindo." The program was memorable and their efforts were well-received at both day and night performances; a highlight was the mentoring community members who came to the microphone one by one to offer brief words on the meaning of the multicultural selections that formed the program's finale.

Two steps forward, one step back. Where music teachers are rushed to meet diversity mandates, or are early on in their sense of how diversity can be communicated through music, experienced in music, and reflected upon for cultural meaning beyond the music itself, the results are superficial.

Careless and light treatment of the study of a musical culture brings artificial or cursory outcomes. Inexperience or a lack of training results in perfunctory experiences that come off as slapdash rather than thoroughgoing. Too often, a supposed experience in musical culture can turn into "material" for musical skill building rather than the joining together of both musical skills and multicultural understanding. Further, a song from Korea or Kenya can sound like a song from anywhere in the world without careful and concentrated listening and a genuine attempt to get close to the music, the musicians, and the musical culture. Tokenistic celebrations of songs from many lands seldom meet the point of experiencing musical and cultural diversity in the comprehensive ways that honor the cultural source of the music; this is when an essentialized sketch is produced instead. Such efforts may do more harm than good, and point to the need for continuous attention to the education and training of music teachers in ways that include ethnomusicological and multicultural underpinnings of music, education, and diversity.

An understanding of pedagogy in music that would serve global goals and multicultural mandates is sharpened by a sense of its grounding in ethnomusicology. Ethnomusicologists study the art, folk and traditional, and popular musical cultures of nearby neighborhoods as well as those of remote and far-flung locales across the globe. They are humanistically drawn to the social process of musical creation and continuation, and they learn through person-to-person encounters in the field the personal and collective meaning of the valued music. Likewise, music teachers are well-served through their study and sense-making of the five dimensions of multicultural education, espoused by James A. Banks, for the theoretical understanding of the ideals that reach all the way to empowering students and the culture of the schools in which they learn. The practical application of Banks's four-tiered system of curriculum reform can support the development of curriculum and instruction in ways that move learners forward from brief glimpses of the exotic to the point of social action where school and community intersections lead to the building of caring human relationships.

Music is intangible cultural heritage, and music teachers are quite logically at the cutting edge of safeguarding heritage in their preserving and transmitting of musical culture. They are facilitators, too, and co-constructors with their students of the learning that transpires in schools. They think musically, and they make music in wondrous ways. Through their careful listening to recordings (and viewing video-recordings for the subtleties of technique), music teachers come a long way in restoring to themselves the lost art of listening, of human learning through the oral tradition, and of convincing themselves, too, of the central place of listening in teaching world music. As they take the plunge into making music outside their cultural comfort zone, they develop skills as well as confidence in the music that they can reasonably share with their students. Their forging of relationships with heritage musicians and culture bearers will reap many benefits for them and for their students, not the least of which is a discovery of culturally based pedagogical processes and eye-opening awarenesses of how and why the music functions as it does.

Music education may be on the brink of a breakthrough to breathing diversity into the curriculum and into the lives of students in the world beyond school. Traditions and conventions die hard, and the challenges are still ahead to step beyond the normative curriculum to an engagement with demographic change. Teaching collaboratively, reaching out to the cultures and communities that surround the school or are accessible via technology (and the media), mixing presentational performance with opportunities to participate (and there is great joy in participatory music experiences that never go on to a staged performance), developing multisensory engagements that invite full-on ear–mind–body participation, telling the stories behind the music and the musicians: These are fresh ways of recharging music education, of moving away from the mentality of "West is best" and "musica exotica," of growing with certainty into study and experience of music in culture and as culture. A community of musicians, teachers (and students), in schools and neighborhoods, living locally and accessible globally, is out there with the power to build bridges, not walls, between people through music. The multicultural question in music education hovers and is answerable by this collaborating coalition, all of them allied in advancing the progress of learners in becoming culturally sensitive and socially responsible citizens through music.

Workshop Worker Bees. From theory to practice can be a *grand jeté,* a "big throw," a stretch out of the comfortable armchair of a philosophizing scholar to the high energy of a teacher's workshop. So that the ideals of policy can reach into practice, and are not detoured, do not disappear into thin air or get lost in translation, workshops and short courses are indispensable pieces of the picture of diversity in school music programs. They happen after school, at a school or elsewhere in the district, as an extra feature at the end of a hectic (if not harried) teaching day, or on a Saturday, often the sixth day of a working week for dedicated teachers seeking fresh material and innovative techniques to fortify and invigorate the teaching of the next week, month, or season. Longer workshopping opportunities happen in the summer, when week-long ventures into the playing out of ideals are demonstrated, experienced, discussed, and given thoughtful reflection. The "worker bees" at these workshops include the workshop leader, the culture-bearing heritage musician, and the teacher-participants who actively engage in singing, dancing, playing, listening, and interactions in the pedagogical possibilities of the new and unfamiliar music that is introduced and sampled.

I am a workshop "worker bee." In my first year of teaching, I searched out every workshop I could find in the hope of garnering materials and advisories on how to teach them, and the interactions were meaningful and essential in pulling me through another week, or designing another study unit, or putting together a school assembly program. The workshop leaders knew their stuff, coming from school-teaching practice and university programs in music education (usually both, in that order), and we all enjoyed the hands-on and applied experiences into which we were suddenly thrust as students, experiencing what we would later teach to our own students. We appreciated the chance to sample the music, to learn of the music's role in culture, to hear the stories of the performers who made the music, to perform it ourselves. Facilitating lead-teachers of these workshops would offer wise words on pedagogical theory and take us into cultural concepts and multicultural principles, but our main interests as teachers was the experiential discovery of the materials, the activities, and the sequences that we could then sort out and feed directly into our own teaching.

As a workshop leader, after school and on weekends I would slip out of my university suit of many words about multiple theories and become the music teacher again. For a quarter of a century, I've enjoyed working regularly with teachers in their districts, on my university campus, and in visits to other university campuses and at annual teaching conventions. In peak periods, I've been on the road for 4–6 weeks in a summer, and at as many as one or two workshops monthly, in locales as varied as St. Louis (MO), Beijing, Tacoma (WA), Johannesburg, Omaha (NB), Munich, New York, Budapest, Tokyo, Austin (TX), Seoul, London, Denver (CO), Bangkok, Rotterdam, Atlanta (GA), Buenos Aires, Limerick, Nashville (TN), and Stonetown, Zanzibar. Sometimes I was sponsored by textbook companies, or by local teacher collectives, school districts, professional organizations, or grant-funding agencies such as the National Endowment for the Arts. I would prep for weeks, even months, to put together the slide shows and overhead transparencies, the listening tracks, video bites, and handouts chockful of notation (which I typically distributed after the chance to experience the music by ear, in our voices, and in our bodies). Depending upon the invitation, my work was centered on several topics: eurhythmics (music and movement), folk dance, Anglo- and African American traditional song, children's singing games, the vocal development of children and youth, world music pedagogy. Depending upon the location, I would make arrangements for a cameo visit of a culture-bearing musician to join us for a session—to sing, play, dance, storytell, talk with us about cultural life. Regardless of the topic (even so far afield as children's voices, for example), the thematic weave across the two-hour, full-day, or week-long workshops was ways in which multicultural, intercultural, and global understandings could develop through the power of musical involvement.

A case in point was a day-long workshop with prospective teachers at the undergraduate level on a California campus. We sang, danced, and drummed three powwow songs—two with recordings, one without—coming in with the pulse-keeping immediately, gradually immersing ourselves in the vocables ("heys," "weys," "yahs," and such), moving in small sideways steps and facing the center of the circle. We engaged in an immersive manner, coming to terms with music by doing it, offering little verbal direction, and students picked up on the model as we performed the phrases, repeatedly, with no breakdown of them, holistically. In less than 10 minutes, this segment allowed for listening, singing, moving, and playing basic hand drums. We followed the experience with a dialogue as to whose songs they were, what messages they were meant to convey, whether we were "permitted" to learn and perform these songs, whether these songs could be re-invented or varied or improvised. The riveting conclusion to the experience was a Skyped-in appearance by a culture-bearing heritage musician, who confirmed our best guesses (and my own previous research) and took us further into a discovery of the powwow event, its music, and its dance.

Workshops with music teachers are alive, because music teachers are live wires themselves, products of daily interactions—planned and unplanned, deliberate and necessarily spontaneous given their charge to listen and react to the questions, comments, and responses of their students. I have learned that it's invariably easier to sit at a desk, at a screen, in an armchair doing my scholarly work, reading and reviewing, postulating and positioning, proposing, positing, and philosophizing, than it is to be "out there" in the everyday world of teaching 8 hours a day, 5 days a week, 35 weeks a year. Teachers are a talented bunch, and they are intelligent in the ways of their subject matter and strategies for communicating it and for drawing learners into their own understandings and skills. They have perseverance and "grit," and they can steel themselves for the unpredictable that comes from working with the sometimes unbridled energy of children and youth. They know about the human elements that make or break the honest impact that lesson plans and curriculum guides can have. They live within the realities of multicultural school populations, and they work in a trial-and-error process to find success in meeting musical and multicultural aims.

There is no question that we desperately need research and theory in the musical education aims we aspire to, and the theories that are confirmed through this research lead to the development of instructional policy. But the ways of the workshop worker bees are critical to the process, too, as they are the facilitating lead teachers of workshops—and the school music teachers themselves—who can turn ideas into best practice. Singing, dancing, playing, and listening, we thoughtfully embrace the potential of music as an Rx for cultural understanding and respect, and as a powerful means for bridging cultures and communities in our world.

References

Abril, C. R., & Gault, B. M. (2008). The state of music in secondary schools: The principal's perspective. *Journal of Research in Music Education, 56*(1), 68–81.

Adams, M. (2007). Pedagogical frameworks for social justice education. In M. Adams, L. A. Bell, & P. Griffin (Eds.), *Teaching for diversity and social justice* (pp. 15–33). New York, NY: Routledge.

Adzinyah, A., Maraire, D., & Tucker, J. C. (1986). *Let your voice be heard.* Danbury, CT: World Music Press.

Allsup, R. E., & Shieh, E. (2012). Social justice and music education: The call for public pedagogy. *Music Educators Journal, 98*(4), 47–51.

Anderson, W. M. (Ed.). (1991). *Teaching music with a multicultural approach.* Reston, VA: Music Educators National Conference.

Anderson, W. M., & Campbell, P. S. (1989, 1996, 2010). *Multicultural perspectives in music education.* Reston, VA: Music Educators National Conference.

Appadurai, A. (1996). *Modernity at large: Cultural dimensions of globalization.* Minneapolis: University of Minnesota Press.

Association for Cultural Equity. (n.d.). *For teachers.* Retrieved from www.culturalequity.org/rc/ce_rc_teaching.php

Atabug, A. C. (1984). Music education in a multicultural society: The Philippine experience. *International Society for Music Education Yearbook, 11*, 103–108.

Averill, G. (2004). "Where's 'one'?": Musical encounters of the ensemble kind. In T. Solis (Ed.), *Performing ethnomusicology* (pp. 93–114). Berkeley: University of California Press.

Baily, J. (1988). *Music in Afghanistan: Professional musicians in the city of Herat.* Cambridge, UK: Cambridge University Press.

Baily, J. (2001). Learning to perform as a research technique in ethnomusicology. *British Journal of Ethnomusicology, 10*(2), 85–98.

Bakan, M. B. (1999). *Music of death and new creation: Experiences in the world of Balinese gamelan beleganjur.* Chicago, IL: University of Chicago Press.

Banks, J. A. (2007). *Educating citizens in a multicultural society.* New York, NY: Teachers College Press.

Banks, J. A. (Ed.). (2012). *Encyclopedia of diversity in education.* Thousand Oaks, CA: Sage.

Banks, J. A. (2013a). Approaches to multicultural curriculum reform. In J. A. Banks

& C.A.M. Banks (Eds.), *Multicultural education: Issues and perspectives* (8th ed., pp. 181–199). Hoboken, NJ: Wiley.

Banks, J. A. (2013b). Multicultural education: Characteristics and goals. In J. A. Banks & C.A.M. Banks (Eds.), *Multicultural education: Issues and perspectives* (8th ed., pp. 3–23). Hoboken, NJ: Wiley.

Banks, J. A., & Banks, C.A.M. (Eds.). (2004). *Handbook on research in multicultural education* (2nd ed.). New York, NY: Macmillan.

Banks, J. A., & Banks, C.A.M. (2013). Preface. In J. A. Banks & C.A.M. Banks (Eds.), *Multicultural education: Issues and perspectives* (8th ed., pp. iii–v). Hoboken, NJ: Wiley.

Bartleet, B-L., & Higgins, L. (2018). *The Oxford handbook of community music.* New York, NY: Oxford University Press.

Baxter, M. (2007). Global music making a difference: Themes of exploration, action, and justice. *Music Education Research, 9*(2), 267–279.

Bell, L. A. (2007). Theoretical foundations for social justice education. In M. Adams, L. A. Bell, & P. Griffin (Eds.), *Teaching for diversity and social justice* (pp. 1–14). New York, NY: Routledge.

Benedict, C., & Schmidt, P. (2007). From whence justice? Interrogating the improbable in music education. *Action, Criticism, and Theory for Music Education, 6*(4), 21–42.

Berliner, P. F. (1994). *Thinking in jazz: The infinite art of improvisation* (Chicago studies in ethnomusicology). Chicago, IL: University of Chicago Press.

Bickford, T. (2017). *Schooling new media: Music, language, and technology in children's culture.* New York, NY: Oxford University Press.

Bicknell, J. (2009). *Why music moves us.* New York, NY: Palgrave Macmillan.

Blacking, J. (1967). *Venda children's songs: A study in ethnomusicological analysis.* Johannesburg, South Africa: Witwatersrand University Press.

Blacking, J. (1973). *How musical is man?* Seattle, WA: University of Washington Press.

Booth, G. (1986). *The oral tradition in transition: Implications for music education from a study of North Indian tabla transmission* (Unpublished doctoral dissertation). Kent State University, Kent, OH.

Bowman, W. (2007). Who is the "we"? Rethinking professionalism in music education. *Action, Criticism, and Theory for Music Education, 6*(4), 109–131.

Bradley, D. (2012). Good for what, good for whom? Decolonizing music education philosophies. In W. Bowman & A. L. Frega (Eds.), *The Oxford handbook of philosophy in music education.* doi: 10.1093/oxfordhb/978019539473.013.0022

Bradt, J., Dileo, C., & Polvin, N. (2013). Music for stress and anxiety reduction in coronary heart disease patients. *Cochrane Database Systemic Review, 2*(12). doi: 10.1002/14651858.CD006577.pub3.

Brăiloiu, C. (1984). *Problems of ethnomusicology* (A.L. Lloyd, Trans.). Cambridge UK: Cambridge University Press.

Bronfenbrenner, U., McClelland, P., Washington, E., Moen, P., & Ceci, S. J. (1996).

The state of Americans: This generation and the next. New York, NY: Free Press.

Buchanan, D. A. (2017). Four strategies for "sound" activities. *SEM Newsletter, 51*(3), 4, 15–17.

Butler, A., Lind, V., & McKoy, C. (2007). Equity and access in music education: Conceptualizing culture as barriers to and supports for music learning. *Music Education Research, 9*(2), 241–253.

Campbell, P. S. (1991). *Lessons from the world.* New York, NY: Schirmer.

Campbell, P. S. (1994a). Bruno Nettl on music of Iran. *Music Educators Journal, 81*(3), 19–28.

Campbell, P. S. (1994b). Music, teachers and children: Research in a time of socio-cultural transformation. *General Music Today, 7*(2), 19–26.

Campbell, P. S. (1996a). Bell Yung on music in China. In *Music in Cultural Context.* Reston, VA: Music Educators National Conference.

Campbell, P. S. (1996b). *Music in cultural context: Eight views on world music education.* Reston, VA: Music Educators National Conference.

Campbell, P. S. (1998). The musical cultures of children. *Research Studies in Music Education, 11*(1), 42–51.

Campbell, P. S. (2001). Unsafe suppositions? Crossing cultures on issues of music's transmission. *Music Eduation Research, 3*(2), 214–226.

Campbell, P. S. (2002a). A matter of perspective: Thoughts on the multiple realities of research. *Journal of Research in Music Education, 50*(3), 191–201.

Campbell, P. S. (2002b). Music in a time of cultural transformation. *Music Educators Journal, 89,* 27–32.

Campbell, P. S. (2004). *Teaching music globally.* New York, NY: Oxford University Press.

Campbell, P. S. (2010). *Songs in their heads: Music and its meaning in children's lives.* New York, NY: Oxford University Press.

Campbell, P. S. (2011a). Musical enculturation: Sociocultural influences and meanings of children's experiences in and through music. In M. Barrett (Ed.), *A cultural psychology of music education.* New York, NY: Oxford University Press. doi:10.1093/acprof:oso/9780199214389.003.0004

Campbell, P. S. (2011b). Teachers studying teachers: Pedagogical practices of artist musicians. In T. Rice (Ed.), *Ethnomusicological encounters with music and musicians: Essays in honor of Robert Garfias.* London, UK: Ashgate.

Campbell, P. S. (2013). Children, teachers, and ethnomusicologists: Traditions and transformation of music in school. In B. Alge (Ed.), *Beyond borders: Welt-Musik-Padagogik* (pp. 13–24). Rostock, Germany: FDR.

Campbell, P. S. (2015). Global practices. In G. E. McPherson (Ed.), *The child as musician* New York, NY: Oxford University Press.

Campbell, P. S. (2016). World music pedagogy: Where music meets culture in classroom practice. In C. R. Abril & B. M. Gault (Eds.), *Teaching general music: Approaches, issues, and viewpoints* (pp. 89–111). New York, NY: Oxford University Press.

Campbell, P. S., Drummond, J., Dunbar-Hall, P., Howard, K., Schippers, H., & Wiggins, T. (2005). *Cultural diversity in music education.* Brisbane: Australian Academic Press.

Campbell, P. S., & Lum, C-H. (2008). Musical America: United yet varied identities for classroom use. *Music Educators Journal, 95*(1), 26–32.

Campbell, P. S., & Scott-Kassner, C. (2017). *Music in childhood* (4th ed.). Boston, MA: Cengage Press.

Campbell, P. S., & Soto Flores, L. (2016). Mariachi music: Pathway to expressing Mexican musical identity. In H. Schippers & C. Grant (Eds.), *Sustainable futures for music cultures: An ecological perspective* (pp. 271–302). New York, NY: Oxford University Press.

Campbell, P. S., & Wiggins, T. (2013). Giving voice to children. In P. S. Campbell & T. Wiggins (Eds.), *The Oxford handbook of children's musical cultures* (pp. 1–24). New York, NY: Oxford University Press.

Cannella, G. S., & Kincheloe, J. L. (Eds.). (2002). *Kidworld: Childhood studies, global perspectives, and education* (Vol. 16). New York, NY: Peter Lang.

Castro, C-A. (2011). *Musical renderings of the Philippine nation.* New York, NY: Oxford University Press.

Choate, R. (1968). *Documentary report of the Tanglewood symposium.* Washington DC: Music Educators National Conference.

Cochran-Smith, M., Shakman, K., Jong, C., Terrell, D. G., Barnatt, J., & McQuillan, P. (2009). Good and just teaching: The case for social justice in teacher education. *American Journal of Education, 115*(3), 347–377.

Conger, R. D., Conger, K. J., & Martin, M. J. (2010). Socioeconomic status, family processes, and individual development. *Journal of Marriage and Family, 72*(3), 685–704.

Corso, D. T. (2003). *"Smooth as butter": Practices of music learning amongst African-American children* (Doctoral dissertation, University of Illinois at Urbana-Champaign). Retrieved from hdl.handle.net/2142/87848

Craft, R. (1994). *Stravinsky: Chronicle of a friendship.* Nashville, TN: Vanderbilt University Press.

Crafts, S. D., Cavicchi, D., & Keil, C. (1993). *My music: Explorations of music in daily life.* Hanover, NH: Wesleyan University Press.

Densmore, F. (2001). *Teton Sioux music and culture.* Lincoln, NE: University of Nebraska Press. (Original work published 1918)

Diamond, B. (2008). The music of modern indigeneity: From identity to alliance studies. In M. Marian-Balasa (Ed.), *European meetings in ethnomusicology* (Vol. 12, pp. 169–190). Bucharest, Romania: Romanian Society for Ethnomusicology.

Dolan, J. P. (2008). *The Irish Americans: A history.* New York, NY: Bloomsbury.

Emberly, A. (2014). Ethnomusicology and childhood: Studying children's music in the field. *College Music Symposium, 54*, 1–15.

Emberly, A., & Davhula, M. J. (2014, Spring). "Proud of who I am": Venda children's musical cultures. *Smithsonian Folkways Magazine.*

Fast, S., & Pegley, K. (Eds.). (2012). *Music, politics, and violence*. Middletown, CT: Wesleyan University Press.

Feay-Shaw, S. J. (2002). *The transmission of Ghanaian music by culture-bearers: From master musician to music teacher* (Unpublished doctoral dissertation). University of Washington, Seattle.

Feld, S. (1982). *Sound and sentiment: Birds, weeping, poetics, and song in Kaluli expression*. Philadelphia, PA: University of Pennsylvania Press.

Fernald, A. (1990). The music of speech to infants: Affective and linguistic functions. *The Journal of the Acoustical Society of America, 88*, S139.

Fletcher, A. C. (1915). The Study of Indian Music. *Proceedings of the National Academy of Sciences of the United States of America, 1*(4), 231–235.

Frierson-Campbell, C. (2007). Without the 'ism: Thoughts about equity and social justice in music education. *Music Education Research, 9*(2), 255–265.

Friesen, D. (2009). That teacher pedestal: How alternative methods challenged my concept of the teacher role. In E. Gould, J. Countryman, C. Morton, & L. S. Rose (Eds.), *Exploring social justice: How music education might matter* (pp. 253–260). Toronto: Canadian Music Educators' Association.

Gaunt, K. (2007). *The games Black girls play: Learning the ropes from double-dutch to hip-hop*. New York, NY: NYU Press.

Goodman, L. J., & Swan, H. (1999). Makah music: Preserving the traditions. In W. Smith and E. Ryan (Eds.), *Spirit of the First People: Native American music traditions of Washington state*. Seattle, WA: University of Washington Press.

Goody, J. (1977). *The domestication of the savage mind*. Cambridge, MA: Cambridge University Press.

Gottschewski, H. (1998). Reception of Western music in Japan. *Toyo Ongaku Kenkyu: The Journal of the Society for the Research of Asiatic Music, 63*, 131–141.

Grant, C., & Portera, A. (Eds.). (2011). *Intercultural and multicultural education: Enhancing global interconnectedness*. New York, NY: Routledge.

Grant, C. A., & Sleeter, C. E. (2013). Race, class, gender, and disability in the classroom. In J. A. Banks & C.A.M. Banks (Eds.), *Multicultural education: Issues and perspectives* (8th ed., pp. 43–60). Hoboken, NJ: Wiley.

Green, L. (2008). *Music, informal learning and the school*. London, UK: Ashgate.

Greene, J. P., Kisida, B., & Bowen, D. H. (2014). The educational value of field trips. *Education Next, 14*(1), 79–86.

Hall, B. J. (1992). Theories of culture and communication. *Communication Theory, 2*(1), 50–70.

Harwood, E. (1998). Music learning in context: A playground tale. *Research Studies in Music Education, 11*(1), 52–60.

Hast, D., & Scott, S. (2004). *Music in Ireland*. New York, NY: Oxford University Press.

Hebert, D. G., & Kertz-Welzel, A. (Eds.). (2012). *Patriotism and nationalism in music education*. Burlington, VT: Ashgate.

Herzog, G. (1950). Song: Folk song and the music of folk song. In M. Leach & J.

Fried (Eds.), *Standard dictionary of folklore, mythology, and legend* (pp. 1032–1050). New York, NY: Funk & Wagnalls.

Hess, J. (2014). Radical musicking: Towards a pedagogy of social change. *Music Education Research, 16*(3), 229–250.

Hicks, C. E., Standifer, J. A., & Carter, W. L. (1983). *Methods and perspectives in urban music education*. Washington, DC: University Press of America.

Higgins, L. (2007). Growth, pathways, and groundwork: Community music in the United Kingdom. *International Journal of Community Music, 1*(1), 39–48.

Higgins, L. (2012). *Community music: In theory and practice*. New York, NY: Oxford University Press.

Higgins, L., & Willingham, L. (2017). *Engaging in community music: An introduction*. New York, NY: London, UK: Routledge.

Hillhouse, A. (2013). Hooks and new tunes: Contemporary Irish dance music in its transnational context. *Ethnomusicology Ireland, 2*(3), 38–60.

Holmes, R. (1990). *A model of aural instruction examined in a case of fiddle teaching* (Unpublished doctoral dissertation). University of Washington, Seattle.

Hood, M. (1982). *The ethnomusicologist*. Kent, OH: Kent State University Press. (Original published in 1971)

Hood, S. (2016). *Ada's violin: The story of the recycled orchestra of Paraguay*. New York, NY: Simon and Schuster.

Howard, K. (1990). *Bands, songs and shamanistic rituals: Folk music in Korean society*. Seoul, Korea: Royal Asiatic Society Korea Branch.

Howard, K. (2014). *Developing children's multicultural sensitivity using music of the African diaspora: An elementary school music culture project*. Retrieved from digital.lib.washington.edu/researchworks/handle/1773/33217

Howard, K., Swanson, M., & Campbell, P. S. (2013). The diversification of music education: Six cases from a movement in progress. *Journal of Music Teacher Education, 24*(1), 26–37.

International Society for Music Education. (1996). *Policy on musics of the world's cultures*. Reading, UK: Author.

Jackson, T. (2012). *Blowin' the blues away: Performance and meaning on the New York jazz scene*. Berkeley, CA: University of California Press.

Janzen, J. M. (1991). "Doing *ngoma*": A dominant trope in African religion and healing. *Journal of Religion in Africa*, 290–308.

Jones, A. L. (2015). "We are a peculiar people": Meaning, masculinity, and competence in gendered gospel performance (Doctoral dissertation, University of Chicago).

Jorgensen, E. R. (1997). *In search of music education*. Chicago: University of Illinois Press.

Keil, C., & Feld, S. (1994). *Music grooves*. Chicago, IL: University of Chicago Press.

Kenny, A. (2016). *Communities of musical practice*. New York, NY: Routledge.

Kincheloe, J. L., & McLaren, P. (2002). Rethinking critical theory and qualitative research. In Y. Zou & E.T. Trueba, *Ethnography and schools: Qualitative approaches to the study of education* (pp. 87–138). Lanham, MD: Rowman and Littlefield.

Kingsbury, H. (1988). *Music, talent, & performance: Conservatory cultural system.* Philadelphia, PA: Temple University Press.

Klinger, R. (1996). *Matters of compromise: An ethnographic study of culture-bearers in elementary music education* (Unpublished doctoral dissertation). University of Washington, Seattle.

Koelsch, S., Offermanns, K., & Franzke, P. (2010). Music in the treatment of affective disorders: An exploratory investigation of a new method for music-therapeutic research. *Music Perception Interdisciplinary Journal, 27,* 307–316.

Lave, J., & Wenger, E. (1991). *Situated learning: Legitimate peripheral participation.* New York, NY: Cambridge University Press.

Legette, R. (2003). Multicultural music education attitudes, values, and practices of public school music teachers. *Journal of Music Teacher Education, 13*(2), 81–93.

Levin, T., (1996). *The hundred thousand fools of God.* Bloomington, IN: Indiana University Press.

Lind, V. R., & McKoy, C. L. (2016). *Culturally responsive teaching in music education.* New York, NY: Routledge.

Lord, A. B. (1960). *The singer of tales.* Cambridge, MA: Harvard University Press.

Loza, S. (1996). Steven Loza on Latino music. In P. S. Campbell (Ed.), *Music in cultural context: Eight views on world music education* (pp. 58–65). Reston, VA: Music Educators National Conference.

Lum, C-H., & Campbell, P. S. (2007). The sonic surrounds of an elementary school. *Journal of Research in Music Education, 55*(1), 31–47.

Lundquist, B. R. (1985). Music education in a multicultural society: The United States of America. *International Journal of Music Education, 5*(2), 49–53.

Lury, C. (2002). *Cultural rights: Technology, legality and personality.* New York, NY: Routledge.

Manabe, N. (2013). Songs of Japanese schoolchildren during World War II. In P. S. Campbell & T. Wiggins, (Eds.), *The Oxford handbook of children's musical cultures* (pp. 96–113). New York, NY: Oxford University Press.

Manes, S. I. (2012). *Songs young Japanese children sing: An ethnographic study of songs and musical utterances* (Order No. 3521529). Retrieved from digital.lib. washington.edu/researchworks/handle/1773/20544

Mapana, K. (2007). Changes in performance styles: A case study of Muheme, a musical tradition of the Wagogo of Dodoma, Tanzania. *Journal of African Cultural Studies, 19*(1), 81–93.

Mapana, K., Campbell, P. S., Roberts, C., & Mena, C. (2016). An earful of Africa: Insights from Tanzania on music and music learning. *College Music Symposium, 56.* doi: doi.org/10.18177/sym.2016.56.fr.11155

Mark, M. (2008). *A concise history of American music education.* Lanham, MD: Rowman and Littlefield.

Mark, M., & Gary, C. L. (1999). *A history of American music education* (2nd ed.). Reston, VA: National Association for Music Education .

Marsh, K. (2008). *The musical playground: Global tradition and change in children's songs and games.* New York, NY: Oxford University Press.

Marsh, K., & Young, S. (2006). Musical play. In G. McPherson (Ed.), *The child as musician* (pp. 289–310). New York, NY: Oxford University Press.

Martin, R. (1998). *The rough-face girl.* New York, NY: Puffin Books.

Mason, L. (1835). *Juvenile lyre (etc).* Boston, MA: Carter, Hendee.

Mason, L. (1844). *Manual of the Boston Academy of Music: For instruction in the elements of vocal music, on the system of Pestalozzi.* Boston, MA: J. H. Wilkins & R. B. Carter.

Mason, L. (1864). *The song-garden: Second book.* Boston, MA: Oliver Ditson.

Mayhew, M. J., & Fernández, S. D. (2007). Pedagogical practices that contribute to social justice outcomes. *The Review of Higher Education, 31*(1), 55–80.

McAllester, D. P. (1968). The substance of things hoped for. In R. Choate (Ed.), *Tanglewood declaration.* Reston VA: MENC.

McAllester, D. P. (1996). North America/Native America. In J. Titon (Ed.), *Worlds of music: An introduction to the music of the world's peoples* (pp. 16–66). New York, NY: Schirmer Books.

McCord, K. (2016, May 12). Update on why we must have diversity, inclusion and equity in the arts. *Alternate ROOTS.* Retrieved from alternateroots.org/update-on-why-we-must-have-diversity-inclusion-and-equity-in-the-arts/

McPherson, G. E., & Welch, G. F. (Eds.) (2012). *The Oxford Handbook of music education* (vol. 1). New York, NY: Oxford University Press.

Merrett, D. L., Peretz, I., & Wilson, S. J. (2013). Moderating variables of music training–induced neuroplasticity: A review and discussion. *Frontiers in Psychology, 4.* doi: 10.3389/fpsyg.2013.00606

Merriam, A. P. (1964). *The anthropology of music.* Evanston, IL: Northwestern University Press.

Miendlarzewska, E. A., & Trost, W. J. (2013). How musical training affects cognitive development: Rhythm, reward and other modulating variables. *Frontiers in neuroscience, 7.* doi: 10.3389/fnins.2013.00279

Miller, J. (1999). *Lushootseed culture and the shamanic odyssey: An anchored radiance.* Lincoln, NE: University of Nebraska Press.

Minks, A. (2013a). Miskitu children's singing games on the Caribbean coast of Nicaragua as intercultural play and performance. In P. S. Campbell & T. Wiggins (Eds.), *The Oxford handbook of children's musical cultures* (pp. 218–231). New York, NY: Oxford University Press.

Minks, A. (2013b). *Voices of play: Miskitu children's speech and song on the Atlantic coast of Nicaragua.* Tucson, AZ: University of Arizona Press.

Moynihan, D. P., Smeeding, T., & Rainwater, L. (Eds.). (2004). *The future of the family.* New York, NY: Russell Sage Foundation.

National Association for Music Education. (2016, May 11). National Association for Music Education announces new executive director and CEO. Retrieved from nafme.org/national-association-for-music-education-announces-new-executive-director-and-ceo/

National Core Arts Standards. (1994). *National core arts standards: A conceptual framework for arts learning.* Reston, VA: Music Educators National Conference.

Nelson, K. (2005). *He's got the whole world in his hands*. New York, NY: Dial Books.

Nettl, B. (1984). In honor of our principal teachers. *Ethnomusicology, 28*(2), 173–185.

Nettl, B. (1986). Improvisation. In D. M. Randel (Ed.), *The new Harvard dictionary of music* (pp. 392–394). Cambridge, MA: Harvard University Press.

Nettl, B. (1996). *Heartland excursions*. Urbana, IL: University of Illinois Press.

Nettl, B. (1998). An art neglected in scholarship. In B. Nettl (Ed.) (with M. Russell), *In the course of performance: Studies in the world of musical improvisation* (pp. 1–26). Chicago, IL: University of Chicago Press.

Nettl, B. (2012). Some contributions of ethnomusicology. In G. McPherson & G. Welch (Eds.), *The Oxford handbook of music education* (pp. 105–124). New York, NY: Oxford University Press.

Nettl, B. (2015). *The study of ethnomusicology: Thirty-three issues and concepts*. Urbana, IL: University of Illinois Press.

Neuman, D. M. (1980). *The life of music in North India: The organization of an artistic tradition*. Detroit, MI: Wayne State University Press.

Nguyen, T. P., & Campbell, P. S. (1991). *From rice paddies to temple yards: Traditional music of Vietnam*. Danbury CT: World Music Press.

Nguyen, T. P., Schramm, A. R., & Campbell, P. S. (1995). *Searching for a niche: Vietnamese music at home in America*. Kent OH: Viet Music Publications.

Nieto, S. (2009). Multicultural education in the United States: Historical realities, ongoing challenges, and transformative possibilities. In J. A. Banks (Ed.), The *Routledge international companion to multicultural education* (pp. 79–96). New York, NY: Routledge.

Oakes, J., Joseph, R., & Muir, K. (2004). Access and achievement in mathematics and science: Inequalities. In J. A. Banks & C. A. M. Banks (Eds.), *Handbook of research on multicultural education* (2nd ed., pp. 69–90). San Francisco, CA: Jossey-Bass.

Ong, W. J. (1982). *Orality and literacy: The technologizing of the word*. London, UK: Routledge.

Perea, J. C. (2013). *Intertribal Native American music in the United States*. New York, NY: Oxford University Press.

Peters, V. (2009). Youth identity construction through music education: Nurturing a sense of belonging in multi-ethnic communities. In E. Gould, J. Countryman, C. Morton, & L. S. Rose (Eds.), *Exploring social justice: How music education might matter* (pp. 199–211). Toronto, Canada: Canadian Music Educators' Association.

Pettan, S., & Titon, J. T. (Eds.). (2015). *The Oxford handbook of applied ethnomusicology*. New York, NY: Oxford University Press.

Powers, H. S. (1980). Language models and musical analysis. *Ethnomusicology, 24*(1), 1–60.

Reilly Carlisle, L., Jackson, B. W., & George, A. (2006). Principles of social justice education: The social justice education in schools project. *Equity & Excellence in Education, 39*, 55–64.

Reyes, A. (1999). *Songs of the caged, songs of the free: Music and the Vietnamese refugee experience*. Philadelphia, PA: Temple University Press.

Rice, T. (1994). *May it fill your soul*. Chicago, IL: University of Chicago Press.

Rice, T. (2003a). The ethnomusicology of music learning and teaching. *College Music Symposium 43*, 65–85/

Rice, T. (2003b). Time, place, and metaphor in musical experience and ethnography. *Ethnomusicology, 47*(2), 151–179.

Rice, T. (2017). *Modeling ethnomusicology*. New York, NY: Oxford University Press.

Richardson, C. P. (2007). Engaging the world: Music education and the big ideas. *Music Education Research, 9*(2), 205–214.

Roberts, J. C., & Campbell, P. S. (2015). Multiculturalism and social justice: Complementary movements for education in and through music. In C. Benedict, P. Schmidt, G. Spruce, & P. Woolford (Eds.), *The Oxford handbook of social justice in music education*. New York, NY: Oxford University Press.

Ross, A. (2016, July 4). When music is violence. *New Yorker*. Retrieved from www.newyorker.com/magazine/2016/07/04/when-music-is-violence

Rowling, J. K. (1998). *Harry Potter and the sorcerer's stone*. New York, NY: A. A. Levine Books.

Santos, R. P. (1996). *Music education in the Philippines*. Perth, Australia: International Society for Music Education.

Sarath, E. W., Myers, D. E., & Campbell, P. S. (2017). *Re-defining music studies in an age of change*. New York, NY: Routledge.

Schippers, H. (2010). *Facing the music: Shaping music education from a global perspective*. New York, NY: Oxford University Press.

Schippers, H., & Campbell, P. S. (2012). Cultural diversity: Beyond "songs from many lands." In G. McPherson & G. Welch (Eds.), *Oxford handbook of music education* (pp. 87–104). New York, NY: Oxford University Press.

Schippers, H., & Grant, C. (Eds.). (2016). *Sustainable futures for music cultures: An ecological perspective*. New York, NY: Oxford University Press.

Schultz, A. C. (2013). *Singing a Hindu nation: Marathi devotional performance and nationalism*. New York, NY: Oxford University Press.

Seeger, A. (1987). *Why Suya sing: A musical anthropology of an Amazonian people*. Urbana, IL: University of Illinois Press.

Sensoy, Ö., & DiAngelo, R. (2017). *Is everyone really equal? An introduction to key concepts in social justice education* (2nd ed.). New York, NY: Teachers College Press.

Sheehy, D. (2006). *Mariachi music in Mexico*. New York, NY: Oxford University Press.

Sijohn, C. (1999). The circle of song. In W. Smyth & E. Ryan (Eds.), *Spirit of the First People: Native American music traditions of Washington State* (pp. 44–49). Seattle, WA: University of Washington Press.

Silverman, C. (2012). *Romani routes: Cultural politics and Balkan music in diaspora*. New York, NY: Oxford University Press.

Slobin, M. (1992). Micromusics of the West: A comparative approach. *Ethnomusicology, 36*(1), 1–87.

Small, C. (1998). *Musicking: The meanings of performing and listening.* Hanover, NH: University Press of New England.

Soto, A. C. (2012). *Bimusical identity of children in a Mexican American school* (Unpublished doctoral dissertation). University of Washington, Seattle, WA.

Soto, A. C., Lum, C-H., & Campbell, P. S. (2009). A university–school partnership for music education students within a culturally-distinctive community. *Journal of Research in Music Education, 56*(4), 338–356.

Standifer, J. A., & Lundquist, B. R. (1972). *Source book of African and Afro-American materials for music educators.* Reston, VA: Music Educators National Conference.

Steptoe, J. (2008). *Mufaro's beautiful daughters.* New York, NY: Lothrop Lee & Shepard.

Takizawa, T. (1997). A new paradigm of world musics in Japanese music education: Japan's learning from ASEAN countries' access roads to world musics. In J. Katsumura & Y. Tokumaru (Eds.), *Report of world musics from Hamamatsu 1996.* Tokyo, Japan: Foundation for the Promotion of Music, Education, and Culture.

Tanglewood II Declaration. (2007). *Tanglewood II: Charting the future.* Retrieved from www.bu.edu/tanglewoodtwo/declaration/declaration.html

Telles, E. (2010). Mexican Americans and immigrant incorporation. *Contexts 9*(1), 28–33.

Theorell, T. (2014). *Psychological health effects of musical experiences: Theories, studies and reflections in music health science.* Dordrecht, Netherlands: Springer.

Titon, J. T. (1992). Music, the public interest, and the practice of ethnomusicology. *Ethnomusicology, 36*(2), 315–322.

Titon, J. T. (2015). Applied ethnomusicology: A descriptive and historical account. In J. T. Titon & S. Pettan (Eds.), *The Oxford handbook of applied ethnomusicology* (pp. 4–29). New York, NY: Oxford University Press.

Treitler, L. (2003). *With voice and pen: Coming to know medieval song and how it was made.* New York, NY: Oxford University Press.

Trimillos, R. (1989). Hálau, Hochschule, Maystro, and Ryú: Cultural approaches to music learning and teaching. *International Journal of Music Education, 14*(1), 32–42.

Turino, T. (2008). *Music as social life: The politics of participation.* Chicago, IL: University of Chicago Press.

van den Bos, P. (1995). Differences between Western and non-Western teaching methods in music education: How can both methods supplement each other? In M. Lieth-Philipp & A. Gutzwiller (Eds.), *Teaching musics of the world* (pp. 169–179). Affalterbach, Germany: Philipp Verlag.

Veblen, K. K. (1991). *Perceptions of change and stability in the transmission of Irish traditional music: An examination of the music teacher's role* (Unpublished doctoral dissertation). Madison WI: University of Wisconsin.

Volk, T. M. (1998). *Music, education and multiculturalism: Foundations and principles.* New York, NY: Oxford University Press.

Wade, B. C. (2004). *Thinking musically: Experiencing music, expressing culture* (Global music series). New York, NY: Oxford University Press.

Waterman, R. (1956). Music in Australian aboriginal culture—some sociological and psychological implications. *Music Therapy—1955, 5,* 40–49.

Wenger, E. (1998). *Communities of practice: Learning, meaning, and identity.* Cambridge, MA: Cambridge University Press.

Weston, J. (2017). Water is life: The rise of the Mní Wicóni movement. *Cultural Survival Quarterly, 41*(1), 12–13.

Wong, D. (2003). *Sounding the essence.* Chicago, IL: University of Chicago Press.

Zhou, M., & Bankston, C. (1998). *Growing up American: How Vietnamese children adapt to life in the United States.* New York, NY: Russell Sage Foundation.

Index

About the Author

Patricia Shehan Campbell is the Donald E. Peterson Professor of Music at the University of Washington, where she teaches courses at the interface of education and ethnomusicology. A singer and pianist, with studies of the Japanese *koto*, Celtic harp, Karnatic Indian *mridangam*, and Bulgarian and Wagogo song, she has lectured internationally on the pedagogy of world music and children's musical cultures. She is the author of *Lessons from the World* (1991), *Music in Cultural Context* (1996), *Songs in Their Heads* (1998, 2010), *Teaching Music Globally* (2004), and *Musician and Teacher* (2008); co-author of *Music in Childhood* (2017, 4th ed.) and *Redefining Music Studies in an Age of Change* (2017); and coeditor of the Global Music Series and The Oxford Handbook of Children's Musical Cultures (2013). Campbell is recipient of the 2017 Koizumi Prize and the 2012 Taiji Award for work on the preservation of traditional music through educational practice, and was designated Senior Researcher in Music Education of the National Association for Music Education in 2002. Chair of the Advisory Board of Smithsonian Folkways and consultant on repatriation efforts of recordings of Alan Lomax to communities in the American South, she is editor of a forthcoming six-volume series on World Music Pedagogy (2018) for practicing and prospective teachers.